SYMBOLIC ANTHROPOLOGY

Series Edited by David W. Crabb

Symbolic Anthropology

Rites of Modernization

James L. Peacock

Rites of Modernization

SYMBOLIC AND SOCIAL ASPECTS OF
INDONESIAN PROLETARIAN DRAMA

With a new Afterword

The University of Chicago Press

CHICAGO & LONDON

The University of Chicago Press, Chicago 60637
The University of Chicago Press, Ltd., London

© 1968, 1987 by The University of Chicago
All rights reserved. Published 1968
Paperback edition 1987
Printed in the United States of America

96 95 94 93 92 91 90 89 88 87   6 5 4 3 2

Library of Congress Catalog Card Number 68–15931

International Standard Book Number 0–226–65131–2

To Louly

Series Editor's Preface

Intellectually we are now in an age when life seems to be holding up the mirror to art, and when anthropology is welcoming a concern with the manifest content of sentient life — the *symbol*. Hence, the present series in symbolic anthropology.

In the course of their scientific pursuits anthropologists are caught up with sentient life as it is lived, as it is thought about or talked about, and as it is acted out. In this book one strand of our concern, the one mentioned last above, is separated out for primary analysis by the author — life as drama and drama as life. He offers a detailed and finely delineated study of the place of acted-out situations in the lives of individuals and of the proletarian community making up part of a modern port city. There are also characterizations which spill over from the stage into domestic and political life, and pieces of plot or dialogue in "real life" settings.

In this work the author also sharpens up considerably our understanding of the phrase "symbolic action" (originally taken from Kenneth Burke). Symbolic action now can surely be considered to include much more than the elaboration of verbal gesture; it has been enriched with connotations of ritual and stage gesture as well. It suggests, indeed, the acting out of social relations, the manifestation of social feedback.

We will all be well served if future volumes on symbolic anthropology — including the analysis of life as experienced (expressive symbols), life as thought about (cognitive symbols), life as talked about (linguistic symbols), as well as more on life as acted out (symbolic action) — rise to the high standards set by this work.

DAVID W. CRABB

Program in Anthropology
Princeton University

Foreword

James Peacock's study of ludruk has impressed me since I first became aware of it. It is a pleasure to find it the first volume in an important series, where it may reach the audience it deserves.

Given the conventions proper to forewords, it is difficult to say more. Interest in the study leads one to want to comment, dissect, expatiate in ways appropriate to other genres, such as the book review and conference discussion. I am thinking now, not of particular results, so much as of the *kind* of study it is. I think that what Peacock has done is of an importance such that anthropologists ought to read his book asking — what can this analysis of interplay between world views, plot structures, life styles, types of performer, channel and audience, teach me to do? What problems in my own study of performances can be approached in similar ways?

Where would different ways be indicated? In sum, *how can I build on this work?* For I believe that anthropologists have a special opportunity, and responsibility, to interpret the meanings in the forms and guises in which peasants and proletarians articulate their struggles for social change.[1] And I believe with Peacock that social scientists often fail to interpret adequately the meanings of such symbolic forms because they seek content or context without sensitivity to the interdependence of both with form itself. One has to do, not with a mirror, an inventory of contents, or some folk equivalent of a projective test — although elements of these may be present — but with something that has a complex integrity of its own. One has to do, then, with form that is an enactment, a symbolic action, manifesting a dialectic between motives grounded in an inevitably changing social order, on the one hand, and the traditions, exigencies, and logic of a partly autonomous genre, on the other. Anthropology's humanistic strain, its ties with folklore and even literary criticism, the example of some of its great figures, all lead one to expect that it take the lead in showing how to be sensitive to form, and yet scientifically responsive too. And so, with such an anthropology in view, and having worked page by page through the present work, one wants to write this book's first serious review, as well as its first recommendation.

Already, though, I have fallen afoul of the proprieties of the genre, foreword. The writer of a foreword is not supposed to be so caught up with a book as to want actually to work with its contents. That would be too intrusive, too instrumental — in terms of one of the world views discussed in the pages to follow, too *kasar*. A foreword should rather advert to some frame of reference, one dear to the writer's heart, if perhaps but indirectly related to the book, and discuss it in a way that invites reader, book, and author into some larger world of significance, the writer's membership in which his style and allusions have been careful to make plain. In short, a foreword should express a certain graceful harmony, it should be *alus*.

Well, the larger world of significance has been mentioned above, is expressed in the title and Series Editor's Preface for this series

---

[1] Cf. an extended critique of Frantz Fanon, *The Wretched of the Earth,* in terms of an anthropological understanding of such forms (A. Norman Klein, "On Revolutionary Violence," *Studies on the Left* 6, 3 [1966]: 62–83); and a trenchant analysis of misunderstanding of retention *vs.* violent destruction of symbols, Ward H. Goodenough, "Education and Identity," in Fred C. Gruber, ed., *Anthropology and Education* (Philadelphia: University of Pennsylvania Press, 1961), pp. 84–102.

and is treated in some detail by the author himself. Let me then merely mention my own slogans for the work anthropologists have to do in this world — *ethnography of communication, ethnography of symbolic forms* — and observe that the surge of interest in studies of myths, rites, performances, both capital-A Arts and the daily arts of communicative conduct, and the structure of speaking can reach fruition if the one requisite, formal analysis, is kept in tandem with the other, the perspective of social (symbolic) action. That said, let me, as unintrusively as I can, invite the reader to watch and reflect on three aspects of the book that are crucial to the larger world in which it takes its place.

Method. Peacock shows us frankly and clearly the problems of one anthropologist studying complex, collective symbolic events. What one euphemistically calls "standard ethnographic field procedures" obviously constitute no adequate guide. Had some one contributory aspect of ludruk been the objective (or had Peacock been a team, one member for each aspect), comprehensive equipment, recording and annotation (the building of a complete documentary record) might have been the entire concern. Work of that sort must indeed be done, and for each aspect of ludruk there are questions one might like to pursue. But very likely we would not now have this book to suggest them to us. At present one field worker has no adequate way both to obtain a comprehensive (and intensive) documentation of performances, and to produce an analytic result within a reasonable time. If anthropologists have often not succeeded in preparing texts for publication within their lifetimes, the use and preparation of shelves of texts, tapes, and films is even less expectable. The training, organizational and support problems of such work have to be faced, if anthropology is to have anything scientifically acceptable to say in coming years.

Peacock provides a model for our present circumstances. Accepting and seeking evidence from every source, he at the same time focussed on the crucial thing — the line of culminations and climaxes, the sequence in which audience expectations are built up and gratified. (In both respects one sees the eminently appropriate examples of Kenneth Burke; see his "Psychology and Form," *Counterstatement* [Chicago: University of Chicago Press, 1957], pp. 29–44.) Under limitations of time and opportunity in the field, a student of symbolic action necessarily goes "where the action is."

Form. The interweaving of contributory genres and modes of expression is one of the special fascinations of ludruk and of the kind of performance tradition it represents. The joining of conventional materials, general structure, and continuous improvisation and adaptation is familiar from jazz, and now, from aleatory music, raga, and so on, but even so, it has seemed odd until recently in our public culture. Yet such forms would seem to have been and to remain a normal thing in much of the world, as accounts of Yugoslav epic, Homeric poems, Chinese storytelling, and, closer to Indonesia, Toda poetry, Indian Rām Līlā dramas, and music such as the raga show.²

Three things particularly engage attention here. One is the formal analysis of the contributory genres and modes of expression, and of their interrelationships. Peacock shows the symbolic importance, and richness, of the joke, the song, the dance, the musical progression and coda, the differential use of verbal and non-verbal channels, the use of a set of socially marked codes and levels of speech, the figures of clown and transvestite. As an input to the drama, each could become the object of monographic study in its own right, pursuing further the definition and writing of rules for proper form and appropriate use. And while the absence of rehearsals, the unstable nature of the performing companies, and the history of the genres, all make clear the considerable independence of the major components of ludruk — the sequence of *ngremo, dagelan, selingan,* and *tjerita* (the last interspersed with elements of the preceding two) — one cannot but wonder if there may not be something more to the syntax of ludruk, if affinities between instances of components might not be found or even implicit rules of selection. One wonders what would result from further study of actors' outlines and from the attempt to write explicit, generative rules for ludruk, as for all other traditional genres within which there is the creativity of producing an infinite set of performances from a finite set of elements and principles.³ (Perhaps too, one could define paradigmatic sets from which choice is made at each point, and find context-sensitive rules for some of the allocation — as between transvestite and clown of topics of songs and jokes.)

---

² Cf. Maurice Bowra, *Heroic Poetry* (London: Macmillan, 1952); A. B. Lord, *The Singer of Tales* (Cambridge, Mass.: Harvard University Press, 1960); Vena Hrdlickova, "The Professional Training of Chinese Story Tellers and Storytellers' Guilds," *Archiv Orientalni* 33 (1965): 225–48; Norvin Hein, "The Rām Līlā," *Journal of American Folklore* 71 (1958): 279–304.

³ The allusion, of course, is to transformational generative grammar — see Noam Chomsky, *Syntactic Structures* (The Hague: Mouton, 1957); *Aspects of the Theory of Syntax* (Cambridge, Mass.: Massachusetts Institute of Technology Press, 1965).

A second interest is comparative analysis, which seeks both con-
trastive sharpening of insight and underlying generalizations. I
trust that no general discussion of the clown or transvestite, of
liminal and mediating figures (which the ludruk clown and transvestite so clearly are), of jokes, of verbal and non-verbal channels
and so on, will neglect the evidence of this study.

A third interest is in what Burke calls "literary species" — the
effort always to define the essential character of the form with
which one is dealing. Such definition serves as a test of one s
understanding and by placing the form in a world of other forms
illuminates both.[4] Peacock's analysis of the popular, modern plots
of ludruk is so full and convincing that I have attempted part of
such a definition, intending it to suggest the difference between the
empathies and emotional effects of ludruk and those defined in the
prototype of such definitions, that of Aristotle for Greek tragedies.
I warn that whatever merit the definition has is taken from Peacock's analysis. It may be of interest to return to the definition
after having read the analysis, perhaps to improve upon it. Before then, the definition, besides illustrating the notion, can only
point one to the book that makes it intelligible.

Tentatively, then, with respect to the plots designated by Peacock
as M-type:

> ludruk is a secular, proletarian drama, through fantasy, mockery,
> and deflected hope effecting a catharsis of the constraints of circum-
> vening life. The catharsis affects at once personal, social, and national
> identities and aspirations. Fantasy and mockery are preliminary to,
> and interspersed with, a culminating dramatization of upward mo-
> bility, fantasy and mockery being focussed in two liminal figures,
> one a seductive, aristocratic transvestite, expressing infantile and
> adolescent sex, and national progress and unity; the other a coarse,
> lowerclass clown, expressing conservative protest and local realities.
> Deflected hope is focussed in a lowerclass girl who (unlike the
> audience, but possibly like their children) is young, unmarried and
> free to choose her spouse, and who by personal attractiveness, and
> seizing of fortunate opportunity, succeeds in marrying into the elite.
> In contrast, a relative or other proletarian comes to a bad end due
> to an increasing personal villainy that implicitly justifies the girl's
> desertion of her original class.

[4] Burke accepts this goal from Aristotle, and practices it brilliantly — see "Three
Definitions," *The Kenyon Review* 13 (1951): 173–92; "Othello: An Essay to Il-
lustrate a Method," *The Hudson Review* 4 (1951): 165–203; and essays on
Shakespearean plays in *Language as Symbolic Action* (Berkeley and Los Angeles:
University of California Press, 1966).

Audience, Modernization, Revolution. The showing of the interdependence between audience and dramatic form is perhaps the
most brilliant feature of the book. Despite government and Communist support of ludruk, the audience to whom a play is presented
is shown to affect its content more than formal political affiliation
of the troupe. This fact is not surprising in the flexible, improvising,
adaptive genre that Peacock shows ludruk to be, but it is an object
lesson for those who would read off the import of a symbolic form
from its sponsorship. Labor union meetings might get class struggle
and political gatherings nationalism, but the proletarians of Surabaja paid for something else. They paid in effect for entertainment
that expressed three facets of their lives — vague concern for national progress and harmony; the pains of progress and of present
conditions; and desires for romantic freedom and personal success
— without demanding change of any sort in themselves. Clearly
ludruk was preparing the modernization that Peacock describes. Its
own history, with respect to types of plot, integrity of plot, profes-
sionalization, attests to this. From static class harmony to decisive
mobility and the punishment of real villains is a major step. But
the villains are not class villains, and indeed, they serve to justify
a mobility that rejects proletarian ties. One can only remark that
that is an odd way for Communists to prepare the Surabaja masses
for revolution. And one cannot read this book without reflecting
that the people who performed and watched these plays may
now, many of them, be dead together with several hundred thousand of their compatriots (killed, such are the ironies of contemporary socialism, perhaps with the aid of Soviet tanks). Peacock
notes that his original analysis, showing bourgeois trends among
the official Communist proletarians, was already complete before
the 1965 massacre.

I cannot trace the interconnections between the events of 1965
and the ludruk participants of Surabaja, but surely it is to be hoped
that information will be obtained, so as to follow through the
implications of the present study. These implications, I think, are
great. On the ways in which ludruk is an enactment of or preparation for modernization, I can only refer to the impressive chapter
in this book. I would like just to comment further on symbolic forms
and revolutions. One cannot say much without knowledge of the
place of commercial ludruk among other forms of ludruk, and
other Indonesian genres, such as *ketoprak,* movies, and so on, and
of the overlap or lack of it in the audiences of each (regarding
genres as a domain and types of audience as a range). But it is

clear that commercial ludruk was preparing, not class struggle, but desertion of proletarian loyalties through opportunistic personal success. Perhaps the policies of the government with regard to promotion of the NASAKOM ideology played a part, but one recalls that before Communist party audiences ludruk did portray class struggle, even, Peacock reports, peasants killing an exploiting landlord. Commercial ludruk, then, was giving proletarians not so much what the party wanted, as what they wanted, and in forms they enjoyed. The audience being shaped by ludruk was itself a factor by which its shaper was being shaped. Transmuted through the component symbolic forms of ludruk, national unity became a lulling song, proletarian realism a debunking clown without solutions to offer, and sexual freedom and elite status the stuff of which daydreams are made. Ludruk would seem to have something to say about the nature of recent Indonesian Communism, and about the place of symbolic action and cultural hegemony in the making and predicting of revolutions.

DELL HYMES

Department of Anthropology
University of Pennsylvania

Prefatory Note

I must acknowledge my debt to David W. Crabb of Princeton University, editor of the series in which this book appears. Professor Crabb was the first person to read the manuscript; I have greatly profited from his enthusiasm and criticism. Dell Hymes, Clifford Geertz, Robert Bellah, and Amelie Rorty offered enormously valuable criticism, encouragement, or aid. W. F. Rendra, a Javanese specialist in theater now studying in the United States, was kind enough to give the manuscript a thorough reading and commentary, and to remark that it told its Javanese jokes well.

Long before the writing had begun, much stimulation and support had already been received. Rufus Hendon, with whom I briefly studied the Indonesian language, was the first to whom I stated my intention of going to Java to study drama and other communication forms; he gave useful advice and strongly encouraged me to concentrate on *ludruk* plays, the subject of this book. Cora DuBois of Harvard University, who was later to supervise the writing of a doctoral thesis which forms a partial basis for this book, supplied guideposts and poignant stimulation at this early stage, as she did during the fieldwork, analysis, and thesis-writing stages.

Once in the field in Java I had the good fortune to find a few bureaucratic paths laid straight. In that regard, I wish especially to thank Djoko Sanjoto of the Indonesian Department of Foreign Affairs, Messrs. Karyono and Moeljono of the East Javanese Inspectorate of Culture, and Hans Burkhardt. Sanjoto Soewito, A. Soetjito, R. Soehartojo, J. Shamsudin, M. Zahir Basalamah, Tjioe Hok Sing, Dr. Ariawan Soejoenoes, and his father, Professor Soejoenoes, all offered invaluable friendship, information, technical assistance, and facilities during my stay in Java.

My debt is especially heavy to Ibu and Bapak Marsosudiro and their family, with whom my wife and I lived. Ibu and Bapak displayed a charity and grace, which we have only now begun to appreciate, in guiding our entry into Javanese society.

After returning from Java, while struggling to make sense out of it, I enjoyed lengthy discussions with a fellow student at Harvard, A. Thomas Kirsch. Mr. Kirsch strongly influenced the views presented in this book and their manner of presentation, as did, in different ways, T. O. Beidelman, Harsja Bachtiar, Eugene Ogan, Claire Helms, Mrs. Robert Raphael Fowler, and the writings of Kenneth Burke and Talcott Parsons.

I also acknowledge the National Institutes of Health predoctoral fellowship (MH–12,186–04) and supplement grant (MH–05,-742–02) which financed my fieldwork. A faculty stipend from the Coordinating Committee of Foreign and International Affairs of Princeton University supplemented my regular teaching salary during the summer of 1966, at which time I wrote this book. I am grateful to C. E. Black for arranging that stipend.

Certain parts of this book are based upon the following previously or concurrently published articles of mine: "Anti-Dutch, Anti-Muslim Drama Among Surabaja Proletarians," *Indonesia;* "Comedy and Centralization in Java," *Journal of American Folklore;* and "Javanese Clown and Transvestite Songs: Relations between 'Primitive Classification' and 'Communicative Events' " in June Helm (ed.) *Essays on the Verbal and Visual Arts, Proceedings of the 1966 Annual Spring Meeting, American Ethnological Society* (Seattle: University of Washington Press, 1967). I am grateful to the editors and publishers of the journals and book in which these articles are found for permission to use materials appearing in them. I am happy to thank Harvard University Press for permission to quote passages from a work to be published by that press, James R. Brandon, *Theatre in Southeast Asia.*

What can be said of a wife and a book? "Without whom, not" sums up the situation. I shall not list all the aids and sufferings of my wife, Florence, but do wish to acknowledge her substantive contributions. The analyses of Javanese music that appear in the book are essentially my paraphrases of analyses she made during our Javanese sojourn. The musical scores were recorded and notated by her.

ON STYLE

Certain stylistic conventions that this book will follow must be mentioned at this time: Javanese words taken from oral sources are spelled in accordance with the system employed by Pigeaud's *Javaans-Nederlands Handwoordenboek,* except that "oe" is replaced with "u" and "g" with "k." Indonesian words from oral sources are spelled according to the system employed in W.J.S. Poerwadarminta's *Kamus Umum Bahasa Indonesia.* Javanese or Indonesian words taken from written sources are simply reproduced as they were written. All reduced-type passages for which no source references are given are transcriptions or paraphrases of my field notes. Following anthropological convention, I have given false names to the natives whose experiences and opinions I report. Although I usually follow the anthropological convention of writing in the "ethnographic present" (reporting situations as if I am observing them while I am writing about them), all that I describe took place, unless I note otherwise, during 1962–63. Foreign words are italicized only so long as it is felt they are still "foreign" to the reader; that is, a foreign word is italicized the first time it appears in each new context, until it has appeared in so many contexts that it is felt unnecessary to italicize it each time it is introduced anew.

J. L. P.

Department of Anthropology
University of North Carolina

Contents

Plates

Tables

Part 1

Introduction

Two Themes

A study of drama in relation to social process could profitably be carried out in many parts of the world. Southeast Asia seems, however, especially fit for such a study since it appears that live theater has an unusually wide and intimate connection with Southeast Asian society. James R. Brandon in *Theatre in Southeast Asia* says that "theatre is an integral part of the culture of Southeast Asia to an unusual degree" in contrast to the modern West where theater is a

> cultural appendage . . . a luxury cultivated by sophisticates, a commercial property exploited by profit-seeking businessmen, a marginal and often desperate way of life for the artist, a haven of comfortable clichés for the bourgeois ticket buyer.

In Southeast Asia, says Brandon, "theatre can be, and often is, much more than this." Several of Brandon's subsequent remarks support this statement.[1] He estimates that Southeast Asia supports at least twenty times as many professional drama troupes per capita as does the United States. He argues that in Southeast Asia drama has been employed from ancient to modern times for deliberate moral education to a much greater extent than has theater in contemporary Europe and America; here drama tends to be just entertainment. He shows that in Southeast Asia theater is still a crucial *mass* medium while in the United States theater is for a minority, the urban elite. In many areas of Southeast Asia, Brandon reports, theater is a more important mass medium than movies, and Southeast Asians think of drama as the most Asian or local of the mass media, while movies exude a foreign odor. Unlike radio, theater troupes in Southeast Asia are almost entirely independently owned and operated, hence less under government control than are government-run national radio networks; therefore, we might expect theater to be related to local social processes in more subtle — perhaps more intimate and important — ways than a medium that is a government mouthpiece.

All that has been said about Southeast Asia theater in general holds for Javanese drama, only more so. For at least a thousand years Java has maintained a vigorous and venerable dramatic tradition in the form of *wajang kulit,* the puppet play that is regarded by Javanese as the most important vehicle of "Javanese religion," that complex of mystical beliefs which most Javanese treasure more than Islam. Wajang kulit has furnished symbols for Sukarno's national myth making [2] (Sukarno's personal feeling for wajang plays is revealed by his taking, in his youth, the name of a wajang character, Bima, as a pen name). Wajang kulit, one of the few "feudal" Javanese institutions venerated by hard-bitten Communists and puritanical Muslims alike, is popular in remote villages, city slums, palaces, and high government circles and evokes remarkable emotional reactions from the usually restrained Java-

---

[1] The "statement" is taken from James R. Brandon, *Theatre in Southeast Asia,* p. 3. The "subsequent remarks" in this paragraph that are attributed to Brandon are found in this manuscript (a preliminary rather than final version), pp. 193, 317, 348, and 359.

[2] For instance, Sukarno publicly applied the label "Srikandi" (name of a brave wajang kulit heroine) to the first woman guerilla of Indonesia who landed in West New Guinea during the 1962 liberation campaign. See Benedict R. O'G. Anderson, *Mythology and the Tolerance of the Javanese,* p. 26.

nese.[3] Yet wajang kulit is only one facet of dramatic life in Java. Java today displays a wide variety of theater — puppet, human, popular, folk, classical, proletarian, religious, political, comic, epic, dance, operatic — and a remarkable amount of theatrical activity. It is estimated that Java in 1963 supported about forty times as many professional dramatic troupes per capita as does the United States [4] (Java's population is about one-fourth that of the United States). With respect to *ludruk,* the proletarian drama on which this book will center, the following gives some idea of its activity: There were, in 1963, 594 ludruk troupes registered (registration voluntary) in the cultural office of the Province of East Java, the area where ludruk is most popular.[5] In Surabaja, the East Javanese port city (population, one million) where I did my fieldwork in 1962–63, I estimate [6] that on eves of major Indonesian holidays such as Labor Day or Independence Day, there were three hundred ludruk troupes performing at once, each with an audience of about four hundred, and every night except on national or religious holidays there were ludruk shows in each of the five commercial ludruk theaters of Surabaja, each with an audience of several hundred.

The sheer amount of dramatic activity in Java and the venerable role of drama there suggest that drama has something significant to do with the lives of Javanese.

This book explores that relationship in terms of one type of drama, ludruk. I view ludruk as a "rite of modernization." Two themes run through this notion. One is that ludruk is a *rite,* a sym-

---

[3] Speaking of a sequence of wajang kulit stories called *Bharata Juda,* Mantle Hood writes, "The deep emotional effect of this series of stories on the Javanese people is indicative of the vital significance of this literature in their lives. Among the many refinements of Javanese society is the ideal of concealing the emotions — it is sometimes said that there is a Javanese smile for every emotion, and it is considered bad manners to speak or laugh too loudly. The deep impact of the tragedies of the Bharata Juda, therefore, is apparent when during the course of these performances unabashed tears streak the faces of the audience." ("Music and Theater in Java and Bali," p. 445.)

[4] Brandon, *Theatre,* p. 193.

[5] *Ibid.*

[6] I arrived at this estimate by observing that in areas of Surabaja that I frequented almost every kampung staged ludruk plays on eves of holidays, such as Independence Day. Therefore, by using a map of Surabaja, I roughly counted the number of kampungs in the city — about two thousand — and conservatively estimated that a sixth of these kampungs staged ludruk on eves of major holidays.

bolic action. The other is that this symbolic action has certain social consequences — it encourages the modernization of Javanese society. I now open discussion of the two themes, outlining, on the one hand, the types of symbolic action involved in ludruk and, on the other, the functions each of these actions serves for Javanese modernization.

LUDRUK PLAYS AS RITES OF MODERNIZATION

I have entitled this study "Rites of Modernization" as a parallel to van Gennep's phrase "Rites of Passage" [7] to underline a similarity between my approach and van Gennep's. Van Gennep was interested in the way rites such as circumcisions, weddings, and funerals enable society to symbolically define persons' movements from one situation to another — from boyhood to manhood, celibacy to matrimony, life to death. I am interested in the way ludruk helps persons symbolically define their movements from one type of situation to another — from traditional to modern situations.

These movements from traditional to modern situations are of several forms. Some occur daily, as when a man leaves a locale ruled by traditional norms (a village) to enter a locale following more modern custom (a factory), then returns to his village at sundown and rises the next morning to go back to the factory. Some occur once in a lifetime, as when a village youth leaves home for good to seek his fortune in town. Some are movements in physical space, like those just mentioned. Others can be thought of as movements from one pattern of thinking to another. Ludruk plays concern themselves with all of these types of movements, aiding, I shall argue, those who are engaged in such movements to make sense out of them and to identify with them. This, ludruk does in three ways: first, it helps ludruk participants (when I use this term, I mean spectators as well as actors) to apprehend modernization movements in terms of vivid and meaningful *symbolic classifications;* second, it seduces ludruk participants into empathy with modes of *social action* involved in the modernization process; third, it involves the participants in aesthetic *forms* that structure their most general thoughts and feelings in ways stimulating to the modernization process.

[7] Arnold van Gennep, *The Rites of Passage.*

I shall now sketch briefly the way ludruk performs each of these functions.

Ludruk Play as Symbolic Classification

"Symbolic Classification" is a term drawn from Needham [8] (who in turn draws on the work of Durkheim and Mauss); [9] I use it to refer to a set of categories, each designated by a native word, into which the natives classify qualities of behavior or thought as well as social groups, natural objects, geographical regions, or other elements which symbolize qualities of behavior or thought.

Javanese proletarians of the city Surabaja, who are the main ludruk participants, think in terms of two schemes of symbolic classification, which, although not the only schemes important to them, seem to be the most exhaustive ones they have. The first scheme might be called a cosmology. It turns on an apparently ancient distinction, expressed in Javanese art and religion, between *alus* (refined) and *kasar* (crude) qualities of behavior and thought.[10] The other scheme could be called an ideology. It is based on a modern distinction, important in Indonesian social and political thought, between *madju* (progressive) and *kuna* (conservative) attitudes toward modernization.

The term "alus" and "kasar" are used by Surabaja proletarians to contrast: castles with villages; a chignon that is smooth, simple, and pliable with one that is stiff and over-decorated with flowers and pins; gods, kings, and aristocrats with peasants and urban proletarians; humans with animals; high Javanese language with low Javanese language; classical puppet plays (wajang kulit) with folkplays such as ludruk; classical Javanese poetry or music with obscene rhymes and songs; *batik* fabric with cheap cloth; a slender physique with a bulbous nose; Ardjuna, hero of puppet plays, with monsters in such plays; restraint in art or etiquette with unrestrained expression of impulses; crooned, measured speech with raucous singsong speech; Central Javanese people and culture with East Javanese people and culture; Javanese people

---

[8] Rodney Needham, *Structure and Sentiment: A Test Case in Social Anthropology,* p. 95.

[9] Emile Durkheim and Marcel Mauss, *Primitive Classification.*

[10] I believe Clifford Geertz in *The Religion of Java,* pp. 232–351, first expressed how deeply and broadly this alus-kasar contrast structures Javanese life and thought.

and culture with Madurese people and culture; feelings of shame with lustful feelings; and so on.

Madju is opposed to kuna to contrast: visible underarms with underarms kept out of sight; hair hanging free with hair in a bun; use of Indonesian language with use of Javanese or other provincial language; playing volley ball with gambling on pigeon races; wearing tight slacks, skirts, and lipstick with wearing sarong and jacket; employing medically trained midwives with employing animistic midwives; feminists with gentle wives of yore; movies with puppet plays; choosing one's own spouse with status-based, parent-arranged marriage; neighborhood cleanups and communal feasts on national holidays with neighborhood purification rites and communal feasts on non-national holidays; being educated with being illiterate; youths with elders; raising children less permissively with raising them more permissively; and so forth. Like the alus-kasar scheme, the madju-kuna system serves to classify a wide range of aspects of Surabaja life; the basic distinction is between objects or actions that symbolize a progressive stance toward modernization and objects or actions that symbolize a conservative attitude.

Ludruk gives expression — in puns, songs, stories, speeches, and dances — to both alus-kasar and madju-kuna symbolism. But, as we shall see, madju-kuna symbolic oppositions are replacing alus-kasar ones in ludruk performances. I shall argue that this is because alus-kasar cosmology served to make sense out of a traditional society that is no more, while madju-kuna ideology imbues the process of modernization with meaning and legitimacy.

Ludruk Play as Conception of Social Action

Not only does each ludruk play present a set of symbols in terms of which actors ·and spectators categorize their experiences, but each play also portrays social action with which spectators and actors can empathize. That is to say, each play draws participants into identifying with actors who are employing means to move toward goals.[11] What is the import of such experiences? To put it melodramatically, in the idiom of the medium with which we are dealing, ludruk invites one to "Fight with a Siegfried! Cheat with a Shylock! Succeed with a Pip! and Love the wild Nana!" Ludruk invites its participants to identify with ludruk characters and

---

[11] My definition of "action" or "social action" parallels that set forth by Talcott Parsons, *The Structure of Social Action*, pp. 44–45, and Kenneth Burke, *A Grammar of Motives*, pp. xvii–xxv.

thus vicariously exercise heroic means ordinarily kept packed away, employ ruthless commercial means traditionally unacceptable, achieve social goals when real-life conditions make it difficult to do so, and enjoy erotic situations not ordinarily at hand. It will be argued that in this way the participants develop a proclivity to favor certain roles, situations, goals, or means on occasions when daily life offers a chance to choose which role one will play, which situation one will enter, and so on. I will also demonstrate that the choices of roles, situations, goals, and means which ludruk promotes are increasingly of a type congruent with the modernization process.

Ludruk Play as Form

How does a ludruk performance lead its participants from beginning to end? By suspense? (Is the spectator led to ask, "Whodunit?" and watch until the end to find out?) Does the literary imagery carry participants along by projecting a mood of going somewhere? Is there much imagery of maturing, traveling, climbing, running, flying? Is somebody killed? (As Kenneth Burke points out, killing somebody is a good way to signal movement from an old to a new phase of a story.) [12] Is the movement cyclical or innovative? (By cyclical, I mean a movement that returns at the end to where it began: a story that began by exhibiting family A ends by exhibiting family A. By innovative, I mean a movement that stops when it has created something that did not exist when it began). How continuous is the movement? Is it disjointed? (Ludruk tends to be disjointed in its climax structure because its narrative climax is so frequently interrupted by jokes — microclimaxes.)

These are questions about ludruk form. By answering them, we arrive at some notion of the formal structure of the plays. But what does that formal structure mean to the participants? Can we make leaps like those McLuhan dares when he concludes that the formal structure of the printed page encourages uniformity, continuity, lineality of thought and action (as well as nationalism) while movies encourage men to think configurationally rather than lineally? [13] I shall argue that ludruk is increasingly drawing its participants into vicariously joining compact, innovative, linear, con-

[12] Kenneth Burke, *The Philosophy of Literary Form*, p. 235.
[13] Marshall McLuhan, *Understanding Media: The Extensions of Man*, pp. 14, 170–178, 325.

tinuous, formal movements that build to climaxes and resolve with successful achievement of a goal; while cyclical, disjointed, non-achieving formal structures are declining in popularity. There is some cause to think that the newer type of form encourages emotional dispositions which facilitate the modernization process.

After a glimpse of the book's first theme, that ludruk performances can be analyzed as symbolic actions (which present certain symbolic classifications, conceptions of social action, and forms), and its second theme, that these symbolic actions encourage Javanese modernization, it is now necessary to say a word about the way these two themes will be displayed as the book proceeds.

Imagine a picaresque ludruk audience composed of social scientists, each of whom suffers from a particular deformity which prevents his perception of all but a single aspect of the ludruk show. There is Mole-face, who can only hear the words. There is Leech, whose sharp but narrow frontal organs are honed to suck from the show its content, while disregarding its form. And there is a covey of creatures whose sensory capacities are numbed in all respects owing to a variety of infections, such as catarrh. These creatures pay no attention to the show at all. Instead, they scurry about before the show begins and after it ends, distributing questionnaires which, when analyzed by means of calculating mechanisms (apparently encased in the creatures' abdomens), reveal that audience opinions have changed as a result of being exposed to the show.

This image is intended to dramatize and malign an approach often used by social scientists, that of restricting one's attention and analysis to a single aspect of a symbolic performance: either its texts or verbal utterances, or its content (such as the social situations it portrays), or its "effects" on a measure of audience attitude. My view, which I shall present in some detail in the final chapter, is that any of these restricted approaches to analyzing symbolic performances results in a distorted conception of the social role of such performances. To avoid such restriction and distortion, and to understand ludruk as symbolic action, I attempt to confront ludruk performances as totalities, consisting of onstage happenings, accompanied by offstage orchestras, responded to by spectators, occurring inside theaters. From the eighty-two ludruk shows which I attended, I abstract patterns. These patterns take account of a wide range of aspects of the shows. They reveal, for instance, that dances appear between scenes of melodrama, audience concentration is fragmented, clowns always wear humble clothes while clothes of transvestites are refined, the drum leads the orchestra, fate is the agency leading to stories' outcome in certain melodramas, the music shows a pitch progression as the performance progresses, heroines of certain stories are always proletarian, and so on. I try to set forth the basic patterns which all ludruk performances follow and the variant patterns which specific types of ludruk performances follow. I try to lay bare the essential nature of the ludruk experience.

The book moves toward perception of ludruk as performance. Following the Introduction, "The Setting" introduces the reader to Surabaja, to the social situation of those who act in and watch ludruk, to the theaters, troupes, religious-artistic traditions, and political forces involved in ludruk, to ludruk's general character. As its name implies, this section is intended as a prelude or background to the main event, and the reader might pay it less attention than the section which follows — "The Show." In this section, I analyze ludruk as a performance. Each of the main acts of ludruk is taken up in turn: the comic prologue, the melodrama, and the songs. Each of these is analyzed as "symbolic action." The concluding chapter defines this term, presents some generalizations about ludruk as symbolic action, and proposes some general points for anthropologists and others to consider, thus completing the presentation of the first theme — ludruk as symbolic action.

The second theme, expanded in the section entitled "The Show," is that ludruk performances encourage the modernization of Javanese society. Interspersed among chapters on prologue, melodrama, and songs are analyses of social trends among ludruk participants: declining neighborhood solidarity and ritual, declining emphasis on refined etiquette, rising social mobility, increasing importance of youth organizations and symbolism, growing interest in romantic marriage, and so forth. I argue that ludruk encourages these trends by aiding its participants to feel at home with them, to get excited about them, to make sense out of them, and, perhaps most importantly, to appreciate by devious psychological processes their children's efforts to join them. Furthermore, I argue that, in terms of most general theories of social modernization, such as that of Marion J. Levy, Jr.,[14] these trends are in the direction of modernization. Thus, ludruk encourages modernization. This argument reaches its culmination in the next-to-last chapter, "Ludruk as a Rite of Modernization," and is carried further by the synthesis of the last chapter.

[14] See *Modernization and the Structure of Societies: A Setting for International Affairs.*

Part 2

The Setting

2

Social Background

Surabaja, a port city, a sailor's town, scene of some of Joseph Conrad's novels, and symbol of Lotte Lenya's famous song, "Surabaja Johnny," is also Indonesia's most industrial and second largest city, having a population of over one million. The sea traveler, sailing between the island of Madura and Java's northeast coast, 150 miles west of Bali, glimpses Surabaja's harbor, ringed with customs offices, import-export firms, and navy buildings, populated with sailboats from Celebes, freighters from Russia, ferry boats, navy vessels, and outrigger canoes. The explorer who penetrates inland and south of the harbor toward the interior of Surabaja discovers industrial-commercial areas, noisy and bustling, composed of Chinese, European, and Indonesian firms, factories, and banks, tiny stores and stands, old-fashioned, dingy department stores from the Dutch era flanked by luxury stores selling jewelry, radios, fabrics, and cameras, and market complexes, the largest, Pabean, being housed in a building the size of an airplane hangar, with stalls selling everything from fruits and vegetables to torn copies of Russian, American, and Red Chinese magazines, and comic books starring puppet play heroes. Surabaja's beggars (of whom it was recently estimated there are 75,000) [1] loll on the sidewalks. On the streets flocks of pedicabs and bicycles pedal along, trolleys rattle past with hordes hanging to their sides, and navy busses flash by at forty miles per hour. The mobs who move about the stores, streets, and sidewalks are mainly Javanese, but also Chinese, Madurese, Indian, Arab, German, English, American, Russian, Balinese, Buginese, Ambonese, Sudanese, and Sumatran — and one may even meet a stranded Filipino or Dutchman.

Surabaja is the capital of the Province of East Java. The Governor's Mansion is on *Djalan Pemuda* (Youth Street) next to *Balai Pemuda* (Youth Hall), where plays, receptions, conferences, and high school graduation ceremonies are held. North of Youth Street, toward the business area, is an open square with a slender obelisk at its center, the Hero's Monument; beside that are the offices of the East Javanese provincial bureaucracy. Not far from the square is the Indonesian National Building, where nationalist and Communist groups have met since Dutch Colonial times; Surabaja was, in 1963, a major stronghold of the Indonesian Communist party and its city government was predominantly Communist. The main city offices of Surabaja are in a quiet residential area. There are some central government offices on the airport road, in North Surabaja, down which President Sukarno, a resident of Surabaja in his youth, parades whenever he returns. In south Surabaja are a complex of streets named for national heroes — Tjokroaminoto, W. R. Supratman, Dr. Sutomo, Diponegoro, and Mother Kartini. The convergence of this network near a market called Wono Kromo is the office of the Regional Inspectorate of Culture Representing the East Java Ministry of Education and Culture, which is across the street from the city zoo.

Surabaja's largest university, Airlangga, and largest hospital, Karamindjangan, are in an eastern part of the town, in an almost rural area of fields and dirt roads. Everywhere are elementary, secondary, and technical schools — Islamic, Chinese, government,

---

[1] "Of Rice and Rats," *Time*, p. 40. Like everything else in *Time*, this figure should be taken with a grain of salt.

or Christian (where many of the elite send their children). There
are also schools for puppet play narrators and classical Javanese
dancers, and there are two or three teachers of Western music,
such as a half-Dutch pianist and a Hungarian violinist, who has
lived in Indonesia since Dutch times. About a dozen newspapers are
printed in Surabaja, many housed together, in spite of their rad-
ically divergent political views, in a row of buildings near the
Hero's Monument. There are perhaps twenty bookstores and a
few publishing firms in Surabaja. There are several large theaters
at which one can see classical Javanese dance-drama and a number of movie houses, the most expensive ones featuring Western
films, the cheaper ones showing Indonesian or Indian films. Mosques
are found all over Surabaja, but are concentrated near a commercial area where many orthodox Muslim traders live. Churches
are mainly in the residential areas.

There are elite residential neighborhoods in several areas of
Surabaja, perhaps the most prominent being not far from the
Governor's Mansion, along Panglima Sudirman street and its tribu-
taries. This is downtown, so the elite houses are mixed in with
stores, traffic, hotels, restaurants, and even flimsy coffee stands.
The elite houses are typically one story with a broad front porch,
small front lawn, and a backyard walled in, with barbed wire
along the top of the wall. Inside are smooth tile floors, Chinese
vases, and heavy Dutch-style furniture. In these houses live the
Indonesian and Chinese doctors, professors, school administrators,
lawyers, businessmen, engineers, and high civil servants, who comprise Surabaja's elite. Some elite are given their status partly by
inheritance: they can trace their ancestors back to a king who
lived during the time of Java's ancient empires, in which case they
have the right to put titles (such as R.A. or R.M.) before their
names, signifying that they are *prijaji* (aristocrats). The elite's
status is also achieved by education, wealth, political success,
and command of style of life partly patterned after the alus central Javanese courts of Djokjakarta and Surakarta and partly modeled on modern quasi-Western ideals. Having a title is not enough
to keep a man living in an elite neighborhood; there are titled, but
poor, prijaji, who live in shantytowns. Perhaps Surabaja, being a
commercial, industrial, and political center, places less emphasis on
title and culture and more on economic and political success than
do the court cities, such as Djokja and Solo, which Javanese say are
alus in character by contrast with Surabaja's kasar but madju
temper.

On the border areas of Surabaja near Chinese, Islamic, and Christian graveyards and within hollowed-out areas that grow inside downtown city blocks like cavities in teeth, are *kampung*.[2] Kampung are linked to one another by a tortuous and extensive network of walkways which criss-cross the streets and carry no traffic but foot. Kampung look much like rural Javanese villages — clusters of bamboo huts and small cement houses. But they are never surrounded by fields as are these villages, although on the outskirts of Surabaja, kampung are often bordered on one side by fields. Each kampung forms a kind of village within the city. Each has a name, a headman, some collective ceremonies, and mutual cooperation of various types among its inhabitants. Kampung dwellers are known as *wong kampung* or *orang kampung* (kampung people) and are distinguished from the prijaji (aristocrats), among whom are found the residents of elite neighborhoods. Kampung dwellers comprise most of Surabaja's proletariat — its artisans, construction laborers, road sweepers, petty traders, and minor clerks. Kampung people are often called, and call themselves, the "little people" (*wong tjilik, orang ketjil*), "low people" (*orang rendah*), "the masses" (*rakjat*), or the "laboring class" (*kaum buruh*); they are a genuine proletariat in that they have class consciousness.[3]

Crosscutting the division of Surabajans into elite and proletariat [4] is a division between *abangan* and *santri*. Abangan do not seriously follow the rules of Islam, but santri religiously adhere to these rules. The abangan do not perform the prayer (*salat*) five times a day, do not fast in the month of Ramadan, have little

---

[2] I use "kampung" here in only one of its meanings — that is, as a low-class in contrast to a high-class city neighborhood. "Kampung" has other meanings, such as "rural village" or "neighborhood in a city" (meaning *any* neighborhood categorized by the municipal government as a "kampung," and ruled over by a headman — *lurah* or *ketua* R.K.). The meaning I employ is the one Surabaja proletarians most often gave to the word "kampung."

[3] I shall use the word "proletarian" throughout this book to refer to kampung-dwelling have-nots with class consciousness, even though these persons are not workers in a highly industrialized economy; they have some peasant as well as proletarian traits.

[4] One can also divide Surabajans into other groups, such as bourgeois (minor officials, middle-level traders, etc.) and beggars (who in some sense are sub-proletarian, and certainly are sub-kampung dwelling since they wander homeless or live in river-bank huts). But the categories "elite" and "proletarian" are the ones most relevant to my study of ludruk drama.

desire to make the pilgrimage to Mecca, and do not abstain from pork. The santri are rigidly committed to all these traditions.[5]

If we think of the Javanese of Surabaja as being divided vertically along an elite-proletariat axis and horizontally along a santri-abangan axis, we can define four main categories: elite santri, proletariat santri, elite abangan, and proletariat abangan.[6] In reality there is a tendency for santri to be of the merchant class (between proletarian and elite), while the abangan tend to be either elite or proletarian. There are many more proletarians than there are either middle or elite groups.

Ludruk participants, whether actors, directors, troupe managers, writers, or spectators, can be described as "Javanese abangan proletarians."

That most ludruk participants are Javanese is indicated by a number of facts, one being that most audience responses to ludruk are in Javanese language. Also, most of about a hundred ludruk participants whom I questioned said they were Javanese. But other ethnic groups do take part in ludruk. Madurese language plays (which will not form a large part of my study) attract many Madurese spectators and feature Madurese actors. A few Chinese attend ludruk and I know one Arab, two Chinese, one Chinese-Japanese, and one man allegedly of Israeli Jewish descent — all of whom act in ludruk.

Ludruk participants are mainly abangan partly because santri consider ludruk forbidden entertainment. Santri say ludruk's female impersonators violate strick rules of Islam by mixing male and female elements in public. "If ludruk is truly oriented toward progress, women will play women," santri say. I have also heard santri criticize ludruk "because ludruk laughs at everything and Islam is serious." I never met a habitual ludruk goer who was santri. Going to the mosque and going to ludruk are mutually exclusive activities — apparently no individual does both regularly. There

[5] This paragraph is patterned after R. M. Koentjaraningrat, "The Javanese of South Central Java," pp. 89–91.

[6] C. Geertz in *Religion of Java* ascribes abangan religious orientation to proletarian-peasant social status. He calls the religious orientation which aristocrats (prijaji) adopt "prijaji." I think there is some empirical justification for this because it is my impression that, in fact, proletarians and peasants are more frequently called "abangan" than are aristocrats. Strictly speaking, however, abangan means simply "not a serious follower of Islam," and it may be linked to a person of any social rank — low or high. (I have heard titled aristocrats call themselves "abangan.")

were some ludruk actors who had been raised by santri parents, but these had rebelled against their santri upbringing — by becoming ludruk actors — and did not consider themselves santri at the time they acted in ludruk.

Not only occupation, residence, and education but also behavior and appearance reveal the proletarian nature of ludruk audiences and actors. From dress alone one can identify many of the ludruk spectators as proletarian. Pedicab drivers wear short pants, enlisted men wear a distinctive uniform, and male proletarians of many trades wear informal sarongs to ludruk, whereas Surabaja elite would not wear such apparel in public. The ludruk participants also exhibit more subtle traits of appearance and behavior that brand them "proletarian." Soetjito, a teacher who often went to *wajang wong,* a dance-drama attended by some aristocrats (*prijaji*) of Surabaja, said the following traits of ludruk spectators distinguish them from prijaji at the wajang wong:

> They have gold teeth, oily hair, and skin disease. Women wear lace too fancy or a sarong with too many pleats for such an informal occasion. Women have too many flowers in their bun. Some even wear a hairnet. Women's hairpins are too elaborate. Men and women go clack-clack with their wooden sandal heels when they walk. They laugh raucously at high pitch; they are the type who sit in the "goat class" [third class] at movies. These people sprawl with their legs stretched out or on somebody else's seat. They talk loudly so everybody can hear them. They scream conversations across rows of seats, for example, "*Lho ngéné* [Hey — sit here]!" "*Gak, Ngono* [No — over there]!" [These words are kasar Javanese.] They have lapses in grammar. Their accent, dialect, and usual level of speech are different from those of the prijaji. For instance, ludruk goers say to one another, "*Tjedak aku* [sit close to me.]." Prijaji wajang wong goers would say, "*Pinarak ngéné waé lho?*" [an alus way of saying, "Sit close to me."]

Though Soetjito is a bit of a snob, his description of the ludruk goers is not very wide of the mark.

By various means [7] I determined the occupation of about two hundred ludruk spectators and actors (most actors work at other jobs in addition to playing ludruk). I never found a ludruk actor

[7] For example, by conversing with spectators sitting around me at ludruk performances, I often learned where they lived and what their jobs were. By the time I had been to 82 performances, a fairly large sample of spectators had been questioned in this way. Also, I asked audience-response recorders (described in Appendix C) to record any fragments of spectators' conversations which revealed their occupation or residence. That procedure resulted in about a hundred record-

or habitual ludruk goer who had a job which put him in the elite strata, though a few were on the border line of the trader "middle" class. Ludruk actors and spectators work at jobs like the following: seller of snacks in the marketplace or on the streets, pedicab driver, prostitute, servant, cook in a private household, cook in a hospital, worker at a Chinese-owned factory, worker at foreign, national, or small Javanese-owned factory, enlisted man, worker at menial job at Surabaja naval base, thief, carpenter, bricklayer, messenger boy, minor clerk in a bank, owner of a small concessions stand (*warung*), junior high school student, seller of cloth in the marketplace.

I never met a ludruk actor or regular ludruk goer who lived outside a kampung in an elite neighborhood, although one actor is now planning to move into such a neighborhood.

No ludruk actor (or director) has gone past junior high school (SMP), and most have not gone past the first three or four grades of elementary school (SR). The educational level of spectators roughly parallels that of actors.

It is the unanimous opinion of actors, theater managers, and laymen — proletarian or elite — that ludruk actors and audiences are "proletarian" (*rakjat, kaum buruh*, etc.). Thus, the objective indexes — occupation, residence, education, behavior, and appearance — that lead me to call ludruk participants "proletarian" are backed by opinions of the Surabaja public.

In concluding this discussion of the position of ludruk participants in Surabaja society, I must say something about the age of ludruk participants. A Surabaja kampung headman gave the following opinion:

> When boys are twelve to eighteen years old, they like *pentjak* [a sport mixing dance and judo]. When they are eighteen to twenty-two years old, they like movies. From age twenty-two until the time they have two children, people like ludruk. By the time they are forty or fifty and on a pension, they prefer wajang wong. After they are sixty, people like wajang kulit [the classical puppet play, which has religious meaning].

This statement reflects the Javanese liking for neat classifications (one moves from "play" to "religion" as one ages), but it also

---

ings such as "Ḍik ['younger sister' or 'wife'], later when I have paid the rent for my pedicab, let's watch ludruk some more", or "I'm going back to Krian [a small town] tomorrow to fetch my things to sell". The first utterance reveals that the speaker is a pedicab driver; the second speaker reveals himself to be a petty seller.

seems to mirror the ludruk audience's true composition. Most ludruk watchers and players do seem to be past twenty and not yet
fifty. They are at the family-raising age. Youths of twenty or less
often said they did not care much for ludruk because, in contrast to
movies, ludruk is old-fashioned (so by contrast to the ludruk
theaters, movie houses are filled with adolescents).

The ludruk participants, then, are proletarian abangan Javanese
parents.[8] What is the nature of this group's social life?

At appropriate places below I shall describe aspects of this
social life. But right away I must characterize two conditions which
underly all that the ludruk participants do, at ludruk and in life.
These conditions are economic and political; the people who take
part in ludruk are rather poor and they are, after a fashion,
Communists.

POVERTY

A striking feature of the kampung population is that few of its
adult males are unemployed. What Hindley says about Java as a
whole — that it lacks a large "socially disinherited unemployed
proletariat" [9] — seems to be true of the Javanese kampung population of Surabaja. The kampung dwellers are, however, under-
employed. The pattern in Surabaja, as elsewhere in Java,[10] is to
give many people slices of a job that could be reserved for one
person. Thus, at the package pickup counter in the post office, there
is one man to receive a claim slip from the customer, another to
stamp the slip, and a third to fetch the package from the shelf
and give it to the customer. A man working in an office will
arrange for a jobless friend or neighbor to be given a job in that
office even though persons already working there do not have
enough to do and spend time sitting around. It seems that an office
or factory can always make room for one more.

Wages paid to any one worker are low. I would estimate that
the average wage earning kampung dweller makes between four
hundred and one thousand five hundred rupiah per month in 1963,
when 1,250 rupiah on the black market or 45 rupiah on the
official market equal one United States dollar. The cost of living in

[8] These are both fathers and mothers; the ludruk audience is about equally
composed of men and women, though the actors are all men.

[9] Donald Hindley, *The Communist Party of Indonesia 1951–1963*, p. 17.

[10] *Ibid.* See also Everett D. Hawkins, "Labor in Transition," p. 255, and Clifford
Geertz, *The Development of the Javanese Economy; A Socio-Cultural Approach.*

Indonesia has increased much faster than wages have. The wage to cost ratio for Indonesia as a whole tripled between 1938 and 1954.[11] From January, 1961 to February, 1963, the price index of nineteen consumer goods in the capital of Indonesia rose 600 percent, while from January, 1961 into 1963, government workers received no wage increase.[12] Between September, 1962 and September, 1963, Surabaja prices of rice and sugar tripled, but wages did not increase to match. The wage to cost discrepancy is offset by government offices and large firms paying their workers partly in rice and sugar; each worker gets a set amount of rice and sugar for himself and a smaller amount for his wife and each preteenage child. Also, rice and sugar are sold by the city at cheaper than open market rates to kampung dwellers, but they complain that they rarely get their full ration.

Kampung dwellers do not eat much meat (it is said that the protein consumption of Indonesians is one of the lowest in the world).[13] They mainly eat rice, supplemented by cassava, sweet potatoes, bananas, mangoes, *témpé* (soy bean cake fried in coconut oil, called "kampung meat"), *sambal* (spicy sauce), heavily sweetened coffee, and small amounts of fish, meat, and eggs. Generally, kampungers seem healthy and active; the women, especially, work incredibly hard and vigorously. Kampung dwellers sleep less than Americans do; they are up at daybreak and stay up until midnight on weeknights or all night at week end celebrations. I did not notice any unusual degree of sickness, although I knew some kampung dwellers who had malaria, tuberculosis, and skin and venereal diseases.

Kampung houses are either cement or a bamboo frame with palm roof and plaited bamboo walls. The largest houses are not much bigger than American motel cottages and are packed very close together, the side of each house about five feet from the side of its neighbor. Except in a few kampung on the outskirts of town, there are almost no backyards. The small frontyard, covered with smoothed dirt (as in many lower-class negro or white neighborhoods in small towns of the American South) rather than grass, is separated from the frontyard of the house facing it by a walkway about five feet wide, unless an open sewer faces it.

Some houses in most kampung have electricity, but none seem to have running water. Although the cement houses usually have an

[11] Stephen W. Reed (ed.), *Indonesia,* 3:893.
[12] Hindley, *Communist Party,* p. 281.
[13] Reed, *Indonesia,* 2:453.

open well, which provides a partial supply of water during the rainy season, all kampung dwellers have to haul water from a central source. There are open sewers. Cement houses have a bathroom furnished with a hole in the floor through which to excrete and, for bathing, a tank full of water which one splashes over oneself by means of a tin cup (Javanese bathe twice a day in this fashion; their bodies and clothes are kept very clean). Windows have no screens, and if they have shutters, these are closed at night. Inside the houses rattan chairs or benches are often infested with lice, which, Javanese say, appeared at the time of the Japanese occupation.

Kampung dwellers enjoy no social security or life insurance and have no savings accounts. Their favorite way of saving is to buy and keep gold objects (such as gold teeth); kampung dwellers do not use banks, which is probably wise in light of Indonesia's inflation of recent years. Some companies and government offices offer pensions after about twenty-five years of service, but these are rarely adequate to support the pensioner. Many families help support aged parents.

COMMUNISM [14]

When Indonesia gained its independence from Holland in December, 1949, it was organized as a federation of states, which by August, 1950, had been transformed into the Republic of Indonesia, organized as a constitutional democracy. The first six years of the Republic were years of a relatively free press, courts fairly autonomous of the government, cabinets accountable to a parliament, and, at first, some economic prosperity. But these were also years of successive cabinet crises, attempted coups, civil war between the central government and outer islands, and bitter competition among political parties, which were split into two blocs — a rather anti-Western bloc, popular among aristocratic and proletarian Javanese and composed of the Communist party (PKI), the Nationalist party, (PNI) and the conservative Muslim party (NU); and a pro-Western bloc, popular among santri entrepreneurs on islands outside Java and composed of the progressive Muslim party (Masjumi), the small Socialist party (PSI), and the small Christian parties.

[14] This section is a synthesis of my own observations and an excellent essay by Herbert Feith, "Dynamics of Guided Democracy," pp. 309–409. Some materials from Hindley, *Communist Party,* pp. 274–304, are also included.

In 1956, amid increasing criticism of parties and cabinets, nationalistic President Sukarno (who, since 1950, had progressively gained power as "rational" and "democratic," hence humdrum Vice-President Hatta had lost it) urged that Indonesia "dream away the existence of so many parties" and replace constitutional democracy with "Guided Democracy." During the next five years, Sukarno and his partner in power, the army, led by Chief of Staff Nasution, proceeded to make that replacement.

The army undertook a great number of "guiding" actions — banning Communist political meetings, labor union activities, and activities of parties opposing Sukarno, such as PSI and Masjumi.

Sukarno dissolved the Constituent Assembly, the elected parliament, the cabinet responsible to parliament — agencies that restrained his power — and instituted a 616-member, seldom-meeting People's Consultative Assembly, a parliament appointed by him, and a cabinet responsible to him. Sukarno also created the bodies to run the Guided Democracy — a 75-member National Planning Council; a 45-member Supreme Advisory Council; and a national front organization enrolling two hundred political parties, mass organizations, and functional groups, and encompassing, by 1962, a membership of thirty-three million.

Manipol-USDEK, a term coined by Sukarno, was the symbol to legitimize and sacralize the new political structure. Manipol-USDEK stands for an exalted goal: to attain, in Sukarno's phrases, the "Just and Prosperous" society organized around "Guided Democracy," "Socialism a' la Indonesia," and the "Revolutionary Constitution of '45," financed by "Guided [centralized] Economy," and in keeping with "The Indonesian Personality." Manipol-USDEK was taught in the schools, preached by the newspapers, and propagated by song and dance, billboards, kampung gates, and printed slogans sandwiched between movies' commercial advertisements. It set the tone for the "spiritual revolution" that Sukarno vowed to bring to pass.

What has been the fate of PKI, the party of the ludruk participant, under Guided Democracy? PKI in 1963, was the largest Communist party outside the Sino-Soviet bloc (with two million members in the party and twelve million in its mass organizations).[15] Yet, by 1963, PKI, like other Indonesian political parties, has been reduced by Sukarno and the army to being a cog of Guided Democracy. Sukarno affords PKI some protection against

---

[15] Hindley, *Communist Party,* p. 285.

army bans. In return, PKI supports Sukarno by drumming up crowds for him to address, crying about the countryside, "Support Bung Karno's Concept [of Guided Democracy] 100%!", strewing quotes from Sukarno among its announcements of programs and policies, ordering and implementing such actions as Sukarno's "New Life Movement," and backing the national front. PKI (publicly) subordinates class-struggle goals to its role in Guided Democracy.

Although PKI's membership was apparently growing during 1962–63, I was struck by the number of kampung dwellers who said that they had formerly been active in PKI or some affiliate organization such as Pemuda Rakjat but had become disillusioned and quit. Of course, my nationality might have encouraged them to make such statements. At any rate, a pedicab driver exemplifies the attitude such PKI dropouts expressed:

> When I lived in Kampung Dinaja in 1954, 75 per cent of the kumpung were PKI. I was active in PKI. Many workers were being "punished" by the government and PKI was the one organization strong among workers. Bung Tomo (Sutomo) was very popular among labor, only that his mouth expressed nonsense. . . . He was a big shot.
>
> When there was to be a PKI meeting in the kampung, the leader would put up posters, but the meeting would be by invitation. The leader would talk about how the "little people" could enjoy better lives. He would give examples of the way it was in Moscow — a foreman and a coolie were the same. Here (in Java) a foreman got 6 rupiah, a coolie 0.8 rupiah. Then members of PKI would confront kampung people at the meeting. "Who do you follow?" "The national government [at that time Masjumi-dominated]." "How's your rice?" "Not enough." "All right then."
>
> In 1952–53, I was working as a laborer at the docks. SOBSI [PKI-linked labor union] had a school, which I and some other laborers a bit cleverer than the ordinary attended. Every night there were meetings and classes. But there were no results. Now most of the teachers are non-active too. They feel pessimistic.
>
> I don't believe in the PKI now. The only person I believe in is the President, to whom I am as child to father. Nowadays people working at a factory make 40 to 60 rupiah per day. How can anybody live on that? None of the laborers care about a leader's politics anymore. We just want a leader who can straighten out the economy and bring rice to us. We believe only in the President.

In spite of such evidences of proletarian disaffection with the PKI, that party is still involved with many practical aspects of the kampung dweller's social life. The PKI-affiliated organizations that

I have heard most about in this connection are RKKS, *Pemuda Rakjat,* and SOBSI.[16]

RKKS (Surabaja City Kampung Association) is virtually an extension of the municipal government of Surabaja, which is PKI-dominated (by 1960, PKI members or sympathizers controlled twenty-six of twenty-seven *lingkungan* [district] offices in Surabaja).[17] RKKS also has direct ties with PKI's central organization. My impression is that many kampung headmen, in addition to being in RKKS, are also active members of PKI (the R.K. [headman] of the kampung in which I lived was active in PKI, and I heard after I left that kampung that he was given a PKI-sponsored trip to Red China). RKKS serves as a bridge between PKI and kampung by helping to draw the more enthusiastic kampung dwellers into PKI.

Pemuda Rakjat (People's Youth), the only mass organization having formal ties with PKI and receiving open assistance from them, works closely with the kampung officials. Kampung youth who are members of Pemuda Rakjat join with the R. K. in organizing the night watch, clean-ups, and celebrations.

The central leadership of SOBSI (All-Indonesian Central Labor Organization) is part of the PKI leadership and it is said that in 1963 virtually all leaders of SOBSI's cadres and unions are members of PKI or have been subjected to PKI schools and courses. Kampung dwellers who work in factories or similar enterprises consult directly with SOBSI officials when they need someone to negotiate on their behalf with management. Kampung dwellers also attend shows and meetings sponsored by SOBSI. Such meetings (one will be described in chapter 4) contain speeches, songs by child choirs, and ludruk shows with Marxist themes.

LOWER-CLASS, SEMILITERATE COMMUNISTS AND LUDRUK

Ludruk is affected by the social, economic, and educational level of both the spectators and the actors, as well as by their Communist loyalties. I shall not belabor this point, but will note here some of the most obvious effects so that the reader can be cognizant of these as he reads on.

Tickets to ludruk are cheap, theaters and costumes are in sorry condition, and actors are poorly paid. Partly because of this actors

[16] The following paragraphs combine my own observations with materials from Hindley, *Communist Party,* pp. 119–230.

[17] Hindley, *Communist Party,* p. 159.

drift in and out of the profession. Because of the fast turnover of personnel, ludruk troupes are not stable; the typical troupe is slapped together quickly, then disbanded after a few months.

The poverty of ludruk's participants is reflected in ludruk's content. Clowns sing about poverty. Down-and-out characters are sympathetically portrayed. Stories starring lowly characters who finally achieve wealth and happiness are popular. Doubtless some of the fatalism, *weltschmerz,* and humor that pervades the ludruk show derives from the poverty and low social status of those who take part in the show. Because ludruk's participants are poor, but also because they are Communist and heir to certain traditions and psychological tendencies, the star of ludruk is a clown who portrays an archetypal proletarian. Some of the fragmented qualities of ludruk acting and of the spectators' mental state during a show (this will be discussed later) may stem partly from disease and malnutrition owing to poverty, as well as from the condition that, since ludruk pays poorly, ludruk actors must work at other jobs all day, so they never have time to rehearse.

The Marxist warp of some ludruk content is partly explained by the fact that ludruk actors and spectators are all more or less involved with Communist organizations and have been exposed to Communist ideas. Some ludruk troupes are affiliated with Communist organizations, but, as we shall see, ludruk is no pure Marxist trumpet. Partly because of its Communist leanings, ludruk often satirizes animistic beliefs which, partly because of their low level of schooling, ludruk participants hold.

In general, because of the social and material situation of its actors and clientele, ludruk is a rather shabby and garish spectacle. Whores, gamblers, drunks, and thieves crowd into the audience. Beggars lie on the grounds outside the auditorium. Ushers are barefoot and shabby. The show itself is wildly comical and often gross, featuring such personages as aging transvestites and harelipped clowns.

CHAPTER

3

Theaters and Animism

Some say that stage shows called *ludruk bandan* and *ludruk lyrok* existed as far back as Java's thirteenth-century Madjapahit empire,[1] but the first eyewitness account of a performance called ludruk that I have found was written in 1822.[2] The performance described in that account starred two men: a clown, who told funny stories, and a female impersonator.

The clown and female impersonator have remained dominant elements in ludruk to the present day, although other figures have been added as ludruk has evolved. At the beginning of the twen-

[1] L. Poerbokoesoemo, "Ludruk dari Segi Sedjarah serta Perkembangannja," p. 4. (The nature of the seminar, at which this paper was read, is briefly described in Appendix C.)

[2] Th. Pigeaud, *Javaanse Volksvertoningen,* p. 322.

tieth century, according to Indonesian scholars and recollections of some elderly informants, there was a form of ludruk called *Besut* which featured the clown Besut, who danced, sang, and joked, and a female impersonator, who danced. About 1920, ludruk Besut underwent several elaborations. The two players became three characters in a story. Besut acquired a wife, Asmunah, played by a female impersonator, and Asmunah's uncle, Djamino, was also brought into the story. Now the show was called ludruk Besutan.[3] Still later, a fourth character was added, Djuragan Tjekep, a man of wealth and standing in the kampung, who was a rival of Besut. After the debut of Tjekep, the play was called ludruk Besep.[4]

In the late twenties Tjak Gondo Durasim organized a ludruk troupe with unlimited personnel and began playing full-fledged drama with characters varying according to the story instead of retaining the same names and roles in all performances. A description of ludruk published in 1930 [5] reports that Durasim had just organized a "new type of ludruk," which performed before the nationalist study club, *Persatuan Bangsa Indonesia,* or "Indonesian Union" (such study clubs were important in the prewar Nationalist movement and, in fact, were where leaders such as Sukarno got their start). According to the report, Durasim was decorated by Dr. Soetomo, a pioneer in harnessing folk plays to nationalism, because "apparently ludruk is a useful means of making ideas penetrate to the masses." Retrospective accounts by Indonesian scholars say that Durasim, sponsored by Dr. Soetomo, performed at Surabaja's National Building until 1936;[6] at that time Durasim's ludruk was banned by the Dutch.

In 1942, the Japanese invaded Indonesia, overcame Dutch resistance, occupied Java for the rest of World War II, and used ludruk as a propaganda device to spread the idea of a "Greater East Asia Co-Prosperity Sphere." Durasim, performing under Japanese control, sang that "living under Japanese rule is like living in a birdcage." [7] For this, it is said, he was tortured by the Japanese and as a result died in 1944.

On August 17, 1945, following initial encouragement by the Japanese and finally their surrender to the allies, Sukarno declared

[3] Poerbokoesoemo, "Ludruk," p. 12.

[4] *Ibid.*

[5] R. Ahmad Wongsosewojo, "Loedroek."

[6] Comment by Soenarto during "Sidang Komisi D" (Session of Committee D). Seminar Ludruk, Balai Pemuda in Surabaja, December 25–28, 1960.

[7] J. Shamsudin, "Prasaran: Peranan Ludruk dalam Masjarakat," p. 5.

Indonesia independent of Dutch rule, thus creating the Republic of Indonesia. Weeks later British forces arrived on Java to take the Japanese surrender and evacuate prisoners of war; not long after that the Dutch began returning. So began the Indonesian Revolution against the Dutch, a series of negotiations and military battles which ended in December, 1949, with the Dutch transferring sovereignty to Indonesia. During much of the Revolution, Surabaja was occupied by Dutch forces while Javanese guerilla bands roamed the inland hills and mountains of Java. Several ludruk troupes traveled about entertaining the guerillas.

Some of the troupes were affiliated with particular political parties. These troups propagandized for their parties when they retrurned to Surabaja in 1950 after the guerillas began to disband. For example, since *Marhaen* (Rural Proletarian) had originated as part of the left-wing youth group, Pesindo (now Pemuda Rakjat), it pushed the Communist line, satirizing such figures as Sjahrir, the Western-oriented leader of the pro-Western PSI. Another troupe, Tresno Enggal (New Love), expressed the views of the Indonesian Nationalist Party (PNI), which was less revolutionary than the Communists and was supported by many civil servants. In the late fifties, with the advent of Sukarno's Guided Democracy and various Army bans on political party activities, it became illegal for ludruk troupes to explicitly express party views or to criticize political figures by name. By the time I arrived in Surabaja, in the fall of 1962, all ludruk troupes were espousing Sukarno's NASAKOM idea — that Indonesia should be a Guided Democracy ruled by a union of its three main factions, Nationalist, Islamist, and Communist — and I never heard any party line explicitly set forth or any political figure criticized by name.

During 1962–63, although many ludruk performances were at meetings sponsored by the Communists, the most frequent performances — and the ones upon which I shall focus — were by commercial troupes in Surabaja's commercial theaters.

LUDRUK THEATERS

Ludruk is performed all over East Java. There are local ludruk troupes as far east as Banjuwangi (on the tip of Java next to Bali) and as far west as Kediri (bordering the Central Javanese culture area). (The island of Madura, off Java's northeast coast, also has a drama called ludruk, but it differs from Javanese ludruk.) Ludruk's center is indisputably Surabaja. Surabaja has more and better ludruk troupes and theaters than any other city. The identity of ludruk with the city of Surabaja is symbolized by Surabaja's emblem, the fish and crocodile, which ludruk dancers often wear on their skirts and which is placed over the stage of the newest ludruk theater.

Surabaja ludruk performances were apparently all held in kampung until the late twenties when Durasim's troupe began playing downtown in the Indonesian National Building. In the early thirties some troupes also began to play on NIROM (Nederlands Indische Radio Omroop) Surabaja,[8] which broadcast ludruk performances weekly. In the forties, during the Japanese and Dutch occupations of Surabaja, commercial ludruk in Surabaja was restricted, but when Dutch forces left Surabaja in 1950, the commercial troupes came alive again. By 1951, they were playing at two commercial theaters, Wono Kromo and Pasar Sore. In the past decade three more commercial ludruk theaters have been built — PBRI, Banguredja, and the theater at the People's Amusement Park. Half-a-dozen troupes now rotate among these five commercial theaters. These troupes and others also play for kampung celebrations such as weddings or circumcisions, for rural village celebrations, political meetings, and they have begun broadcasting on the radio again; RRI (Radio of the Republic of Indonesia) Surabaja broadcasts ludruk performances on Saturday nights.

The five commercial theaters of Surabaja vary in size and construction from Banguredja, a huge shed with rattan walls, to the newest and best theater at the People's Amusement Park, which has cement walls and floor. Every commercial theater has a wooden stage, open to the audience only at the front and raised several feet from the floor upon which the audience's chairs are placed. Nobody but a performer is supposed to come onstage during a performance in commercial theaters; in contrast, at kampung shows where the stage is open at all sides children collect on the stage during the performance (see Plate 20). A *gamelan* (percussion orchestra) that accompanies ludruk shows is placed in the dressing area (backstage) at all theaters except in the People's Amusement Park, where the gamelan sits in an orchestra pit at the front of the stage, thus furnishing a new buffer between stage and audience. Children and adults constantly filter into the gamelan pit and lean over the edge during the performance. Sometimes friends of the gamelan players sit among them as they play, and they all drink palm wine together.

[8] Soemady, "Kesenian Ludruk dan Siaran Radio," p. 7.

Tickets are bought at the box office just before the show begins; they cannot be bought in advance. Prices range from ten rupiah (about twenty-five United States' cents at the official rate of exchange and less than a penny at the black market rate — a couple of hours pay for many ludruk goers) for fourth class seats to thirty-five rupiah for first class seats. This is much cheaper than the real price of tickets at the better Surabaja movies, since almost all such tickets must be bought from scalpers at prices up to 175 rupiah. Unlike at the movie houses, where highest priced seats are at the back of the theater, ludruk seats increase in price as one moves toward the front.

The theater at the People's Amusement Park is owned by the city. Others are owned by private businessmen. Every ludruk theater is in a market area and is therefore surrounded by stands selling snacks and trinkets, except for Banguredjo, which is in a red-light district. No theater is in a residential kampung, a fact which has great significance for ludruk performances, as we shall see.

The atmosphere in ludruk theaters is bawdy. Spectators eat during the show. Sometimes ludruk spectators eat a whole supper of rice or chicken curry with beer and coffee. Others content themselves with chewing *kwatji* nuts and drinking a sickening sweet soft drink called *limun*. Infants quench their thirst with mothers' milk. There are always a few children defecating or urinating on the floor during performances — suitable responses to ludruk. Foot-long rats run about eating refuse. Actors are greeted with whistles, raucous laughter, and screams of "Hoohoohoohoohoohoohoohoohoo-hoo!" Spectators express their disgust at a performer by muttering "fuck" (*djantjut*) or screaming derogatory remarks such as "Your voice is like shit [*taèk*]!" or just "Ludruk is like shit." Knife fights occur. Whores and pickpockets ply their respective trades. Hoodlums or hordes of raggedy children constantly sneak past the ticket-taker or through holes in the wall. One ludruk troupe printed blurbs advertising its performance as

SENSATIONAL! UPROARIOUS! HORRIFYING! AND RAMAI!

The last word meaning "noisy or crowded" sums up the general atmosphere of the ludruk theater. It is not an alus place. It is a kasar place, a bawdy, loose, hedonistic place where one can indulge sundry impulses of body and mouth. It seems symbolically fitting that in the People's Amusement Park, where all manner of Javanese entertainment is found, the ludruk theater is placed in a back corner, next to the toilets.

LUDRUK TROUPES

The main troupes which circulate among the commercial Surabaja theaters are *Tresno Enggal* (New Love), *Enggal Tresno* (Love Will Come Quickly), *Massa* (The Masses), *Sari Rukun* (Kernel of Co-operation), also *Irama Enggal* (New Rhythm), and Mari Katon (Noisily Watch). Occasionally a super-troupe, such as *Marhaen* (Rural Proletarian), which ordinarily plays at benefit performances for the political and cultural elite, appears at a commercial theater. Sometimes unaccomplished groups such as *Massa Rukun* (Coopera-tion of the Masses) or *Rukun Enggal* (New Cooperation) appear when better troupes are unavailable. Each troupe is all male, composed of about fifteen actors who play major character roles, four or five female impersonators who sing and dance between scenes, and half-a-dozen extras who play bit parts. All troupes are privately owned and managed with the partial exception of Tresno Enggal, which has a contract with the troop entertainment unit of the Brawidjawa army of East Java. When Tresno Enggal plays commercially, it is managed by its lead clown, Toebi. Every troupe has a manager (always of the working class), who arranges con-tracts with theater owners or other agents (troupes get a set fee for each performance, regardless of the box-office take). Unlike dramatic troupes elsewhere in Southeast Asia, which are owned by elite businessmen (or businesswomen), ludruk troupes are "owned" by proletarians. All pay is divided among a troupe's actors and manager (who in lesser troupes gets a huge share of the money).

In most troupes the manager directs every aspect of a perform-ance — moving scenery, telling actors when to go on and get off the stage, and deciding who will play what role.

The most highly organized troupes such as Tresno Enggal have a formal roster of officers. Tresno Enggal has several secretaries, in-cluding a "general secretary" who serves as manager, and a "sec-retary of finance" who keeps up with the troupe's funds, allocating some for equipment, some for transportation, some for members' pay, and so on. These secretaries make decisions among them-selves; but members can appeal decisions, and the whole troupe meets to decide some issues. Since Tresno Enggal is under contract to the army a certain lieutenant must be consulted on any impor-tant decision.

Actors in lesser troupes say they make only enough money (75–100 rupiah per performance) from playing ludruk to "buy ciga-rettes." Partly because of their low pay, partly because there are

frequent squabbles and scandals involving managers' financial tactics, actors are constantly quitting the profession or moving from
one troupe to another, and ludruk troupes frequently break up.
Only four of 1960's dozen best-known troupes still existed in
1962, and five of the seven major ludruk troupes of 1962 did not
exist in 1960. Almost none of 1950's famous troupes were performing in 1962. One manager of a lesser ludruk troupe said he
had known a manager who "encouraged homosexual liaisons
among members of his troupe in order to hold the troupe together;
at least such liaisons increased the chances that if you got one
actor to show for a performance, you would get his lover as well."
True or not, the remark suggests a certain instability among the
lesser troupes.

Given this tradition of instability, it is remarkable that Tresno
Enggal and Marhaen have each managed to develop fully professional, cohesive, stable troupes. Both Marhaen and Tresno Enggal
have had the same name and core personnel for over twenty
years, although splinters from the two troupes have formed other
groups — Warna Warni, Warna Sari, Djilmaan Massa, and Massa
from Marhaen, Enggal Tresno and Tresno Kangen from Tresno Enggal. Marhaen and Tresno Enggal have a gentleman's agreement
that neither will accept actors from the other group. Each has
established a small pension which it pays its aged actors. Each
pays its members enough so that they need not work at jobs other
than acting; the troupes are fully professional. Each has made
rules against homosexuality among its members. The two troupes
together are trying to form a ludruk association which will set up
rules (for instance, against plagiarism) guiding conduct among all
major ludruk troupes. Each troupe has a definite office locale: Marhaen's manager has a sign outside his home indicating that this is
Marhaen headquarters and Tresno Enggal has its "office" at a
downtown combination office and pool hall of the Brawidjawa
army. With Marhaen and Tresno Enggal, ludruk is becoming professional: ludruk acting is getting to be defined as a full-time
occupation carried on as part of a stable organization that is
guided by an explicit professional ethic.

ANIMISM

Ludruk Besut was involved in the *abangan*, Buddhist-Hindu-
animist ritual complex of which the *slametan* (a commensal rite)
is a part. Around the Besut stage were placed *sadjèn* (offerings

to spirits) which included precisely the same items (comb, tobacco, mirror, betel nut, and 18½ Dutch cents)[9] found in sadjèn at slametan and at puppet play (wajang kulit)[10] performances. Like the puppet play, which, like the slametan, is supposed to have the power to keep participants *slamet* [safe] from spirits while it is being performed, ludruk Besut played all night and was performed at weddings, circumcisions, and other passage ceremonies.

Besut wore a red Turkish cap, black short pants, a white sash (supposed to have some connection with the sadjèn), and was naked from the waist up. It is said that the colors red, white, and black had magical significance.[11] Besut began his performance by lighting torches placed at the four corners of the stage, an act supposed to have ritual significance.[12] Besut then took part in a rather curious story, involving symbols which may have had mystical as well as oedipal meanings.[13]

Present-day ludruk when it is performed inside kampung retains a few animistic elements. Like Besut and Wajang it is performed at passage ceremonies such as circumcisions or on occasions such as *sedekah bumi* (honoring the guardian spirit of a kampung). As with wajang, a slametan ritual is sometimes given in connection with the performance, yet I have never seen a slametan at commercial ludruk performances in downtown theaters. Actors say, "It just doesn't feel right to have a slametan in a commercial theater." Commercial ludruk performances rarely even depicted the slametan on the stage. The two times, out of eighty-two performances, that they did so, they made fun of it; reprobates in a comic skit burlesqued the slametan custom of saying "Amen," and clown-servants gobbled up slametan food in uncouth fashion as a zombie lumbered in from the side of the stage.

Examples of magic in kampung performances given by lesser ludruk troupes: an aged lead clown meditates (*tapa*) and fasts before going on stage in order to be clever at joking; rival troupes employ sorcerers to stiffen each other's dancers; to protect themselves, dancers go through motions such as blowing on their hands; to insure everyone's security, charms are placed backstage and offerings made to *danjang* (guardian spirits). All of this seems to reflect an idea that the stage is a magical place which can be made

---

[9] Wongsosewojo, "Loedroek," p. 204.
[10] Clifford Geertz, *Religion of Java,* p. 42.
[11] H. Hadiwidjojo, "Fungsi Seni Ludruk dari Zaman ke Zaman," p. 21.
[12] *Ibid.*
[13] Wongsosewojo, "Loedroek," pp. 205–07.

dangerous by magical forces or safe by ritual. None of this magic goes on in extra-kampung commercial ludruk, and some of the more madju troupes, Marhaen in particular, satirize animistic habits. Among kampung dwellers commercial ludruk enjoys a reputation as "a weapon for enlightening the masses by destroying their beliefs in magic."

THEATERS, TROUPES, ANIMISM, AND LUDRUK

Since commercial ludruk theaters are outside kampung, in centrally located commercial areas, people from different kampung come to the same theater. Therefore, many of the spectators are strangers to each other. They know that when they leave the theater, their fellow spectators will play little part in their daily affairs and will have little control over them. Furthermore, the commercial ludruk audience is no sect or political cell; there is no roll call or compulsion to stand up and be counted. The theater is dark and nobody knows who is there and who is not. Anyone can enter simply by buying a ticket and can leave when he wishes. In general, ludruk offers a good deal of anonymity and a free atmosphere.

Social freedom and anonymity is combined with high density — strangers' bodies are crowded together to a degree a Westerner would find oppressive. Prostitution and pocket-picking — bodily relations — abound in this place of social freedom. Crowded bodies and noise combined with social freedom create a Javanese variety of beer-hall *gemütlichkeit* called *ramé* that involves high spirits and humor — qualities which, as will become clear later, pervade the ludruk performances. Perhaps the high spirits encourage both the romantic fantasies and irreverent jokes of ludruk. The mob atmosphere probably encourages a herd-aggressiveness; as we shall see, ludruk mobs scream at scapegoats in a manner more violent than that customarily exhibited by the individual Javanese.

Commercial ludruk is relatively free of animistic elements that saturated Besut shows and are still present in kampung ludruk. Whereas Besut and present-day kampung ludruk treat the stage as a magical domain, commercial ludruk sees it as purely secular (which may relate to the fact that commercial ludruk uses physical devices to separate the stage from profane realms, whereas Besut and kampung ludruk, with ritual acts for separators, use fewer physical separators). That the commercial ludruk stage is not regarded as a magical place may encourage commercial players to feel less inhibition about varying stories, roles, and onstage arrangements than they would feel if they saw the stage as pervaded by some kind of magical atmosphere which would be set into turmoil if onstage actions varied from prescribed, traditional forms. Besut's stories were much more stereotyped or ritualized than today's stories are.

That ludruk is "secular" and commercial probably encourages its flexibility in another way. If ludruk were a rite whose audience would come, regardless of how entertaining the rite because of social and religious obligations, it might be less concerned about responding sensitively to audiences' changing tastes and interests than it is; but as a commercial show, ludruk's existence depends on its entertaining its audiences enough so that they continue to buy tickets.

Commercial ludruk acting is turning into a kind of profession. Today, largely due to Tresno Enggal's and Marhaen's example, ludruk acting is — while hardly a prestigious profession — something in which a man can legitimately specialize full time. That is, a man can legitimately specialize in acting — expressing, dreaming, idealizing, criticizing — while leaving practical work to other specialists. Being free of responsibility for applying one's ideals probably removes some of one's inhibitions about championing new ideals and breaking with old traditions.

In sum, various aspects of ludruk's immediate setting — its theaters, the organization of its troupes and status of its performers, its apartness from the kampung and from kampung animism — would seem to encourage the freewheeling, antitraditional attitudes which, as will become clear, are expressed during the ludruk show and passed on to the ludruk participants.

4

Politics and Art

Strictly speaking, I am concerned with the kinds of attitudes ludruk encourages, and with the way it promotes such attitudes, but not with influences on ludruk. Therefore, I need not treat such matters as central governmental control over ludruk or classical artistic influences on ludruk. Such matters are, strictly speaking, external to my argument.

It seems wise, however, to pay some attention to these "influences," partly to get a wider picture of the setting within which ludruk exists, but mainly to gain some notion of just how strong — or weak — the influences are. It is easy to see how such things as government controls or artistic traditions affect a dramatic performance; therefore, it is easy to overestimate their importance and to underestimate some of the more subtle factors. The brief survey that follows expresses my view that ludruk is no servile mouthpiece of government, compulsive plagiarist of the classics, or stereotyped rendition of hoary folk forms; it is a flexible response to its performers' and spectators' attitudes and situation.

POLITICAL INFLUENCES ON LUDRUK

Central Governmental Control

The Indonesian Ministry of Information (*Kementerian Penerangan*) does not have direct control over the commercial ludruk performances with which I am concerned. The Ministry has tried to indirectly influence such performances. About two years before my arrival in Surabaja in 1962, they sent an official around to the major troupes to give lectures on national policy and to hand the actors sheets on which were typed slogans such as "Support Pantjasila!" or "Build our Nation!" The actors were encouraged to work such slogans into their performances, to do patriotic stories, and to stage nationalist dances. Because funds were short, the Ministry cut its activities in 1960; officials apparently have not contacted ludruk troupes since about 1960. This means that many of the troupes playing at the time of my study had not had direct contact with the Ministry, since many of these troupes had been in existence for only a few months.

It is interesting to observe how government propaganda gets incorporated into the structure of ludruk performances. For example, clowns and female impersonators, who do most of the ludruk singing, had equal access to slogan sheets handed out by "Information" officials. But, since ludruk clowns have traditionally specialized in social and political criticism, they continue to sing songs criticizing the government while almost all the idealistic nationalist slogans appear in songs sung by the female impersonators.

I do not believe the central government censors ludruk performances very strictly. I have heard that the police (DPKN) are supposed to examine ludruk scenarios, but so far as I know, they do not.[1] I have heard of a few cases where ludruk actors were lectured by the police for stinging too sharply with some particular ad-lib satire (such as a satire on brutal police methods).

---

[1] Brandon, *Theatre*, p. 334, had the same impression of governmental censorship of ludruk. Governmental censorship in general in Indonesia is looser than it looks on paper; see Feith, *Guided Democracy*, p. 377.

The "drama inspector" of the Regional Inspectorate of Culture Representing the East Java Ministry of Education and Culture (*Inspeksi Daérah Kebudajaan Perwakilan Departemen P.P.D.K. Djawa Timur*) told me that he had the power to stop a "disloyal" performance of ludruk, but that he had never stopped one yet. This man, an extremely intelligent and widely read artist-philosopher, was perhaps not an ideal censor since he is famed for his belief in free artistic expression.

Factional and Party Loyalties

Ludruk Marhaen came into existence in 1945 as part of the drama wing of Pesindo (Indonesian Socialist Youth), the group which became Pemuda Rakjat. Although Marhaen does not now have official ties with PKI or Pemuda Rakjat, many of its actors have been exposed to communist ideology through lectures, attending Pemuda Rakjat congresses, or taking part in the PKI mass organization LEKRA (Institute of Mass Culture), which sponsors plays, art exhibits, orchestras, and publications of stories and poems (LEKRA, it is said, exerts little discipline on its members but does bring them into contact with PKI propaganda). Some of Marhaen's stalwarts are avowed Marxists.

In 1961, the URIL (troop entertainment unit) of the Brawidjawa army of East Java asked the drama inspector of the Regional Inspectorate of Culture to interview actors in Tresno Enggal to judge their artistic talent and "national consciousness." This inspector told me that he asked each actor, "Do you know that by playing ludruk you can be part of the national struggle, that ludruk is not just an art form?" "What did they reply?" I asked. "Yes," said he. After passing this examination, Tresno Enggal signed a three-year contract with URIL. Now having been "indoctrinated" through hearing lectures by army officers stressing the themes "fight against Imperialism and Colonialism" and "Carry out Sukarno's multi-level Revolution by building the country morally, economically, and culturally," Tresno Enggal divides its time between giving commercial performances for its own profit and performing at army camps for URIL.

Marhaen and Tresno Enggal are the two troupes most famed for their factional or party loyalties — Marhaen to PKI, Tresno Enggal to the army. What influence do these loyalties have on the content of performances by Marhaen or Tresno Enggal? "Great influence," one would assume. But the evidence suggests

41

that performances are more affected by their audiences than by political loyalties of the performing troupe.

Consider the following three performances:

"Bitter Sugar Cane" (*Tebu Pait*) The performance, sponsored by the East Javanese Committee of PKI and two subunits, a youth organization and a branch of SOBSI, was held at the National Building of Indonesia on Bubutan Street. The stage was decorated with flowers and a large hammer and sickle on a red felt banner. The audience appeared to contain no elite. Workers and their families were dressed up and seated toward the front, officers of the sponsoring organizations sat in chairs near the stage's side, and a crowd of roustabouts drifted into the back seats. Actors were drawn from several ludruk troupes; two stars were from Tresno Enggal, one from Marhaen, and others were from Enggal Tresno, Massa, and other troupes.

After songs and comedy not very different from those of commercial ludruk, the story opens. A peasant is having a hard time growing enough to eat because the headman (*lurah*) of his village has rented the village fields to a sugar cane factory. The lurah and his assistant are depicted as contemptuous of the peasant's troubles and interested only in gifts they will receive from the Dutch government if they get more taxes from the peasants. The lurah's attitude is illustrated by this scene:

> The lurah is sitting at home when his wife enters, saucily swinging her hips at him and informing him that he's not popular in the village. Two peasants enter. The lurah makes them sit on the floor. He then makes them put their thumbprints on a paper signifying that they will pay taxes. All of this is comical, the lurah bopping the peasants' fingers with a ruler when they don't get their thumbs in the right place. They leave and a peasant hero enters. The lurah asks him why he won't pay taxes and then makes him give his thumbprint, grinding his thumb into the paper.

Finally the peasants organize. One kills the *tjarik* (lurah's assistant), then all go to the office of the lurah, where they find, also, his superior and a manager of the sugar factory, a man from Ambon (Ambonese are famed as Dutch tools). After much argument, during which the peasant depicts his sufferings to the callous officials, the Ambonese reprimands the peasant hero for his impudence and pushes his head down. Now, though they have been respectfully squatting, all the peasants stand up! The officials draw guns. The peasants whip out sickles and rush at the officials, killing them. As the curtain drops on the confusion of dying bodies, about forty children suddenly rush onto the stage and grab the flowers and hammer and sickle as the audience and gamelan players sing "The Blood of the People is still Running!"

"Wave of the Three Commands" (*Gelombang* TRIKORA)[2] The performance, by Ludruk Marhaen, was held in Surabaja's largest auditorium, the main auditorium of the city-owned People's Amusement Park, a building that has housed events such as a national youth conference, a weight-lifting contest between Indonesia and Red China, and an exhibition displaying Indonesia's industrial growth. Tickets were by "invitation" for as much as 150 rupiah each, four times the price of first class tickets at ordinary commerical ludruk. There appeared to be few proletarians in the audience. University students served as ushers. The front row was occupied by dignitaries from Djakarta. Spectators looked rich (many looked new rich). Near me sat law students from Airlangga University clad in sweaters and button-down collars.

After a dance about girls learning to read, and a clown song with more nationalist content than in ordinary commercial shows, the story begins. A poor peasant woman with a sick child is brusquely dismissed by her husband, Darta, who is a high government official, and interested only in cornering a beautiful young girl, Miriam. Meanwhile, Dr. Sudibjo, Miriam's aristocrat sweetheart, leaves for battle against the Dutch in West New Guinea.

Miriam and her parents have arranged for her to marry Dr. Sudibjo, when news comes that he has died a hero's death in West New Guinea. Darta bribes Miriam's father to let him marry Miriam. Now comes the wedding scene:

> The wedding throne is set. Darta, dressed in tails and white gloves, is seated on the wedding throne eager to grasp his prize. Suddenly Miriam appears, dressed in army fatigues, accompanied by a female army officer. She kneels at her mother's feet and says, "You have arranged for me to marry. But my duty to my country comes first. If you refuse to let me go as a volunteer to West New Guinea you oppose TRIKORA!" The mother replies, "Next time we'll go together!" Miriam runs off with the army woman to West New Guinea. The police arrive to arrest Darta for embezzling funds. Then, standing beside the empty wedding throne destined for their daughter and surrounded by the guests who had come to witness the wedding, the parents raise their hands to the sky and shout, "Long live TRIKORA! Long live West New Guinea!" as the curtain drops.

---

[2] TRIKORA symbolizes three commands (acquire food, security, and West New Guinea) that the Indonesian people are supposed to have voiced to the government.

"Revenge in the Night" (*Pembalasan dilarut Malam*). The theater is the ordinary commercial ludruk theater in the People's Amusement Park. The atmosphere is raucous and bawdy. All spectators are paying customers, but at cheap rates — 35 to 10 rupiah each. They are of the working class — carpenters, small traders, and so on. The troupe is Tresno Enggal.

The performance opens with a dancer who sings mystical songs and songs about forgotten love. Then a clown sings a few verses about the people's duty being to help the government develop the country, after which he shifts to a critique of the modern female's immodest dress and promiscuity. After his song, a comic skit is presented in which two scoundrels steal a trunk and find a ghost inside. After this, a female impersonator sings a song telling of broken love and urging all Indonesians to unite. Now the story begins.

A village girl and her husband leave for the city because they cannot support themselves in the village. Meanwhile in the city a young aristocrat, Bijantoro, has been running around so much that his parents have married him to his cousin, whom he treats cruelly. In the city, the village girl, Inem, becomes very madju and immoral in her ways, dressing in skirts and slacks and wearing her hair in a four-foot-long ponytail. She meets Bijantoro. She and Bijantoro run away together, leaving their respective spouses behind. In the final scene it turns out that the two abandoned spouses have met, married, and are living very comfortably together. They are seated in their living room when two wretched blind beggars crawl up. These turn out to be Inem and Bijantoro, who skitter away when they see whose house they have come upon. The happily married pair shout "revenge in the night" as the curtain drops.

How can these three plays be compared? "Bitter Sugar Cane," has a Marxist theme. It begins with oppressed masses and ends with revolution. "Wave of TRIKORA" begins with the theme, "evil official" and "oppressed village girl" but does not follow that theme beyond the first act. The wronged wife of Darta disappears after the first act and is never mentioned again. Beginning with the second act, the story turns toward the theme "imperialism and nationalism." The Dutch imperialists hold West New Guinea, and a doctor (an aristocrat, who by narrow Communist tenets should be a villain) becomes a national hero by dying in the War of West New Guinea. In the final scene, the arrest of Darta is a minor incident, quickly passed over, and the primary focus is on Miriam's sacrifice of marriage and family ties to commit herself to a national cause. "Revenge in the Night" depicts the domestic trials of two families, one elite, the other proletariat. The bad spouses, one from each family, run away together and suffer in the end while the good spouses, one from each family, marry and live happily ever after. This is a rather bourgeois story, with evil and good spread among both high and low classes.

The first play, with the most blatant Marxist theme, was presented by a combination of actors, including two stars from Tresno Enggal, the troupe with formal ties to the army (most formidable foe of the Communist party). The second story, playing down class struggle and accentuating nationalism, was performed by Marhaen, the ludruk troupe with the strongest formal Communist tie. The third, rather apolitical, domestic play was by Tresno Enggal.

Since the army (or central government) and PKI express many-faceted ideologies, it is possible to see Tresno Enggal's performances as expressive of army ideology and Marhaen's as expressive of PKI ideology. On the face of it, however, the Marxist play in which Tresno Enggal actors star does not give the most direct possible expression to the army's rather fascist line, and Tresno Enggal's domestic play does not give much explicit attention to any political ideology at all. Marhaen's "Trikora" play can be seen as an expression of PKI's National Front stance, but this stance is not distinctively PKI.

Linkages between each play's content and audience are not conclusive, but at least are more obvious than linkages between each play and the performing troupe's political affiliation. The first, a class-struggle play was presented to workers at a labor union meeting. The second, a nationalist play de-emphasizing class struggle was presented to elite and near-elite of Surabaja as well as to government dignitaries from Djakarta. The domestic, relatively apolitical play was presented in a commercial theater to lower class married people. It appears, judging from these three examples, that the audience to whom a play is presented affects its content more than the formal political affiliation of the performing troupe does. These three examples are not exceptional. Contemporary nationalist stories are almost never presented in commercial theaters but were presented at almost every benefit performance attended by political elite that I witnessed. Stories about domestic affairs (called *tjerita rumah tangga*) were more popular than any other type of story at commercial theaters. Class-struggle stories are apparently common fare for audiences at communist meetings.

Nationalism and Personal Ambition

In the minds of the Javanese public, wajang (in puppet or dance forms) and ludruk occupy diametrically opposed corners of the cosmos. Wajang is alus; ludruk is kasar. Inevitably if I mentioned for the first time to a Surabaja Javanese that I was studying ludruk, he would say, "Ludruk is kasar in contrast to wajang, which is alus." When I was about to leave Surabaja, Javanese said, "Now you have studied the most popular kasar art, ludruk; you must return and study the most significant alus art, wajang." The following comments by Javanese catch the sentiments that surround ludruk, in contrast to wajang:

> A woman born in Central Java: "Upon hearing wajang wong (classical dance-drama) songs, one feels peaceful even though there is competition in the economic world. With *djula-djuli* [the ludruk theme song], I feel no peace in my soul, but feel, I must sing!"

> A teen-age boy of Central Javanese origins: "Wajang wong is religion, while ludruk is just entertainment. Wajang wong serves to teach polite restraint. It portrays proper manners of the wife in relation to her husband. Ludruk doesn't teach anything, for in ludruk the wife yells at her husband anytime she feels like it."

> A kampung headman who teaches classical dance: "The opening dance of ludruk [*ngremo*] has as its purpose opening the performance, just as the *srimpi* dance does when the king walks into his palace. But I feel like laughing inside — though I don't laugh out loud — because the negremo is just cheap imitation [*palsu*]."

> A school teacher of low-aristocratic parentage: "When I see the wajang wong, I conjure up visions of castles in India, but when I see ludruk I think of a village."

All of these comments are by persons who pride themselves on their alus ways, look down on that which is kasar, and therefore look down on ludruk.

Although Javanese rank ludruk low on the alus-kasar scale, they rank it higher in terms of the madju-kuna scale (assuming madju at the top). Ludruk looks better to them when they think of it as a source of madju values than it does when they see it as a kasar version of alus art. The same headman who said he felt like laughing inside when he saw ludruk dances said ludruk was useful in that it taught *kemadjuan* (progress) to the masses and helped them lose their belief in magic. Intellectuals at the Ludruk Conference (described in Appendix C) were rather dubious about ludruk's artistic value and went along with a Mr. Boeradi's statement that ludruk's "only hope is to harness itself to Manipol-USDEK." I have heard both kampung persons and elite say that ludruk can help uplift the masses: "ludruk is sprung from the womb of the people and therefore can be a weapon to raise them." Several said that ludruk's domestic stories could teach madju domestic ideals such as "marriage should be free, not forced" and "the fit between spouses' spirits means more than that they are of the same rank."

Ludruk actors and directors are not oblivious to the fact that ludruk looks better from a madju than from an alus standpoint. The most madju-minded of all ludruk personages, Shamsudin of Marhaen, gave a thirty-page speech at the 1960 Ludruk Conference entitled "The Role of Ludruk in Society" (*Peranan Ludruk Dalam Masjarakat*) which can be interpreted, I think, as an attempt to deny the validity of judging ludruk in terms of classical aesthetic criteria and show the influential men at the conference that ludruk's greatness lies in its contribution to national revolution and progress.

Shamsudin begins by saying that ludruk is "a form of people's art, not classical art" such as the alus arts like "wajang that is part of Hindu culture and which depicts the superiority and heroism of the Brahman and Ksatriya classes." Wajang, says Shamsudin, is part of a "culture that is born from those gentlemen who are in control" and can be used as "a tool to suppress those people who are gripped." Thus Shamsudin discredits wajang, in terms of current Marxist and national Indonesian ideology, by seeing it as an instrument of feudal tyrants.

Shamsudin then sneers at purely aesthetic standards: "Of course some like the taste of the phrase 'art for art's sake' but for the ludruk world this phraseology is weak and abstract. Some accuse ludruk of not being art, of just being propaganda. They look down on ludruk players because these seek (through performing) day-to-day living — or a bit more kasar — a handful of rice. But our work has an honorable end. Let them talk. It doesn't hurt us!" Shamsudin asks that ludruk be judged by its political end, not by its beauty (or state of alus).

The rest of Shamsudin's speech tries to show the ways that ludruk has contributed to the development of the Indonesian nation. He begins with a metaphorical interpretation of Besut:

47

Torches were lit in every corner of the ludruk stage; his eyes still closed, Besut came out from behind the stage. Around the dancing place were hung bunches of food. So from the beginning the ludruk stage hummed as a baby being born where the natural wealth of the land was full; torches opened eyes; thus all of Besut expressed the philosophy of freedom.

Shamsudin then recounts how Gondo Durasim helped build the Indonesian Nationalist Building and nationalist schools during the colonial period. Shamsudin also says that Durasim wrote the story, "Djoko Dollok," (summarized in chapter 5) "which told about the superiority of a child of the people, a child of Mother Rondo Praban, who succeeded in killing a prince." For such revolutionary expressions, says Shamsudin, Durasim was "muzzled by the Dutch government." Under "Japanese tyranny," Shamsudin says, Durasim played the same revolutionary role, and for this was tortured and killed.

Then came the Revolution, during which ludruk "shouldered weapons" and moved "close to the front," entertaining the troupes. "The role of ludruk in the revolutionary movement was, of course, very dynamic," says Shamsudin.

Shamsudin talks about a film which Marhaen made after Indonesian independence: *"Kunanti di Djokja"* ("I Wait for You at Djokja"). This film rivals foreign films, says Shamsudin; thus ludruk Marhaen

carries out its duty by opposing vulgar foreign culture which is anti-nationalist by means of the white screen. Although it is not a spear stuck in the ground, only a needle, the above-mentioned ludruk film jabbed its tip into the heart [*djantung*] of capitalist films. According to the terminology now in favor, *Kunanti di Djokja* is a ludruk film that supports MANIPOL and USDEK. In terms of proposals by Bung Karno as leader of the Revolution or as Honorable National Head, certainly the steel strength assembled in this view of culture [Marhaen's film as an expression of MANIPOL and USDEK] shatters that culture which stinks: rock 'n' roll!

Shamsudin concludes by saying that Bung Karno coined the term "politics phobia" for those who are afraid to engage in politics and that people suffering from this "sickness" are "Colonial Agents who fear the victory of the Revolution of 1945. Ludruk must oppose complaints, all trifling, from those sick with the above fever . . . ludruk is already politicized! The ludruk stage no longer floats only ludruk but is already a tool of political propaganda." Those who criticize ludruk for not being art "do not dare talk about how ludruk was muzzled by the Colonial Government, how Pak Gondo was tortured by the Japanese for his criticism of those who ruled. . . . For us in ludruk that was born and made great in the cauldron of Revolution, ludruk drew a heroic heritage from generations of the past — such as the late Pak Gondo. Ludruk is a child of the revolutionary uterus!"

Shamsudin is an extremely ambitious man of about forty. He says his favorite ludruk role is *"Sawunggaling"* (the peasant who become a prince). Shamsudin has only an elementary school education but has studied English on his own via Australia radio and knows quite a few English words. He writes pieces for newspapers, paints, is writing a history of ludruk Marhaen, gives lectures to actors of Marhaen on English language and art appreciation, wants to start a ludruk academy, and is organizing a union of ludruk troupes. It was Shamsudin who staged a "revolution" that caused Marhaen's female impersonators to cut their long tresses and improve their morality. Shamsudin also hired a psychiatrist to lecture to the impersonators on "homosexuality as a disease," and has managed to get three of the impersonators to marry and become fathers. Under Shamsudin's stimulus, Marhaen has made three movies ("Kunanti di Djokja," "Duty of Youth," and "My Sergeant Major") for Radial Film Company and several records for Irama and National Record Company. Other ludruk troupes are satisfied with inserting a few nationalist slogans in songs between scenes of stories, but Shamsudin has organized nationalist group dances, a choir of transvestite sopranoes and male basses to sing nationalist songs such as Resopim, and Shamsudin has written stories with nationalist themes, such as "Gelombang TRIKORA."

All this activity and nationalist exhibitionism has paid off for Marhaen and Shamsudin (as well as for other Marhaen leaders such as Bawa, who has a brand new motorcycle). Marhaen has given seventeen command performances at Sukarno's Freedom Palace, is in demand at political meetings in Surabaja, Djakarta, and Medan, was the only ludruk troupe vocally represented (by Shamsudin) at the mainly elite-attended Ludruk Conference of 1960, and is slated to receive a bus from the government as a gift in appreciation of its contribution to the national struggle. Shamsudin has flourished sufficiently to buy a lot in an elite neighborhood. He may soon become the first ludruk actor in history to live in a neighborhood of a higher class than a kampung.

The case of Marhaen and Shamsudin shows how an artistic group and a man can rise in the nationalist atmosphere of Indonesia by becoming a mouthpiece for nationalist, madju values, even though the man and his art are proletarian in origin and kasar in style. No other ludruk personage has exploited the political market to the extent that Shamsudin has, although a few younger directors have made moves in that direction (for example, Basman, who wrote the poems cited in chapter 13, organized a new politically oriented ludruk group, and won a trip to Moscow).[3] Most of the ordinary ludruk troupes playing in Surabaja's commercial houses are, as a politically ambitious actor in Tresno Enggal put it, "not interested in joining the national struggle; they just want to attract customers." It appears that a troupe's involvement in nationalist politics depends in large part on the ambitions of actors in the troupe. The troupes are not simply blank pages onto which inculcators of national propaganda press their stamp. Troupes go out looking for political opportunities as much as propaganda agencies seek troupes. That Marhaen's plays have more nationalist content than plays of other troupes do is due to Marhaen, not to some omnipotent bureau of propaganda.

ARTISTIC INFLUENCES ON LUDRUK

Alus Art of Java

Flat, buffalo-hide, wajang kulit puppets are manipulated by a man seated cross-legged below a light that casts the puppets' shadows on a white screen, creating a mystical play of flitting shadows which has strangely moved alus Javanese emotions since

---

[3] Basman, thirty-one years old, an extremely bright and energetic son of a bricklayer, was a leading organizer of the 1960 Seminar Ludruk. In 1963, Basman organized the ludruk troupe "New Voice," composed mainly of young men in his kampung and surrounding kampung. He then incorporated "New Voice" into a larger group, Oetera, which he had organized and which also included modern drama players and an orchestra. Next he incorporated Oetera into a still larger group, which he also had helped organize, Okra Djatim (East Javanese Organization of Mass Culture). At the time I left Surabaja, Okra had held its first two sessions. The first was at the Inspectorate for Regional Culture Representing the Ministry of Education and Culture in East Java. At that meeting the Inspector of Culture expressed his pleasure that Okra had come into being in Surabaja, and Oetera's modern drama group performed (unfortunately not completing the performance because the heroine could not remember her lines and ran away weeping). The second meeting was at the National Building; it featured the orchestra and ludruk group. At this meeting the Master of Ceremonies went through a ritual, before the ludruk performance, of inviting each of about a dozen non-present officials to come up and speak. Each time he would invite an official, the presi-

ancient times, as is shown by a thousand-year-old quotation from a play called "Ardjuna's Wedding Celebration": "There are those who weep as they watch the puppets, being sorrowful and perplexed in mind, although they know it is only from pieces of leather that the words come!" [4]

All ludruk participants, being Javanese, have seen the wajang kulit at village or kampung performances or as children crouching all night on the steps of an aristocrat's porch during a wedding celebration. Undoubtedly wajang kulit has molded the aesthetic and moral values — and therefore ludruk performances — of the ludruk participants in deep and subtle ways; but I see only one obvious and pervasive influence of wajang kulit on ludruk — the clown.

The wajang kulit clowns may have originated in Java during pre-Hindu times (before A.D. 600),[5] and therefore may be additions to the Hindu myths, from which wajang has drawn some elements of its stories of Ardjuna and the Pandawas. According to legend the main wajang kulit clowns, Semar and Togog, were originally gods, brothers of Batara Guru. But because of their bad conduct they were banished from heaven to live among mortals — Semar and his three sons, Pétruck, Garèng, and Bagong, becoming servants of the Pandawas, princes of the Kingdom of Amarta. These kasar clown-servants, with their grotesque shapes, uncouth speech, and clumsy movements, bring the alus princes down to earth (Geertz [6] compares Semar's relation with Prince Ardjuna to Falstaff's relation with Prince Hal). Yet the clowns are more than they seem. Apparently stupid, really they are wise, and Semar is in truth a god:

> When one of the gods visits the Pandawas, all of the princely heroes assume positions of respect, so that their heads are lower than his, and address him in the highest level of language and are answered by him in low Javanese. The only exception is Semar who remains standing and speaks to the god in Ngoko (low Javanese) and is

---

dent of Okra would rasp, "He's Sick." and the Master of Ceremonies would express his regrets, then invite the next absent official to speak. I do not know how Oetera and Okra fared after their seemingly troubled beginnings, because I left Surabaja soon after the second meeting. But apparently these activities helped Basman win the Moscow trip.

[4] B. Alkema and T. J. Bezemer, *Concise Handbook of the Ethnology of the Netherlands East Indies*, p. 435.

[5] Hood, *Music and Theater*, p. 443.

[6] C. Geertz, *Religion of Java*, p. 277.

answered in high Javanese. This respect and veneration shown for Semar — god that he was, but servant that he is — makes a profound impression on the Javanese people.[7]

As we shall see, clown-servants in ludruk play a role similar in many ways to that of the clown-servants of wajang kulit.

Classical Javanese dance is extremely alus, with graceful, controlled, stylized motions and gestures of arms, hands, and fingers related to the *mudras* of India. The main forms are *srimpi* and *bedaja* (stylized portrayals of courtly stories at one time performed only in the courts) and *wajang wong* (invented in the middle of the eighteenth century by Sunan Mankunegara of Surakarta, a drama danced by humans [*wong*] imitating the wajang kulit puppets and depicting wajang kulit stories).[8] Ludruk dances have incorporated some stylized srimpi or wajang wong motions.

Some marginal classical dance forms are supposed to have influenced ludruk. Poerbokoesoemo[9] argues that the ngremo (opening dance at ludruk) is derived from a *topèng* (masked) dance in its original East Javanese version, since both ngremo and topèng dancers wear bells on their ankles that jangle when they stamp their feet. Some say the ngremo was influenced by the *kiprah,* a Central Javanese dance performed without a mask, by characters representing angry or enraptured warriors and monsters.

Ludruk in all phases of its known development has featured a male dancer impersonating a woman. This dancer was apparently called *ronggèng* or *talèdèk* at the time of Besut and may have been connected with other Javanese dancers called *talèdèk* or *ronggèng*. Geertz mentions a street dancer of this type who dances "poor imitations of the srimpi and bedaja with elements of folk sources mixed in."[10] Such a dancer is a woman, often a prostitute, or a man impersonating a woman. Alkema[11] says that the Javanese equivalent of a royal corps de ballet, the bedaja dancers at the court of Djokjakarta, included not only girls but also boys of noble birth impersonating girls; Wilken adds that the ronggèng or talèdèk street dancers, like those mentioned by Geertz, occasionally performed in the courts as singers or dancing girls and that such dancers, though prostitutes, were "more refined" than

[7] Hood, *Music and Theater,* p. 443.
[8] Alkema and Bezemer, *Handbook,* p. 450.
[9] Poerbokoesoemo, *Ludruk,* p. 7.
[10] C. Geertz, *Religion of Java,* p. 296.
[11] Alkema and Bezemer, *Handbook,* p. 434.

the average prostitute.[12] These dancers also performed during short pauses of alus performances such as wajang; just as today's female impersonator performs between scenes of ludruk. The style of the talèdèk, Javanese informants say, resembles the dance of the ludruk impersonator, and Wilken's description bears this out: the talèdèk, he says, slings a shawl alternately around the body and out, contorting hips, arms, and hands, but hardly moving the feet, and singing very shrilly. All of this points to some historical connections between the present-day ludruk transvestite dancer-singer and the talèdèk, who in turn has connections with alus dance. This historical link is suggestive since, as we shall see, to-day's ludruk transvestite dancer wields more alus symbols in his performance than does any other ludruk character.

Classical dance and drama are accompanied by an ensemble of instruments, the gamelan, which, like other alus art forms, is an-cient (prototypes of modern gamelan are depicted on bas-reliefs of the Borobodur and Prambanan monuments erected in the ninth century A.D.),[13] venerable (it is a sacrilege to step over a gamelan),[14] and exotic to Western senses. Unlike Western music, which is com-posed of "vertical" harmonic blocks, gamelan music is composed of numerous "horizontal" strata or voices; many streams ripple simultaneously.[15] *Balungan* instruments (*sarons* or metallophones) play the main melody. *Panerusan* instruments elaborate on the melody, and include various metallophones (*gendèr barung, bonang*), a kind of xylophone (*gembang kaju*), a two-stringed vio-lin (*rebab*), a flute (*suling*), and a zither (*siter*). Interpunctuating instruments (the gongs) divide the nuclear melody into phrases. Rhythm instruments (the double-ended drum, *kendang tjiblon*) set the basic beat and elaborate it. These instruments and this musical structure have been taken over by ludruk gamelan.

There are two main tuning systems for the classical Javanese gamelan: *sléndro* and *pélog*. Sléndro consists of five tones which are almost equidistant, pèlog of seven tones which are not equi-distant. Each tuning system can be arranged into three basic scales, each of which has a different gong tone as its principal tone. The three basic scales of sléndro are *patet nem, patet sanga,* and *patet manjura*. Like wajang, ludruk uses only the sléndro

---

[12] G. A. Wilken, *Manual for the Comparative Ethnology of the Netherlands East Indies,* p. 115.

[13] Hood, *Music and Theater,* p. 450.

[14] *Ibid.,* p. 451.

[15] *Ibid.,* p. 452.

tuning system. Also as in wajang, as a ludruk performance progresses the ludruk gamelan moves successively through the three scales of sléndro — nem, sanga, and manjura — each of which is higher in basic tonality than the one preceding it.

Ludruk music differs especially in two ways from classical gamelan music. Ludruk music is louder, since the drum (one of the instruments Javanese classify as "loud") leads ludruk while the rebab (one of the instruments Javanese classify as "soft") leads the classical gamelan. Ludruk music reflects Balinese influences; note the sudden changes in ludruk music from loud to soft (as when a curtain is raised for a scene) and the ludruk gamelan's use of two players playing interlocking parts on the gendèr, each playing as fast as he can, the result being a performance twice as fast as a single man could play.

A final classical influence on ludruk is *tembang*. Tembang is a form of classical Javanese poetry which can be sung; to *nembang* is to sing. Tembang, which flowered in the seventeenth and first half of the eighteenth centuries, are of several forms, each with a rigidly fixed metrical pattern defining the number of syllables each line shall have, the final vowel of each line, and the number of lines. The main tembang sung in ludruk is *kinanṭi,* one of the simplest of the tembang forms.[16] Female impersonators sing the ludruk kinanṭi, imitating the thin, high, front-of-the-mouth nasal tones, trills, and ornamental flattening of tones that female singers of kinanti have traditionally displayed. Kinanṭi songs in ludruk, as in classical art, are usually about unrequited love: for a prince dying in battle or a man whose image cannot be forgotten.

Kasar Art of Java

Poerbokoesoemo thinks that ludruk originated as a dance that lowly people performed at weddings and other "noisy" celebrations.[17] He suggests that the term "ludruk" may have come from the Javanese word "nggedruk" which means "to stamp one's foot on the ground during a dance" as in the "noisy" wedding dances and the present ludruk ngremo dance.[18] Poerbokoesoemo stresses that in its earliest form, ludruk was simply a song and dance plus a few jokes; a story was not added until recent times. Both

[16] C. Geertz, *Religion of Java,* p. 282.
[17] Poerbokoesoemo, *Ludruk,* p. 4.
[18] *Ibid.,* p. 2.

Poerbokoesoemo [19] and Pigeaud [20] see resemblances between ludruk and *lerok,* a folkdance from the town of Situhardja, near
Surabaja, that features female impersonators wearing long shawls
like the sampur of today's ludruk ngremo dancers, and a male
dancer (lerok) dressed completely in red, with face half-red
and half-white, who causes a band of little bells around his
ankle to jangle when he stamps his foot, as in today's ngremo.
Poerbokoesoemo [21] also notes resemblances between ludruk, *gam-
buh* of the Gresik-Pasuruhan-Surabaja area, a dance-judo (*pentjak*) exhibition, and *gemblak* which begins with a woman who
presents a masked dance and then, in a mixed Javanese-Madurese
monologue, tells of her part in a story to come (in the story, her
role is played by a man). Such a monologue, but by a male, is
the way the present-day ludruk begins.

There are some similarities, which may indicate mutual influences, between ludruk and *ketoprak,* [22] a popular play staging ancient Javanese legends as well as, occasionally, contemporary
romance, stories of the 1945 Revolution, and even "Hamlet" and
"Quo Vadis." Ludruk began staging full stories in the twenties,
when ketoprak, which began as a portrayer of stories, was invented. Ludruk and ketoprak are both found in commercial theaters: in fact, a few theaters alternately present ludruk and ketoprak
performances. Both ludruk and ketoprak have a gamelan prelude,
a prologue featuring semi-alus dancing and/or clowns, a main
story that is a realistically acted seriocomic farce, and reversal of
sex roles (in ludruk men play women while in the ketoprak I saw,
as in wajang wong, women played men). The clown-servants in
ketoprak are, like ludruk and wajang servants, low complements to
elite characters. The manner of alus dancing by ketoprak girls
is similar to that of ludruk transvestites. Songs of the ketoprak
girls contain some refrains (for instance, "lay-lo-lay-lo-lay-lo") like
those of ludruk transvestite songs.

Many verses sung by ludruk singers take the form of Malay
pantun. Pantun are poems of four lines, the first two presenting a
metaphor, the second two describing baldly an event or situation
to which the metaphor alluded; the first and third, second and
fourth lines rhyme. At the time of ludruk Besut, ludruk songs

[19] *Ibid.,* pp. 4–5.

[20] Pigeaud, *Javaanse Volksvertoningen,* p. 322.

[21] Poerbokoesoemo, pp. 4–5.

[22] Many of the parallels noted here were noted earlier by Clifford Geertz, *Religion of Java,* p. 289. In a few respects my observations differ from his.

were apparently more strictly of pantun form than now,[23] when the lines to a verse are not always four, do not always rhyme, and are usually called *parikan* instead of pantun.

Various bits of kasar art now and then get loosely inserted into ludruk performances. Occasionally a folktale such as "Red Onion and White Onion" is performed. Sometimes a few motions from the *djaran kèpang,* a vulgar street dance by a man who rides a bamboo horse, appear. Wild Madurese dances and songs, Balinese dances, and, owing to nationalist influences, Sumatran folk dances are presented from time to time by ludruk.

Pan-Indonesian Art

Geertz describes art forms of the pan-Indonesian type as follows:

They are not confined to Java; nor is there much of anything characteristically Javanese about them as compared to other areas of Indonesia such as Sumatra or the Celebes. Insofar as they are literary, they are in the national language, Indonesian Malay, rather than in the "regional" language, Javanese. They are in part presented over the mass media, which of course extend all over the islands — the radio, movies, and nationally circulated magazines. They are practiced and appreciated by the same groups, mostly the urban youth, who have always been in the forefront of nationalism. They are the form of art common in the large port cities — Surabaja, Djakarta — where indigenous forms of art have been weakened in the general deracination of culture; and they are especially popular among the new political elite which is in power in these cities.[24]

Among such art forms, Geertz numbers the *orkès,* an orchestra of stringed instruments such as guitars and banjos tuned to the western diatonic scale rather than to sléndro or pélog scales, *lagu,* Indonesian hit tunes sometimes resembling Latin American songs, and short stories or plays written in Indonesian language (Bahasa Indonesia) and set in "big-city Djakarta-Surabaja-Medan asphalt jungles."[25]

The orkès and lagu have not affected ludruk musical form in any profound way since ludruk still uses the gamelan and follows the sléndro tuning system instead of the Western scale. There are some resemblances between the sentimental content of ludruk songs and lagu, but the resemblances between ludruk songs and

[23] H. Overbeck, "Pantoens in het Javaansch," pp. 208–30.
[24] C. Geertz, *Religion of Java,* p. 303.
[25] *Ibid.,* p. 306.

kinanti or Malay-influenced pantun sung by ludruk Besut thirty years ago are more striking.

It is easy to buy Indonesian novels, short stories, poems, and plays in Surabaja book stores or stands, but ludruk actors do not seem to read them very much. Ludruk actors mentioned only two plays that they had taken from Indonesian literature. A cursory survey of Indonesian writings does not reveal any striking similarities between the "asphalt-jungle" stories and ludruk tales, although it is true that ludruk does include stories which focus around themes (forced marriage) which concerned Indonesian novels of the twenties or events (The Revolution) which were important in later novels.

Live performances of "modern drama" (*drama modèren*) are popular among Surabaja students. I have seen such performances at high school culture shows, high school graduation ceremonies, Islamic Youth Meetings, and meetings of IPPI, the Communist student association. The only ludruk actor who displayed much interest in modern drama was, significantly, the only one who had finished junior high school.

In prewar times there was a "Malay Opera" (*stambul*) which Geertz describes as something like a Victor Herbert-type operetta with plots taken from folktales and from tales such as the "Thousand and One Nights." [26] It is not clear to me what influences stambul had on ludruk stories, but I have been told that ludruk took some costume elements from stambul; for example, the red cap of Besut and a rose backdrop which transvestite singers use today are supposed to have come from stambul.

Indonesian language films that I saw or heard about in Surabaja in 1963 were love stories (a blind Sumatran youth goes to a big city, is seduced by a flashy city girl, but reclaimed by his faithful village sweetheart), Indonesian equivalents of America's "Beach Party" film epics (teenage romance sandwiched between shots of water-skiing and swimming), and tales of the Revolution. I did not see any striking resemblances between these films and ludruk stories. Several Javanese said that certain ludruk love stories are adapted from Indonesian movies produced before the war. Ludruk actors and directors clearly contrast, however, ludruk form with movie form. They point out, for instance, that movies sometimes end with a single figure on the screen whereas ludruk "must" end with a crowd on stage.

[26] *Ibid.*

American films are very popular among ludruk actors; "Gone with the Wind" is a film about which they speak with feeling. Yet aside from superficial imitations (actors utter "I love you" for comic effect) and isolated borrowings (one ludruk story starring a zombie was taken from an American horror movie), it is hard to pin down effects of American movies on ludruk; in terms of plot development, characterization, and underlying ethic, the contrasts between ludruk and American movies are strong, although they have lessened since the time of Besut.

I have tried to show that ludruk troupes do not simply parrot political propaganda. Nor are ludruk performances carbon copies of other art forms. Ludruk actors actively mold that which comes to them from other sources so that ludruk performances will fit their situation and thoughts and those of their audiences. This conclusion is supported by several facts aside from some already mentioned in this chapter:

Profits and popularity of ludruk troupes other than Marhaen and Tresno Enggal depend on proletarian audiences. These audiences loudly react during performances and also make formal requests for certain stories or songs. Thus the troupe can tell what is popular and what is not. Actors are concerned about audience responses; some have even had nightmares of hostile or absent audiences facing them while they were performing.

Ludruk is uniquely fitted to respond to audience reactions or to actors' impulses. There are only sketchy scenarios to guide actors during performances of ludruk stories. There are no scripts. Actors make up their lines as they go along — although lines tend to get stereotyped when a story has been performed repeatedly. Clowns consciously emphasize spontaneity — saying what pops into one's mind in a given situation — as part of an East Javanese tradition. Clowns' jokes change considerably from performance to performance.

There is no tradition which demands that a troupe literally copy a story, song, or joke that they see or hear. In fact, artistic directors are proud of their ability to modify stories and songs which come from outside ludruk to make them "fit ludruk style." Some actors are known for their skill at varying songs and skits to fit different audiences.

Ludruk actors often speak of having "written" some ludruk story themselves. Sometimes they say the story came to them in a dream or that it was drawn from their "own experience." A few even described the creative process. One man relates that one night he wandered around his kampung, unable to sleep, overcome with impressions of his neighbors' miseries. He finally went to bed. When he awoke, a story about a kampung character was clear in his mind. He wrote the story down and later his troupe performed it.

Perhaps because of the traits of ludruk noted above, there are similarities between many ludruk stories and certain fantasies rife among Surabaja proletarians. For instance, kampung dwellers, recounting stories of their own love affairs or love affairs that allegedly involved neighbors, constructed stories very much like ludruk love tales.

If, as I have argued, ludruk is flexible, responding to its audiences' and actors' needs and ideas, molding external political and artistic resources to fit these needs and ideas, then ludruk has an advantage over such canned forms as American movies; ludruk can more successfully attune itself to Javanese proletarians, drawing them into empathy with it, and in this way luring them into taking on the attitudes which it expresses. We turn now to ludruk itself, to begin to see how ludruk fosters these attitudes.

5

The General Character of Ludruk

PREFABRICATED STRUCTURE

James Brandon compares Southeast Asian and Western theater as follows:

> In the West, the *play* is the measure of all things. Each play is thought of as a unique creation, an artistic entity complete unto itself. It is especially created by a writer — the playwright — and it may be totally unlike any other play ever written. In the two main systems of production in use in the West — repertory and the producer system — the play is the unit of production. In the production system, the system we have on Broadway, theatre artists are brought together on a one-shot basis to produce a single play; after it is finished, they disband perhaps never to work together again. In

repertory, though actors work together on a series of plays and a play may be revived, still each play is prepared and mounted as a separate work of art. The focus of Western dramatic art, that is, is on the *uniqueness* of each play. Above all we prize individual creativity, newness in theatre. And our production systems are geared to provide just that: they are systems for "hand-crafting" each production.

In Southeast Asia the aim of production is not to produce one play, or even ten or a hundred separate plays, but to stage examples of a genre. The *genre,* not the play, is the unit of production. Production is organized around permanent troupes of from ten to a hundred and fifty actors, writers, producers, musicians, singers, technicians, and administrative staff. It is not at all unusual for actors to have performed together in the same troupe several thousand times. Since a troupe performs in a single genre (with few and minor exceptions), dancers are expert in the dance patterns of the genre, musicians and singers know all the traditional melodies and songs, actors know backwards and forwards the stories on which plays are based, they know the standard dialogue patterns, and the style of performance. A troupe will perform a different play every night as a rule. Actors play the same type of role night after night, and in some cases they play the same character all their lives (actors who play the clowns, for example). A few standard types of scenery, costumes, and make-up satisfy the production needs of any play that might be given. In short, the theatre troupe, like a good jazz group in the West, is skilled in the basic artistic patterns of the genre, is used to working together, and can produce a play at the drop of a hat, with no more special preparation than a jazz group needs to belt out a number.

If theatre productions are "hand-crafted" in the West, they are "pre-fabricated" in Southeast Asia. In successive performances the standard parts of the genre are shifted, rearranged, put into different combinations. Each of these particular combinations is, of course, a "play." Like the patterns of a kaleidoscope, all the combinations of plays are regroupings of the same basic elements. No two patterns are exactly alike; none are totally different.[1]

What Brandon says for Southeast Asian theater holds true to a great degree for ludruk. Every ludruk performance is a collection of examples of the following genre: ngremo, dagelan, *selingan, tjerita.* Every ludruk performance opens with a dance called the "ngremo" that is performed by a man dressed in bizarre black men's or women's clothes. ("Ngremo," which means "rapture dance," represents, in classical versions, all phases of lovemaking,

[1] Brandon, *Theatre,* pp. 155–156.

from preparation to consummation; so it is fitting that ngremo opens ludruk, as one Javanese said, "by seducing the spectator into the show.") After the ngremo, the dagelan begins; a single clown sings, soliloquizes, then engages in a dialogue with a second clown, all of which leads into a comic skit. After the dagelan a female impersonator sings and dances. This is the selingan. After the selingan the tjerita begins. That is usually a melodramatic story with many comic episodes. Selingan (interludes) by female impersonators are presented between scenes of the melodrama. In commercial performances the ngremo lasts about half-an-hour, dagelan about an hour, melodrama about two hours, and all the selingan together consume another hour; so the total performance lasts about four and a half hours.

Although every ludruk show contains an example of each of the basic genre — ngremo, dagelan, selingan, tjerita — the content of the ngremo, dagelan, selingan, and tjerita varies from show to show, and the content of each of these elements varies almost independently of the content of the other elements. A troupe, let us say, performs six different dagelan routines (*A, B, C, D, E,* and *F*), six different tjerita (*M, N, O, P, Q,* and *R*), and three types of ngremo (*X, Y,* and *Z*) during a series of twenty performances. Show number one might consist of dagelan *A*, tjerita *N*, and ngremo *X*. Show number two might consist of *A, M,* and *Z*. Show number three might be *CMX*. Show number four might be *CPZ*. Show number five might be *BQX*, and so forth. Any combination of examples of the dagelan genre, tjerita genre, and ngremo genre will do, but one example of each of the three genres usually is included in a show. If there were set combinations such as *AMX* and *BOZ* or *BPZ* that should always be performed together, each combination would form something like a "hand-crafted" show of the West. But each of the elements (e.g., a given tjerita) of a ludruk show is "prefabricated," perfected as a unit in itself, and each "show" is composed of an apparently random combination of these prefabricated elements. There is never a rehearsal of a ludruk show as a whole. Each element has been worked up as a separate unit, so the director decides which elements to put together for a given "show" just before the show begins — or while it is in progress.

It is as if a summer theater group knew a number of songs and dramas, the names of which they keep in a hat. Every night they draw out a combination. That combination is the night's show. Monday night they begin by singing "Oh What a Beautiful

Morning," followed by "My Favorite Things," which is followed by a performance of "Hamlet," with "Summertime" and "Edelweiss" sung between acts. Tuesday night they begin with "Bess, You is My Woman" followed by "Silent Night," which is followed by "The Tempest," with "Jingle Bells" and "The Ballad of Mack the Knife" sung between the acts. Wednesday night begins with "Indian Love Call," followed by "Silent Night," after which a performance of "Hamlet" is again presented, with "I Could Have Danced All Night" and "Oklahoma" between the acts; and so it would go.

Parts *within* each ngremo, dagelan, tjerita, or selingan performance are more integrally connected than are the ngremo, dagelan, tjerita, and selingan that compose a given ludruk show, but such parts vary fairly independently of one another. Each dagelan consists of a song, monologue, dialogue, and comic skit. The last two parts are fairly tightly fused to one another but the first two vary more or less independently of each other and of the last two parts. Let us say that during a series of twenty performances, a troupe does skits *A, B, C, D,* and *E,* dialogues *A', B', C', D',* and *E',* monologues 1,2,3,4, and 5, and songs *X, Y,* and *Z.* Skit *A* might usually (but not always) be preceded by dialogue *A',* Skit *B* by dialogue *B',* and so on. But any combination of monologues and songs could appear and any combination of monologues and songs with the skit-dialogue pairs would do.

Ludruk songs, whether forming part of selingan, ngremo, or dagelan all have a similar structure, which is unlike that of the typical western song. A typical western song is a custom-made package of words plus melody. One does not ordinarily hear a "song" that is a potpourri of lyrics from "Auch Kleine Dinge," "Yes, We have No Bananas," "Mother Machree," "Jesus Loves Me," "Jezebel," and "Die Gedanken Sind Frei." But this is the way ludruk songs are. At any given time there are about two hundred different quatrains or couplets popular around the ludruk circuit. Each "song" in a ludruk performance consists of five to fifteen such quatrains or couplets. From one singer one night we hear a song composed of couplets 1, 5, 3, 4, 8, 9, 57, and 176. From another singer (or the same singer) on another night, we hear a song composed of couplets 189, 2, 79, 5, 2, 11, 67, 95, 45. From still another singer, we hear a song composed of couplets 200, 1, 3, 5, 67, and so on. It does not seem to matter in what order the couplets or quatrains are presented, although the order of lines within a couplet or quatrain (and certain longer verses of clown songs) does matter. It does not seem to matter which quatrains or couplets go with which in the sense that sugar, not salt, should always go with coffee.

Each melodramatic story (tjerita) is more handcrafted than is a dagelan or song, though there are some stock scenes and characters which crop up in varying combinations in stories. This story handcrafting may signal a trend in ludruk form since the stories are the most recent addition to ludruk performances, coming in with Durasim in the late twenties.

It seems to me that the "prefabricated" nature of the ludruk show makes one mode of description more appropriate than others. Each individual ludruk "show" (e.g., the "show" of July 10, 1963) is not so crucial a unit as is each genre (e.g., ngremo or tjerita) that goes into the show, for the examples within each genre are more integrally connected to one another than are the ngremo, tjerita, dagelan, and selingan of each show. So I shall treat each genre separately. Chapters 6 and 7 will deal with the dagelan, chapters 8, 9, 10, and 11 with the tjerita, and chapters 12, 13, and 14 with ngremo and selingan. Each chapter or set of chapters will treat the variant examples of the genre on which it focuses.

An alternative mode of presentation would be to select a few "representative" texts of total four-and-a-half-hour ludruk performances and analyze each of these texts as a unit. I think it is more useful to lay bare the distinctive features of each genre, since ludruk participants themselves apparently regard each genre as a more crucial unit than any single "show" composed of examples of such genre. Taking account of variant examples of each genre also has another advantage; this procedure forces one to publically come to grips with the variations in one's corpus of examples. It does not allow one to vaguely survey a corpus of texts, pick a few texts and present them as "representative" of the not-yet-analyzed corpus.[2]

[2] C. Geertz, "Form and Variation in Balinese Village Structure," pp. 791–1012, and E. R. Leach, *Political Systems of Highland Burma,* argue that it is useless to search for a "representative" village in either of their Southeast Asian societies (Balinese or Kachin). A better procedure, each says, is to define categories (e.g., of temples) instances of which are found within every village in the society — although playing a different role in each. Their conclusion on Southeast Asian villages resembles Brandon's on Southeast Asian drama — that a spatiotemporal unit (a show or a village) which appears to the Westerner as the basic unit is not so basic to the Southeast Asian as is each category or "component" (e.g., a song-genre or temple-type), an instance of which is one of the elements composing the spatiotemporal unit. It is interesting that two of the most famous anthropological analyses

FLICKERING ATTENTION

In wajang kulit performances, the gamelan changes "key" as the evening wears on and characters move from one level of mystical achievement to another. In one story, Bima, a son of King Pandu, searches for living water and kills two giants as part of his search. This signals the death of Bima's earthly desire to sin. At this point the gamelan changes from a lower key (patet nem) to a higher one (patet sanga). Then Bima overcomes a monster, signalling his mastery over sexual appetite. At this point the gamelan changes to a still higher key, patet manjura, and Bima proceeds to achieve a *unica mystica* by entering the body of god.[3]

Ludruk has borrowed the pitch progression (but not the mystical progression) from wajang kulit along with a musical composition called Talu which consists of three parts, *Ajak-ajakan, Srepegan,* and *Sampak* (Ajak-ajakan, a prelude, is usually omitted by ludruk). Before the performance begins ludruk plays Srepegan followed by Sampak, in the key of nem. In the middle of the performance, usually about ten-thirty in a commercial theater, the gamelan plays Srepegan and Sampak in the key of sanga — approximately a Western scale half-step higher in pitch than nem. About eleven-thirty the gamelan plays Srepegan and Sampak in the key of manjura, approximately a major third higher in pitch than sanga. Thus pitch rises as the performance progresses. The pitch rise is not constant but accelerated. There is a larger jump from ten-thirty to eleven-thirty than there was between seven-thirty and ten-thirty.

There are also other progressions during the ludruk performance. Tempo and volume increase. The drum gets louder and wilder in its rhythmic patterns. Although the gamelan music is ordinarily a complex of loosely connected "stratified" improvisations, as the performance approaches its end, the instrumental parts move toward unison; all begin playing the same principal melody. This is because Sampak is played more toward the end than are other gamelan compositions, and Sampak is played more nearly in unison than they are.

---

of the "component" (as opposed to "representative village") type and one of the few "component" analyses of drama should have been done in Southeast Asia. This coincidence suggests one direction in which the search for distinctive pan-Southeast Asian culture traits might go.

[3] Moerdowo, *Reflections on Indonesian Arts and Culture,* p. 132.

After the final ludruk curtain falls, the music shifts to a popular folk or children's melody that is softer, slower, and in a key about a major third below the key (manjura) in which Sampak-srepegan was played just before the final scene.

Consolidating in our minds all these musical progressions, we can see that the ludruk performance has a musical climax structure.

Not only the performance as a whole, but also each playing of the Srepegan and Sampak shows a formal climax. If we divide Sampak and Srepegan from beginning to end into two-note blocks and classify each block as repeated tones (both notes of a block are the same), step-progression tones (one note varies from the other one step up or down the Javanese sléndro scale), or skip-progression tones (one note varies from the other more than one step up or down the Javanese sléndro scale), we find that the Srepegan has no repeated tones while the Sampak has 29 repeated tones and the Sampak has only two step-progression and four skip-progression tones in contrast to eighteen step-progression and sixteen skip-progression tones for the Srepegan. That is, the majority of Sampak tone pairs (eighty-three per cent) are repeated while all srepegan tone pairs (100 per cent) are either step or skip progressive. Therefore, since Srepegan always precedes Sampak, every time Srepegan-Sampak are played there is a shift from a progressive tonal pattern to a series of repeated tones. As this shift occurs, tempo and volume increase. Srepegan tempo gradually increases until after several minutes of playing it has doubled, at which point it moves into Sampak which is played very fast. At this heightened tempo, the heavy bronze saron, not being able to play every note, hits every other note thus producing many repeated note pairs. These repeated tones are beaten into the listener's head; the heavy saron and bonang, the loudest and most strident instruments of ludruk, pound out the repeated tones while high, medium, and low saron beat out the tones on strong beats (second and fourth beats of a measure), and medium and high bonang play the tones in octaves on syncopated beats, making an echo against the saron. The sampak is repeated in this manner again and again at top volume. Each Srepegan-Sampak sequence, then, builds in tempo and loudness with skips and steps up and down the scale until a high level of tempo and loudness is reached at which point the sampak tones are loudly repeated again and again. One can see why Talu (Srepegan-Sampak) is considered one of the few Javanese compositions with a strong climax.[4]

---

[4] Jaap Kunst, *Music in Java,* 1:341.

There can be no question but that the ludruk performance as a whole and in certain of its parts manifests a formal climax structure (the musical climax structure is the most clear-cut, but there are also parallel non-musical progressions). Ludruk participants do not get involved, however, in sustained and concentrated fashion with ludruk's formal climax. Like the string of twinkling lights surrounding the ludruk stage, their attention flickers on and off. They wander in and out of the theater throughout a performance, and this physical movement is paralleled by mental. Spectators and actors have their eyes on the action one instant and stare blankly away the next. Spectators are looking at the stage then suddenly are talking with their neighbors. Players in the gamelan, even as they beat out the loud climax to the sampak, suddenly look around and talk to other players or even, by all appearances, fall asleep for a second. These mental flittings are paralleled by comings and goings onstage. The following is an outline of entrances and exits in a typical scene, lasting about fifteen minutes:

Curtain opens.
Mother, father, daughter, and son onstage.
Son leaves.
Mother leaves.
Father leaves.
Daughter is alone.
Father returns.
Father leaves.
Two soldiers enter.
Mother returns.
Soldiers leave.
Father returns.
Father, mother, daughter talk, then all leave.
Curtain drops.

The quick shifts of attention during performances are paralleled by a quick shift of mental focus after the performance is done. When the performance is over, the ludruk participants are able to turn their attention sharply away from the stage. There is no leveling-off period like that we see in American athletic or show business dressing rooms. Ludruk actors leave immediately after the final curtain drops and are out of the auditorium as soon as the audience is; I remember leaving the theater once and suddenly realizing that the man walking beside me had just died a violent death onstage seconds ago. Spectators too get out of the theater quickly, and several whom I questioned said they had no post-final-curtain feeling of hating to leave the onstage fantasy world. All of this may reflect that "punctuate" sense of time which Geertz attributes to the Javanese which allows them to "shift sharply from one kind of activity to another with very little transition." [5]

Margaret Mead described Balinese responses to drama as follows: "A Balinese audience at any performance is a group of people who are technically interested; they are uncaught by the plight of the princess lost in the forest, blown away on her silken cobwebs, but they are very deeply concerned with the twist of her little finger." [6] This description to a degree fits the Javanese ludruk audience. Auditors often comment "technically" on a dancer ("Still stiff, this one") or on dramatic action ("This fits." "That crying sound effect is poor." "His pistol did not go off." "He forgot his moustache!"). There is also a tendency, apparently, for audiences to center on particular motions or words instead of the total plight and orientation of a character. Audiences imitate a single word or gesture of an enraged man instead of empathizing with his situation and response. Occasionally somebody does get carried away, such as the insane villager who leapt onto the ludruk stage to aid a heroine in a fight with her husband's second wife, but Javanese seem to regard too much involvement as gauche: a woman spectator forgets herself when a son is killing his father and screams, "Waduh Allah! The father is being choked!" and her husband has to remind her, "It is only a character in a story, a performance (*digawése*)." Standing aloof and technically evaluating or casually imitating small pieces of the action such as words, gestures, or twists of the dancer's little finger would seem to encourage flitting concentration; it is easier to jump back and forth from observing a small and visible part of behavior than to leap in and out of empathy with a character's total situation, personality, and development.

I must stress, though, that while ludruk participants empathize in flitting fashion, they *do* emphathize; and although, according to my impression, ludruk audiences make more "technical" comments than do, say, ordinary American movie audiences, that is not the major type of comment made at ludruk. Eight reports (written by Javanese audience-response recorders) [7] of audience

[5] C. Geertz, *The Religion of Java*, p. 12.

[6] Gregory Bateson and Margaret Mead, *Balinese Character: A Photographic Analysis*, p. 28.

[7] These "audience-response recorders" were Javanese students whom I hired to record the audience response heard at ludruk. Their work is described in Appendix C.

responses to ludruk melodrama were analyzed, revealing that the most frequent type of response (51) described or imitated physical motions, sounds, or onstage objects (for instance, an onlooker imitates the remark, "Wah she doesn't have a house . . . babah."). The next most frequent response (47) expressed empathy with a character's role or feelings (a spectator says, "What a pity. They pay him no attention."). Thirty-one responses passed moral judgement on a character ("Oh this one is evil!"). Sixteen responses were technical comments, twelve were aggressive shouts ("Hit him!"), seven were admiring ("How beautiful she is!"), and by far the most frequent response was simply laughter.

"Introspection reports" [8] reveal a good bit of empathy; while watching a lower official yield to a superior, a man writes, "I feel the emotion 'fear of giving in to an opponent' — something we have often experienced." As a fight starts, a clerk, Supii, writes, "We feel horror, with heart beating fast, because a quarrel starts. . . . I fear, for Si Pitung (the hero) is a quiet man who doesn't want to fight." Then, as Pitung's wife goads him into fighting: "Inside (*batin*), I am glad she goads him." A villain evokes the remark, "He is extremely unfit, for he lends money only with interest. We feel very embarrassed." Other comments report sad feelings, happiness at outcomes, nostalgia, and so on.

Other signs that ludruk spectators empathize with ludruk: A male servant at work imitates a ludruk woman, a child at play imitates a ludruk fighter, teen-agers greet each other with a phrase made popular by a ludruk clown. A mentally disturbed boy draws pictures of ludruk characters, telling stories about them as he draws; the Madurese fighter, Pak Sakera, fills the page with a swirl and leer, as the boy tells of his gambling.

The flitting quality of the participants' empathy can be linked to the "prefabricated" structure of the ludruk show. Except for the broad structure of a ludruk performance — which never changes and so would not require the sustained attention of those who have seen ludruk again and again — the parts of a ludruk show are not connected to one another in a tight sequence such that involvement in one part draws one's attention on to the next part. Instead, the parts are loosely connected to one another, often varying independently of each other. Therefore, participants' attention can be organized in chunks rather than as a sustained flow, yet still be in step with the performance.

---

[8] These "introspection reports" were written, at my request, by spectators at ludruk; they described their thoughts and feelings during the plays. See Appendix C.

Javanese artistic traditions might encourage fragmented concentration on onstage sequences. Ludruk spectators are sophisticated theater goers in that they not only perceive each onstage action; they also compare it with other members of the genre that it exemplifies. "That dance step is like X step in wajang wong" or "He talks like so-and-so in ketoprak" are comments which spectators make about onstage acts. Their attention is drawn from the sequence of which X act is a phase to a genre of which X act is an instance.

The classical wajang kulit tradition of paying attention not only to onstage sequences but also to mythological-philosophical meanings of discrete onstage acts or elements ("The lotus eyes of this puppet symbolize alus qualities while the pop eyes of that symbolize kasar qualities") may have encouraged habits of flickering attention to onstage action which carry over to ludruk. Attention is drawn from the onstage sequence of which X act is a phase to the philosophical category of which X act is a symbol.

Some of the younger ludruk directors have expressed a desire to make the ludruk plays more sustained pieces of action. Basman said he could not get impassioned about stereotyped stock sad scenes that were not joined with a larger dramatic structure even though older people, like his kuna mother, could; his mother, Basman said, could weep upon hearing a stereotyped musical phrase of a few notes. Soetjipto, of Tresno Enggal, said that when he manages a performance at the People's Amusement Park, he glues his eye to his watch and keeps things moving and connected. When a part takes people's attention from the whole, he cuts it. It is true that performances directed by Basman and Soetjipto did achieve unusually sustained climaxes.

Probably switching from all-night kampung celebrations to four-hour commercial shows has forced ludruk directors to think, more than they once did, of a ludruk show as an integral, tightly packed unit. In some cases the shorter time appears simply to have forced them to schematicize to show many events in a short time; the following scene took about four minutes to perform:

> Boy and girl meet on the street, the first time they have laid eyes on one another. Boy greets girl in polite Javanese. She replies in kind. He moves closer. They switch to familiar Javanese and utter approximately three sentences each. He says, "Let's get married." She says, "All right." They walk away arm in arm.

Perhaps the director was stimulated by the knowledge that the

1 The clown—soul of ludruk

2 The gong player

3 Transvestite singer, onstage

4 Transvestite singer, backstage

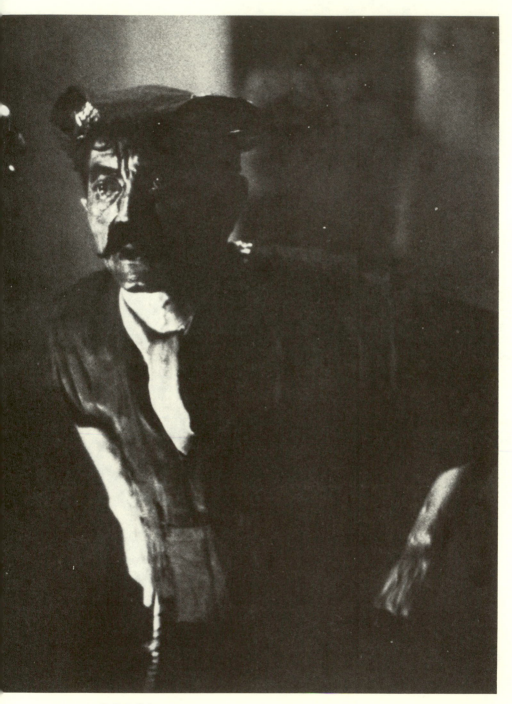

5 Pak Sakera

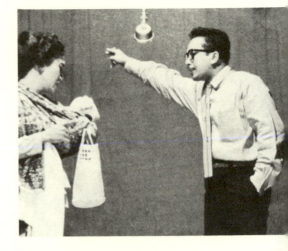

5 Darta's village wife with her sick child

7 Darta drives his wife and child away from his offic

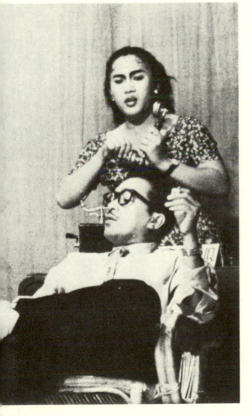

8 Darta relaxes with his secretary

9 Actors in Tresno Enggal about to embark from Brawidjawa Army Headquarters

10 Transvestite singers backstage with Florence Peacock

11 Ludruk audience

manager of the ludruk theater always cuts off all lights at midnight, whether the show is finished or not.

One Javanese intellectual complains that no sustained climax can develop in ludruk because "all pleasures and releases are spilled out in jokes" [9] and another agrees: "We cannot compare ludruk to Western drama for there is nothing in the West which comparably mixes laughter and sadness . . . ludruk, of course, is far from perfect in terms of such Western categories as 'climax.'" [10] Indeed, in ludruk, tragic scenes usually become comic. A village headman's daughter has just been killed by a zombie. The village headman begins weeping but starts wiping his face with his necktie and suddenly is laughing. A family has just been informed that their son was killed in action. The mother cries out in horror, the sister weeps on the mother's skirt, the father stands silently to the side, but suddenly everybody is laughing as the father gives all his son's belongings to the son's comrades-in-arms who accept them with lecherous eagerness and speed. A daughter returns home to find her father dead in bed and is so overcome with grief that she falls to the floor throwing her bowl of rice onto her brother's head. (Not all ludruk goers laughed at this; one man complained in his introspection report that the actors should be sad when the father dies, but they make it funny.)

All ludruk characters are slightly ludicrous regardless of their social position. A ludruk tyrant may occupy the same position in fictional society as a tyrant does in a German film, but the ludruk tyrant lacks the heavy, demonically concentrated quality of the German one. [11]

The principle jokesters in ludruk are the clowns (called *pelawak, punakawan,* or *badut*). These do not have the divine origins and power of Semar (who in court dramas is usually portrayed by a man who is in real life the most powerful or oldest of the court's princes), but they dominate ludruk even more than Semar dominates wajang. Ludruk in its beginning was hardly more than a clown, Besut. Ludruk's most famous hero, Durasim, was a clown. Most managers of ludruk troupes today play the clown role. Lud-

[9] Poerbokoesoemo, *Ludruk,* p. 14.

[10] Comment by Boeradi, "Diskusi Komisi C" [Discussion of Commission C], Seminar Ludruk, Balai Pemuda in Surabaja, December 25–28, 1960.

[11] Siegfried Kracauer, *From Caligari to Hitler,* pp. 77–79.

ruk performances proper begin with a clown song (the ngremo is danced while the audience filters in). The only characters in the dagelan are clowns. During stories (tjerita) clowns, unlike other characters, use their own names, so they are the only story-actors whom audiences always know.

The clown is the character whom ludruk spectators must deeply regard as "one of us." The clown plays lowly roles such as servant, laborer, or tramp. He speaks *ngoko* (low) Javanese, Surabaja dialect. He wears humble clothes. He is superstitious, provincial, and penniless. He stumbles along with his master's bags, and he squats below the gold tip of an official's cane, carrying on a kind of below-waist-level conversation with the audience.

Since the clown has a peculiar identity with the proletarian ludruk goer, a portrait of the clown's personality might illuminate our understanding of the Javanese proletarian's personality. Partly for that reason, I present the following brief sketch (keeping in mind, of course, that the clown is no simple projection of proletarian character; he takes the form he does in order to fulfill certain aesthetic functions within the ludruk plays).

The clown is childlike.[12] Like Peter Pan, he never grows old, although other ludruk characters do. The clown cries like a child, uses babytalk, and is orally focused: he is shown sucking a pacifier, greedily gobbling up food, requesting milk and bananas (babyfood). Clowns are not genitally-oriented. They shrink from potential sexual partners with remarks like, "She'll be my enemy under the blanket." While a clown-servant's master stares at a girl, the clown talks about his breakfast. Clowns joke about their inability

---

[12] There are several features of Javanese proletariat family life and child rearing to which one might loosely relate the clown's "child-like" features as well as other traits of his personality. For instance, Bateson and Mead note that because Balinese make each child responsible for looking after the one just below it in age, the Balinese baby is raised by a child nurse (p. 212). Therefore, to follow the implications of Bateson's remarks (p. 212), the baby is given an unusually good opportunity to internalize the superego of a child, rather than adult, authority figure. Lower class Javanese rarely have adult servants to look after them, and a "child nurse" pattern similar to that of the Balinese is present among these lower classes. Perhaps this mode of child care encourages lower class Javanese (whom the upper classes sometimes explicitly label "children") to grow into adults who have traits that in some ways are childlike, or to grow up feeling little guilt about occasionally acting childlike. But this is a very gross chain of reasoning; one must ask about the total family context within which the child is raised; for instance, does the Javanese father give the child a model of great dignity which compensates him for looking to his child nurse as a model of behavior?

to use phallic objects such as guns, which recalls the fact that Besut wore a broken sword that Wongsosewojo called "the soul of ludruk." [13]

Clowns have only flitting commitment to any person or group. They are always double-crossing one another. Two clowns are arrested. "Who did it?" asks the policeman. "He did it!" shout both clowns at once, each pointing his finger at the other. Clowns tell people that they are somebody whom they are not and make promises which they do not keep ("Just said it, didn't feel anything about it [*gak ngerasa*]," they say). Clown-servants are celibate, a state that is not a literal reflection of the servant's status in Surabaja, but, I suggest, a literary device to signal the clown's detachment from any group, including families. Clown-servants do not show any particular loyalty to their masters. Clowns' social lives are just a series of face-to-face encounters, quick and fleeting. Their weapons are not institutional or personal loyalties but clever patter aimed at checkmating the other for a moment, placating him for an instant.

Clowns have little sense of self, little ego identity. The clown owns no property and so is sometimes shown wandering homeless, but unlike Western literary tramps such as Hesse's Knulp, the clown never wanders by himself; he is always with a partner, yet he never appears to empathize or identify with his partner and will betray him in an instant. The clown who finds his home in another's home, his master's, does not identify with his master. He just mocks his master's external signs — sounds and motions. The clown's favorite game is to imitate gestures and words of somebody other than himself — a creditor when he is actually a debtor, a master when he is a servant, a girl when he is a man, a policeman when he is a thief.

Clowns are reductionists. Machfoed, a pedicab driver, said ludruk clown humor is based on the idea of *nglètèk* (to reduce high to low, to peel away pretense). Clowns' jokes reduce high status to low, culture to biological drives, alus to kasar, cosmopolitan to provincial. A clown begins to say something in a high-pitched voice using cosmopolitan and intellectual Indonesian language but suddenly drops to a low growl in Surabaja dialect, ngoko Javanese. By compulsively revealing his low side, the clown becomes invulnerable; no one can reduce him lower than he reduces himself.

[13] Wongsosewojo, "Loedroek," p. 205.

MOTHERS, WIVES, AND TRANSVESTITES

Kinship among Surabaja Javanese is no more important a basis for organizing social life than is kinship among urban Americans. As in America, descent is traced through both mother and father and the most important kinship unit is the nuclear family, consisting of mother, father, and children. The nuclear family has rather loose obligations to extra-nuclear kinfolk. On occasions such as weddings a nuclear family's extra-nuclear kinship bonds become fairly important.

I deal here with the household group, which is often the nuclear family, since the nuclear family tends to live apart from kinfolk. I emphasize one feature of the household: its affairs are organized around the mother (wife).

The matrifocus [14] of the Javanese household can be seen first in the fact that persons from outside the nuclear family who move into the household are usually related to the mother, not to the father. For instance, in the household where my wife and I lived, two boys and one girl came (at different times) to live in the household, and all were related to the mother, Ibu Marsosudiro, not to the father, Bapak Marsosudiro. In turn, Ibu followed the Javanese practice of "lending children" to relatives who did not have children. She lent her two youngest sons to two of her sisters, each of whom lived in towns other than Surabaja. Thus, in these sisters' households, they, not their husbands, were the ones whose nephews came to live with them; again, the relatives who moved to the household were related to the mother, not the father. Not only relatives who move in, but also those who visit, are more likely to be related to the mother than to the father. Ibu Marsosudiro's relatives paid several visits. But Bapak's relatives never came to visit, although they did not live much farther away than did Ibu's relatives and were visited several times by Bapak; the oldest daughter used to joke about how Ibu's relatives always came, at which time Bapak would resignedly go off and take a nap. A final example: when a Javanese parent is old, it is expected that he or she will go to live with his or her daughter, not son (all informants considered this pattern ideal, though I know several cases where a mother is living with her son). This means that the daughter, viewed

---

[14] Hildred Geertz. *The Javanese Family,* p. 78, applies the term "matrifocal" to the Javanese family, using the term in its strict sense — that is, to signify that households are linked by bonds between their female heads.

now as mother in her own household, is the one who attracts relatives, not her husband.[15]

The mother manages all household financial affairs. Often the father just turns his paycheck over to his wife, and she doles out an allowance to him. "Men can't keep money," said a Javanese woman working as a cook, "that's true of 100 per cent of them." I heard several kampung women say that on payday they went to the factory where their husbands were working and got the husband's paycheck direct from the paymaster. A son in need of money does not write "Dear Dad" as in American jokes. He goes to his mother or even to his mother-in-law. (A Javanese psychiatrist, Professor Soejoenoes at the Karamindjangan Psychiatric Ward, said that in his ward the number of female mental patients had increased faster than the number of male patients during the time prices were rising so rapidly in Indonesia. This, he explained, was because in Java women are more concerned with household finance than men are.) Tresno Enggal, like all ludruk troupes comprised only of men, always elects as treasurer a man who plays female roles on (and sometimes off) the ludruk stage, perhaps reflecting the Javanese idea that women are good at money matters.

Mothers do a great deal toward making as well as managing money for the household. Professional women traders dominate the markets [16] and almost all kampung housewives do some trading in their spare time. ("Buying and selling," the Javanese equivalent of the American child's "playing store," is considered a girl's game.) To get capital for trade, women organize *arisan:* a group of women pool their funds, and take turns using the pool for entrepreneurial ventures. In addition to trading, kampung women work as cooks, servants, midwives, and construction laborers.

The mother is seen as a source of magical strength. Surabaja billboards advertise a medicine called "Mother Medicine" (*Djamu Ibu*) that cures all ills. But most powerful of all medicines, said a ludruk director, is fluid from the mother's womb. When all else failed to cure his malaria, said he, his mother gave him her fluid, and he recovered, for the mother is "the wellspring of mysterious health." In ludruk plays the mother sometimes provides the proletarian with magical strength which enables him to cope with threatening bourgeois or elite male forces. In one play, a fierce prince has no mother, only a father. He encounters a proletarian who

[15] *Ibid.,* pp. 44–46, describes similar patterns.

[16] *Ibid.,* p. 122, emphasizes women's strong role in trade. See also Alice G. Dewey, *Peasant Marketing in Java.*

has no father, only a mother. The prince brutally beats the proletarian, who runs away weeping to his mother, Mbok Rondo Para-
ban. She comforts him and gives him an enchanted stick, with
which he flails the prince, who falls dead. In another play Sarip
Tambakjasa, the hero, his mother's favorite, is pitted against his
brother, whom his mother hates, and who is a fanatical Muslim
(Islam has a number of masculine connotations). The Muslim
brother shoots silver bullets, made super-potent by prayer to Allah,
at the hero. But each time the hero is hit, his mother cries out, and
he is revived — until the Dutch police muzzle his mother. She cannot cry out and the hero dies in agony.

The child is closer to his mother than to his father. After the first
five years of his life, during which time he is very intimate with the
father, the child begins to approach the father with formal manners and to speak to him in formal (*Krama*) Javanese, as he
would to a high official. The father steps down from his pinnacle
to discipline the child only in case of the most drastic misdeeds.
The mother is the one who punishes the child for ordinary offenses.
(Several mental patients whom I interviewed had delusions of
being hit by their mothers; none had such delusions regarding their
fathers.)

Because the mother is such an important focus of household life,
Javanese reason that it is more important for a newcomer to a
household to get along with the mother than with the father, who
is marginal to household affairs. That is why a Javanese mother
who wishes to lend her child to someone tries to lend it to one of
her sisters.[17] It would do no good for the mother to lend the child
to her brother since his wife, not he, would have daily power over
the child. The brother is marginal to the household. A stepfather is
not so much a threat to a child as is a stepmother, which may explain why ludruk plays are full of tales of evil stepmothers, but
lack tales of evil stepfathers.

The male's external position in the household is symbolized at
weddings and circumcision ceremonies by the strict custom that all
men must sit outside the house, under an awning, while all women
get inside the house, sitting in the front room or jabbering and
working back in the kitchen.

We see, then, a matrifocal household pattern: mother (or wife)
at the center of the household, father (or husband) hovering

---

[17] See also H. Geertz, pp. 36–41.

around the edges. What connection might this social pattern have to ludruk?

All female characters in ludruk stories are portrayed by transvestites. These characters include the following types:

The hero's mother (for instance, the mother of Sarip Tambakjasa): When a woman is characterized as a mother, but not as a wife (Sarip's mother's husband is never shown), she is invariably sympathetically portrayed. Sometimes she is almost worshipfully portrayed, as in a story entitled "A Mother's Tears," a maudlin tale of a mother who sacrificed all for the sake of her sons.

The middle-aged nagging wife: Every ludruk troupe has an actor, usually of effeminate but aggressive personality offstage, who specializes in this role. (President Sukarno deems this figure his favorite ludruk character: Sukarno has asked a famous portrayer of this character to give repeated performances at his palace, and he has given the figure a nickname "Meddlesome Mouth," referring to rapid and predatory mouth movements which she exhibits.)[18] The nagging wife is always coupled with a submissive husband, played by a clown. The wife knocks her husband around, taunts him about his sexual impotence, and rants on and on (at such high speed that her mouth finally turns into a kind of meatgrinder, spewing out spittle but no words) about the husband's general sorriness. The husband just sits passively. But occasionally (since he is always played by a splendidly witty clown), he drops a sly comment that makes the wife look ludicrous, at which point loud laughter issues from the audience. The male spectators and the actors who play the clown-husband greatly enjoy this scene, which is inserted at some point into almost every performance, regardless of whether it fits the story or not.

The thirtyish villainess wife: A good example of this type of character appears in a melodrama called "Sin" (*Dosa*), a story performed about four times as often as any other domestic tale. The villainess, Mariandel, wears flashy clothes, has an aggressive, forward manner. She takes a lover, kills his wife, gets her husband sent to prison for the crime, and lives a life of sinful delight for about twenty years. Then, just as her husband is released from

---

[18] There are various rumors connecting Sukarno with ludruk. For instance, it is said that during Sukarno's teen-age years, spent in Surabaja, he sometimes played roles in ludruk plays — ludruk being at that time more intimately linked to the nationalist movement than now. Sukarno, it is said, played roles such as heroine, "tough guy," and so on.

prison, she kills her lover; again, she tries to get her husband to take the rap. He refuses, and with great delight and contempt turns her over to the police. After she is in jail, the husband takes her children to see her. He points his finger at her, as she crouches weeping in a dark cell, and says, "Do not weep for her. She is a sinner!" The curtain drops and spectators scream vindictive comments such as "serves you right!"

The beautiful young mistress: We shall see some evidence that this type of transvestite is a kind of wish-fulfillment fantasy for kampung men; she is a nice symbolic substitute or compensation for a man's domineering wife.

In addition to these story characters, ludruk presents transvestite singers who personify the beautiful mistress or parody the aggressive woman. The linkages are not perfect, but it appears that by exhibiting the types of transvestites that they do, ludruk actors either protest against or compensate for the male's position in the matrifocal household. The middle two characters parody or blacken the image of the domineering wife; the first and last glorify the opposite of that type — the sweet mother or romantic mistress.

THE LUDRUK COMPLEX

The various features that we have presented seem to be functionally connected to one another. Ludruk's prefabricated structure is related to its participants' flickering attention; flickering attention is related to ludruk's tendency to break up climaxes by jokes; the frequency of jokes in ludruk is related to the dominant position of the clown; the clown reflects the lower class male personality; the lower class male's personality is probably related to his postion in the matrifocal household (here I would be very cautious, since there are so many different lower class Javanese male personalities); and the male's position in the matrifocal household is related to the characters which ludruk transvestites depict.

Just how tightly these elements of "the ludruk complex" fit together is a matter for further debate. What I wish to stress here is how basic these elements or features are to ludruk. Every ludruk show, regardless of its story content, exhibits a prefabricated structure, is watched in fragmented fashion, features clowns and nagging transvestites. All parts of each ludruk show — prologue, melodrama, and songs — display these features and characters. Thus, before turning to a separate analysis of each part of ludruk and of different types of ludruk shows, I have sketched those elements and features common to all of these parts and types.

Part 3

The Show

6

Prologue

Phases of the dagelan (comic prologue to the melodrama) always occur in the same order: song, monologue, dialogue, and victimization. In this chapter I set forth the main features of each of these phases except the song, which will be considered in connection with other ludruk songs in later chapters. Unless I state otherwise, the features I describe for each phase of the prologue hold for all or virtually all of the seventy-five prologues that I watched.

MONOLOGUE

A lone man, a clown, dressed like a servant or other lowly worker, sings a song and then begins a monologue. Often he begins by saying "If I think and think about myself. . . ." Then he describes himself as "confused," "in despair," or "depressed." He complains, "All of life is stirred up." He laments, "O Allah . . . why is my fate like this? Why are my soul and body confused like this?" Eventually he gets around to describing his failure to make a living. He says, "The government program (TRIKORA) offers education, position, food, and clothes. But I can't get anything. Why did I get married? After three years already eight children." A listener rejoins, "That's not nice, pal; if you have diarrhea, go defecate." He tells about his household financial problems. A listener shouts, "Your house, younger brother is in a pipe!" to which somebody else adds, "in a *waru* root." He whines that his salary is tiny. A listener screams, "Big enough to buy a G-string and brassiere!" He says he looked for work and found no vacancies. A listener tells him, "Go on out, pal. Stop by my place. Not enough workers there to kill the mosquitos." He moans that he has four children and a salary of fifty rupiah per day, not enough for one kilogram of rice. A listener responds sarcastically, "Just buy an ounce and eat it a grain at the time." He groans that his pay is fifty rupiah per day, just enough to buy fish (to put on the rice). A listener says cynically, "Just eat *bubur* (porridge given to children) and drink a lot, then you'll be full."

The monologue, then, consists mainly of complaints. Listeners respond by heaping abuse on the complainer. Yet, although they abuse the monologuist, listeners reveal in some of their responses, interviews, and introspection reports, that they feel quite a bit of identity with that figure, who presents himself as a kampung person like themselves, with their clothes, speech, and problems. Said Machfoed, the pedicab driver: "His talk recalls to me my own life history."

DIALOGUE

The dialogue begins with the appearance of a second man, whose presence is unwelcome to the monologuist. A monologuist, coming to the close of his monologue, whines, "I'd like to see Meler, but I hope I don't meet Arli, for he always regards me with contempt." He continues looking to the front, but extends his arm to the side. It touches something and begins to tremble. "Lho!" he explains. He slowly rotates his eyes around toward the outstretched trembling hand, his face still straight ahead. The hand is in contact with Arli, slanted eyes accentuated by paint, smile of scorn on his lips.

In some dialogues, three figures appear. A monologuist, lips contorted as if in pain, whines on and on about his troubles. Suddenly a second man appears, equipped with a raucous voice and a mouth alternately protruding forward in the shape of a megaphone and opening to reveal large teeth. This second man, Slamet, touches the monologuist, Amat, who shrivels at his touch, hunching his shoulders as if to fend off a rain of painful stimuli. Slamet says Amat is insane because he has been talking to himself. Amat snivels that Slamet is always trying to humiliate his friends "and that's not our (the Javanese) way." Slamet repeatedly addresses Amat as "boy" and Amat asks Slamet to be more polite. Slamet keeps slapping Amat's back as Amat shrinks away; Slamet meanwhile loudly insisting that back-slapping is Surabaja custom (it's not alus Javanese custom). At this point a third person, Dojo, who like Slamet is loud and grinning, appears. Everybody greets him. He then shakes hands with each of them again and again. He says loudly to Amat, "I heard you were in jail!" "Yes," replies Amat, "I killed your son." (These are typical ways kasar Surabajans greet each other said an alus spectator from Central Java.) Dojo continues shaking hands. Finally Amat slaps Dojo's hand and pulls away from the group. His face assumes a look of pain. He jerks his cap off in frustration.

Usually there are just two figures in the dialogue. After they meet, they engage in a duel of wit. At machine gun speed the two spit riddles at each other:

A asks B, "How many turns between here and Gresik [a city near Surabaja]?" B: "75." A: "Wrong!" B: "How many?" A: "Two." B [in disbelief]: "Two!" A: "Yeah, left and right. How many traffic lights in Surabaja?" B: "Maybe twenty." A: "Wrong! Three." B: "Three!" A: "Red, green, and yellow."

The questioner asks, "How *many* lights or turns?" He then supplies, as the correct answer, an answer to the more general question, "How many *kinds* of lights or turns?" He misleads the answerer as to the level of generality at which he expects an answer.

Another favorite type of dialogue begins when one partner arouses the expectations of the other; then, when the other bites, he disappoints these expectations. Anton tells Amin in glowing words about a job. At this job, says Anton, they give you coffee when you arrive for work; then at midmorning you stop by the brewery, and they give you beer. Amin, a fat buffoon, becomes excited. Then Anton asks Amin, "Well, can you give me that job?" "Waaah, I thought you were offering it," says Amin. After this Amat and Amin decide to practice asking for jobs. Anton pretends to be an employer. Amin asks for a job. Anton reels off a string of qualifications required for a certain job: experience, literacy, ability to speak Indonesian, and so on. Finally he reveals the nature of the job: "There's an opening for a *babu* (woman servant)." (This is very funny because Anton, who is skinny, short, greasy, and mustachioed, rasps the word "babu" in a totally repulsive manner.) Amin is indignant and Anton mutters that there truly is an opening for a babu in Central Java. Then the tables are turned. Amin pretends to be a Dutchman who is hiring Anton. Amin blusters in an over-resonant, back-in-the-throat voice, striding about with his chest puffed up and chin resting on his chest, expounding interminably the details of the job — what time Anton should appear at work, what tools he should bring, what rate of pay increase he should expect, and many other details with which Dutch employers would apparently be expected to concern themselves. Finally Anton asks Amin to what place he should report for work. "Work!" blusters Amin, "I myself have no job."

Another type of joke frustrates expectations linguistically. It turns out that one partner has misled the other by an ambiguous word:

A claims to be a *tukang* (artisan). B asks: "Are you a tukang stone (stone worker)?" "No," replies A. "A tukang wood (carpenter)?" asks B. "No." "A tukang electric (electrician)?" "No." And so it goes through a long list of tukangs until finally it comes out that A is a tukang *tjopét* (pickpocket).

In another popular dialogue, one man is striving to get another to pay back money which he (the first) lent to the other:

The creditor asks, "What about your debt?" The debtor replies, "My debt is my business." The creditor then threatens to report the debtor to the police. The debtor says it is very complicated nowadays to report to the police. Therefore, he and the creditor should practice reporting. He offers to play the role "policeman" so that the creditor can practice reporting to him. The creditor then attempts to report to the "policeman" the delinquent debt of the man who is playing the role "policeman." This gets him nowhere, so he appropriates the role policeman. But now the debtor is playing the role "creditor" and reporting his own debt.

This skit involves Gilbert-and-Sullivan-like piling up of nonsense by logical deductions from overly narrow premises — as when the Lord Chancellor in "Iolanthe" argues that since he wants to marry his ward, Phyllis, and since anyone who wishes to marry a ward must get permission from the Lord Chancellor, he must get permission from himself. The premise in the ludruk dialogue is that there are only two roles available: "policeman" and "man reporting a debt." Assuming this premise, the creditor has lost the duel before it begins; whether the debtor plays the role "policeman" or "creditor" he is exempt from the role "debtor."

It is interesting to note the rapidly shifting body positions that parallel the quick logical shifts which lie at the base of these duels of wit. Here is a typical sequence of body positions (during a duel of about four minutes):

> The two partners lean toward one another.
> A leans way back, looking forward.
> B looks toward A.
> B moves away and looks back over his shoulder at A.
> A turns away and both A and B look over their shoulders at each other from a distance.
> Both come back closer to each other until they almost rub shoulders.
> Each moves away and looks back at the other. . . .

When someone is bested in one of these duels, spectators laugh and say the loser is "sprayed," "checkmated," or "one-upped."

Some spectators, in their introspection reports, indicated that a carefree mood crept over them during a duel: a pedicab driver says, "This reminds me of the time when I still kept sheep and my heart was gay." A clerk: "My inner feelings join with this as if I did not yet have a family. I forget everything that involves responsibility and risk." Perhaps such a mood flows partly from the artificially delimited but rather clear-cut system of nonsense logic in terms of which the word and role play of the duel is organized; such logic sets the duel distinctly apart from everyday society.

Also the dialogue is separated by its visual setting from daily life in household and kampung. The backdrop for the dialogue never depicts a kampung or household. It is either blank or it portrays downtown Surabaja, showing the central square, Hero's monument, post office, and streets leading toward business and market areas. Characters in the dialogue often allude to the fact that they are meeting "on the street." Spectators sometimes describe the encounter of monologuist and second figure by the word *kepetuk* which means "chance meeting" such as might occur on the street in contrast to "planned visit" as to somebody's house which is denoted by another word. A youth describes "kepetuk" in the dialogue: "It's like I'm walking along the street, run into a friend, and exclaim, 'Lho!' [in surprise]." The conventional symbolism of the dialogue signals that a street scene rather than a domestic scene is being displayed: in ludruk, domestic scenes are always presented on the full stage while street scenes are presented on the front half of the stage, with the back half covered by a curtain or mural; the dialogue is always on the front half of the stage.

The dialogue is concerned almost entirely with non-domestic, downtown matters — getting jobs, streetlights, routes out of town. Spectators' responses indicate that they imagine themselves in a commercial rather than domestic realm when they listen to the dialogue. A pedicab driver says in his introspection report, "I remember the confusion of seeking a job."

The rhythm of the dialogue parallels the rhythm of Surabaja commercial encounters rather than that of domestic visits. Domestic visits, among Javanese, are marked by a slow, smooth, crooning kind of rhythm. The rapid-fire thrusts and retreats of the duel are much more like the rhythm of bargaining in the market place. There buyer and seller exchange a few fast words about the price, the buyer steps away a few paces, the seller calls him back with a new price — and the duel begins again.

The dialogue characters, then, are of the street and market, not the home or kampung. This is indicated by the form of their dialogue — its content, rhythm, logical structure — and the physical setting of the dialogue. An informant supported the impression that these dialogue characters are cast as jobless reprobates hanging around the streets and bazaars rather than as family men at home in the kampung household: "We call this type of character, in ludruk or in life, *peleta*. In real life, Paiman [who plays a dialogue character in ludruk] lives as a peleta. He is a bachelor, he drinks, gambles on pigeon races, plays cards at night, has no job. When he is broke, he gets money from his parents. I think ludruk was born when this kind of person decided to depict his life onstage."

THE VICTIMIZATION

After the dialogue, the prologue unfolds in various directions. Out of the seventy-five prologues that I watched, the most frequent single type of sequel to the dialogue was a skit, which I shall call "the victimization." Forty of the sequels to the dialogue were of this type. The other thirty-five sequels were splintered into about a dozen types of which no single type occurred more than five times. So the most popular single type of dialogue sequel is the victimization.

The victimization is marked off from the dialogue in that it always begins or ends in an urban kampung or rural village domicile, whereas the dialogue is always outside these locales, usually on the street or in the market, as we have seen. The victim is always shown at home in his kampung or village, whereas the reprobates of the dialogue are almost never shown at home. We may divide victimization sequels into two kinds: those that begin at the victim's home and those that conclude at the victim's home.

Consider first some victimizations that begin at the victim's home. The stage is set for the event by the last words of the two reprobates during their dialogue. They say that they have decided to rob or swindle somebody. The curtain drops, then reopens to show the victim-to-be sitting alone. He is dressed in black, contrasting with the white jackets which reprobates usually wear; the black indicates the rural origins of the victim, while the white jackets of the reprobates are those of urban servants and waiters. The victim-to-be delivers a soliloquy which reveals that he has a responsible position in his village or kampung, that he owns some property, and that his neighbors consider him a little queer. Following are four typical scenes introducing a victim to be:

> The victim is sitting alone, hands folded primly in his lap. He says nothing for several minutes, then rasps, "I never talk with neighbors." He goes on to say that all his windows are locked because he expects thieves. He has worked hard since childhood to get his possessions. . . .

> The victim is a headman (lurah) of a village. He says, "Being lurah here is sometimes hard. People are afraid of me. When I pass through the village, every window is shut . . . but, after all, I was once insane. I can make myself disappear but unfortunately can not become visible again. I expect thieves. . . ."

> The victim sits with shoulders hanging dejectedly: "I am rich, but cannot sleep. I just change from one bed to another. I dream of police. I fear them. . . ."

> An old man, whom the thieves describe as "rich and stingy" is doing an anal dance. The gamelan plays a dirty-sounding, rolling

tune with much drum-slapping, while the old man wiggles his buttocks to each slap of the drum.

Victims are robbed or duped in various ways:

Case A: Slamet, a reprobate, breezes into the victim's house while the victim's back is turned. The victim, Amat, turns and sees Slamet. A quarrel develops because Slamet entered Amat's house without asking permission to do so, thus breaking a traditional rule of Javanese (and kampung) etiquette. Amat is confused (since traditional rules specify no tactics for dealing with a guest who does not follow the traditions). Slamet asks for food and drink, brazenly exploiting Amat's hospitality and then even asks Amat for money, threatening to kill himself if Amat will not give him the money. Amat becomes very anxious, for he has a phobia about getting into trouble with the police. Slamet suddenly dies. Amat frantically waves money in front of Slamet's face, and Slamet revives. But then he dies again. Amat waves a larger amount of money in front of Slamet's face. Suddenly a second reprobate, Amari, enters. Upon glimpsing the dead Slamet, Amari screams that Amat has committed murder and threatens to summon the police. Amat hastily slips Amari some cash, which Amari receives with one hand while refusing with the other. He then ambles over, revives the dead man with a touch and rides him out the door pickaback. ("Amat was afraid to tickle the dead man," said an informant, "because he is afraid of disturbing the peace of his house. He's a typical kuna villager.")

No sooner are Slamat and Amari gone than a third man enters Amat's house and immediately falls dead upon the table with a noose already around his neck. Again Amat is dismayed. Again Amari enters, accuses, and is bribed, after which he pretends that the noose is an air hose and pumps up the corpse, which rises slowly while dancing a coarse dance.

Now, back on the street, the two dead men and Amari begin splitting the bribe-money. But Amat comes upon them unseen. One by one the plotters see Amat looming behind Amari and slip away, leaving Amari fondling the money. Amari says, "I'll just give this money to my. . . ," wheels about, and the waiting hands of Amat receive the money.[1]

Case B: As the victim is sitting in his house, reprobates intrude, one after the other. None ask permission to enter. Each does a different type of dance. The victim cannot resist joining in each dance. Each time, while the victim is rhythmically sucked into dancing with the victimizer, the victimizer's hand snakes out, and the victim can-

---

[1] Almost the same skit as this one is described by C. Geertz, *Religion of Java,* p. 293.

not resist putting money into it, although he grimaces painfully as he does. Later, as the dancers divide their spoils, the victim comes upon them unseen and gets his money back. As the victim lectures the thieves about their misdeeds, they all slip laughing away.

Consider now two victimizations which end at the victim's house:

Case X: One reprobate, Slamet, pretends to die on the street. His friend, Amat, covers him with a cloth and sits on the ground beside him weeping. An older man comes by and asks Amat who the dead man is. The "dead" Slamet is the older man's nephew. The uncle makes a few coarse remarks about the generally sorry character of his nephew, then asks to look at the body. The weeping Amat protests that the nephew "died of plague, not of god." The uncle walks around the body anyway, trying to get to it, but Amat walks frantically inside the uncle's path, blocking the uncle from the body, speeding up when the uncle speeds up. Finally the uncle is persuaded much against his will to hand over some money to Amat to pay him for his trouble in carrying the nephew to the uncle's house. Amat tries to continue weeping but giggles gleefully upon getting the money. The uncle leaves. The two swindlers stand up and construct what looks like a coffin, each taking one end of the covering cloth and sticking the nephew's shoes out of one end of the cloth so that it looks as if the nephew is under it. In this fashion they proceed to the uncle's house. There the nephew lies down and Amat recovers him with the cloth and then leaves. The uncle enters, sees the body, says a few more ugly things about his nephew, and then prepares to burn his body since it is diseased. The nephew dashes away as the uncle searches for kerosene. Now the usual "getting back" scene follows, with the uncle sneaking up behind the culprit with the money, who wheels around, only to push the money into the uncle's waiting hands.

Case Y: Amin, fat and gross, accosts his stepmother and tells her he was just out looking for Anton (who is greasy and skinny), her true son, but found him dead. He says he thinks Anton had been drunk because he was dead in the street. The mother bursts into loud wails. Amin exploits her grief, prodding her to give him money to take care of Anton's burial. As she wails louder and louder, he presses her for more and more money.

Now Anton accosts his stepfather, calling "Father! Father!" and beating himself to make himself weep. "Amin is dead!" Anton asks for money to fix Amin's burial. The father shows no grief at his son's death, just fury at having to pay out money, of which Anton asks more each time the father grudgingly pulls out a tiny sum. Finally Anton leaves with a large sum and laughs a wild laugh of joy.

Anton and Amin meet and strut around together, laughing, fingering their money, and sticking bills all over their caps. But the parents catch them and get their money back. The father is crudely joyous over this, as he and the mother settle down again in their house.

How can the victimization be interpreted? Cases *A, B, X,* and *Y,* as well as most of the other thirty-six victimization skits that I saw (see Table 1) exhibit the following pattern: the victimizers are

TABLE 1

REPRESENTATION OF AGE AND PLACE OF ACTION IN
"VICTIMIZER" AND "VICTIM" SKITS
(40 Skits)

	AGE		PLACE OF ACTION	
	Young	Old	Home	Eleswhere
Victimizer	40	0	4	36
Victim	7	33	34	6

young and never at home, while the victim is old and at some point in the skit at home in his village or kampung domicile. This contrast can be linked to the fact that the victim is often constrained by traditional kampung or village norms ("The victim is always kuna," said an actor who always plays the victimizer), while the victimizers treat such norms in cavalier fashion, manipulating them to seek their own advantage. In case *B,* for example, the victimizer brazenly intrudes in the victim's house. The victim is taken aback since traditional Javanese etiquette decrees that a visitor must go through a ritual of asking permission to enter the host's house before he is allowed to enter. But the victimizer ignores the traditional rules. He just barges in. Then he begins to dance. The victim cannot resist moving in rhythm to the dance. Suddenly the victimizer's hand snakes out and the victim cannot resist handing over his money. Several kampung dwellers said they had a fear of somebody drawing them into a harmonious interaction of some kind and then suddenly asking them for something; they would be unable to refuse the request. This is what the victimizer does in case *B.* He exploits the kampung dweller's tendency to get drawn into harmonious interaction and to do anything to maintain such interaction, even when it is damaging to his long-term interests. The kampung dweller is wedded to the traditional norm, *rukun* (social harmony). The victimizer, fresh from the downtown streets which are relatively "free" (*bébas*) of traditional norms, exploits for his own self-interest the kampung or villager elder's enslavement to traditional norms. The victimizer turns a traditional social end (avoidance of disharmony) into a means toward individual profit.

In case *A* a similar conflict appears. The victimizer intrudes, violating traditional norms of etiquette. The victim is kuna in his fear of police — the machinery of bureaucracy and law — and in his fear of "disturbing the peace of the house"; the kuna quality is the weakness that the victimizers exploit.

In cases *X* and *Y,* which are of a much rarer type than *A* and *B,* the victims are not so explicitly kuna as are *A* and *B* victims, but they are the victimizers' elders and are shown in a kampung domicile; their age and habitat automatically brand them as more kuna than the victimizers, who are young and hang around the streets. And the weakness which victimizers in *X* and *Y* exploit is the victim's kuna concern with funerals. *X* and *Y* seem to be mild renditions of the conflict which the more common *A* and *B* type skits express.

We cannot ignore the fact that the victim in every case gets back what the victimizers took from him — his money. Thus, in the end, the kuna figure wins. Or does he? The last scene, in which the victim gets back his money seems to be only a formality. The actors do not dwell upon it as they do on the rest of the prologue. Only a moment is spent on it, and then the curtain drops. It is a schematic and stereotyped scene. This "giving back" scene can be viewed as a legitimizer. It is tacked on, after everybody has had an hour of glee at the victim's expense, to restore an air of legitimacy to the skit. The crime was the focus of the victimization. And even though the victim gets his money back, it is the victimizers who dash happily away while the stodgy victim tries to lecture about morality.

One peculiar feature of the victimization is that in almost every case a man is chosen to represent the kampung household; the victim at home is almost always male. Yet in real life, as we have seen, the woman is the pillar of the household and the man is marginal to it. This means that the victim has an unusually weak position. He is marginal to the place which must serve, in the skit, as his citadel. Therefore, victimizers appropriately attack him in that place. It is significant that the only victimization of the *A-B* type, which I saw, that featured a woman victim failed. In the skit two reprobates accost a woman and threaten her with a *kris,* the ceremonial dagger explicitly regarded as a phallic symbol. But the woman grabs the kris and threatens the would-be thieves with it, who back away trembling with fear. The woman makes the men take off their shirts; both turn out to have on women's underwear. They mince a few steps and then stalk angrily away. This skit was performed, interestingly enough, in a kampung rather than in an extra-kampung commercial theater. In the kampung the victimizers' attack on the true pillar of the kampung — woman — fails.

BASIC THEME

There are many prologue themes that could be elaborated upon. I have stressed a theme running through most prologues — conflict between kuna norms and anti-kuna young reprobates. During the monologue one reprobate more or less draws the audience into identifying with him. During the dialogue the reprobates establish their character and locale; they are creatures of the streets and markets, guided by cognitive "nonsense" norms of word and role play, rather than by moral norms of kampung and village tradition, and they are jobless but interested in profit. During the victimization these characters, guided by self-interest more than by kuna village morality, take advantage of a man who is, in ambiguous fashion, embedded in kampung and village domestic society and who is older and more committed to tradition than they are. This victim is duped or robbed and ridiculed. A few spectators express indignation at the victimizers' gall,[2] but most laugh at their antics and the plight of the victim.

---

[2] For instance, a kampung headman criticized the comic prologue, saying that it taught bad morals, taught people to swindle and steal. It is interesting that the victim, who is swindled in the prologues, is often a village or kampung official. Perhaps the head sees the skit as threatening a symbol of his vested interests.

7

Social Correlates of the Prologue

KAMPUNG

Every group of a dozen or so kampung households comprises a *rukun tetangga* (association of neighbors) under the leadership of a *kepala rukun tetangga* (head of an association of neighbors) or R. T. The R. T. is elected yearly by the household heads in his association. His duties are to "serve the social needs of the households." He registers births, marriages, deaths, and guests of houses within his jurisdiction. He assesses his households to finance collective projects. He organizes a night watch against thieves. The R. T. receives no salary, his house is his office, and his office hours are from early evening to about nine o'clock at night.

On certain occasions a family will invite neighbors from the ten or so households surrounding its household to celebrate the communal feast known as "slametan." The slametan sanctifies and symbolizes mutual dependence and mystic unity of neighbors. During the slametan, few gestures signifying rank are used. Every participant feels part of one body, without ill-wishes or fears. Everybody's heart feels peaceful, so it cannot be penetrated by evil spirits; therefore everybody is *slamet* (safe).

Each "association of neighbors" is part of a larger unit, the kampung association (*rukun kampung*), which is composed of about twenty associations of neighbors. The kampung association is headed by an official called an R. K., who is elected yearly but often serves longer. Like the R. T., the R. K. receives no salary and has office hours in the evening. The R. K. coordinates his R. T.'s and mediates between kampung and *lingkungan* (a municipal government unit composed of several kampung).

Each kampung has a name, such as "Margo Rukun" (Way of Cooperation), whereas each rukun tetangga does not. When asked where they live, kampung dwellers always give the name of their kampung.

There is one spiritual being and one ritual that focuses around sacralizing the kampung community. The spirit, *danjang,* is the spirit of the founder of the kampung. A stone in some quiet spot marks the grave of the founder, dwelling place of the danjang. The ritual, *bersih désa,* performed on a certain month of the Javanese calendar, involves offering food to the danjang and thus sanctifying the kampung area by cleansing it of dangerous spirits.

Most people who live in a kampung work elsewhere, at factories, stores, markets outside their kampung. Even kampung officials usually hold a job outside the kampung, since they receive no salary for their duties. (For instance, the R. K. in the kampung where I lived worked as a clerk in the central post office downtown.) In most kampung there is a small store and small concession (coffee and soft-drink) stand. Except for the women who run these, storekeepers work outside the kampung. Kampung on the outskirts of Surabaja have some small fields beside them, but I never knew of anybody who subsisted on yields from these fields. Those who grow crops in them have jobs elsewhere and just reap from their fields, as one pedicab driver in my kampung put it, "enough sugar cane to pass around to the neighbors."

The work of rural Javanese villagers is more intimately linked, spatially, organizationally, and conceptually with the government of the village in which they live than is the urban kampung dweller's work linked to his kampung government. This is so partly because the village (*dukuhan*) acting as a corporate unit headed by a *kamitua* and his assistants holds ownership rights to much of the land (usually surrounding the village) on which villagers farm.[1] Individual villagers are granted rights only to use that land. The village government also controls the irrigation system. Thus the village government controls the villager's work — the land and water with which he works — in a sense that the R. T. and R. K. do not control the work of the urban kampung dweller. The R. T. or R. K. has no control over the downtown factory or store in which the kampung dweller works or the implements he uses at his work.

The kampung dweller not only works outside the kampung, he also shops outside it, in the markets or stores scattered around Surabaja. Each market brings together people from various kampung on a rational "business is business" basis, rather than as neighbors in a moral community. In the market formal etiquette is not emphasized as much as in the kampung. Rapid-fire bargaining in kasar language (it is said that "kasar" is related to the word for market, "pasar") is the typical market pattern.

Kampung dwellers also play outside the kampung, usually in the downtown streets or market areas that are Surabaja's bright lights of Rialto. Prostitutes roam the streets, markets, river banks and open squares but are never allowed in respectable kampung (they only enter certain kampung that specialize in prostitution). Most shows — movies, theater, trance dancers, fire-eaters, and patent medicine spiels — appear outside the kampung. Restaurants, coffee shops, and ice-cream parlors are outside the kampung.

In the streets and markets outside the kampung, kampung dwellers say, life is "freer" than inside the kampung. On the streets youths can wander about all night; while in the kampung overnight guests must register with the R. T. If a youth dallies at a girl's house past midnight, the kampung guards and youth gang up on him and force him to go home. On the streets people do not unfailingly act polite to each other, but he who enters the kampung must act polite in proper Javanese fashion:

A group of boys are sitting around the entrance to our kampung. Some fellow wants to ride a bicycle hard through the entrance. He doesn't want to ask permission in an alus way to enter with his

---

[1] H. Geertz, "Indonesian Cultures and Communities," pp. 45–47.

bicycle. We beat him up, then tell him, "You are Javanese but have not yet learned to understand Javanese manners!"

Much can be observed which supports kampung dwellers' perception that life on the outside streets is freer and brasher than in the kampung. In the kampung there is still emphasis on control over individual impulses to insure harmonious interaction with neighbors and proper deference to elders. The croon of polite Javanese still marks many within-kampung exchanges. On the streets the rhythm is different: Beggars wheedle. Packs of jostling pedicab drivers scream. Trucks and busses race forty miles an hour through the streets. Young hoodlums roam about shouting taunts. Hordes clamber onto trolleys, while pockets are picked and breasts fondled in the melee. I recall one visible transformation from a "street" to a "kampung" role. A teen-age hoodlum, dressed in tight pants and ducktail haircut, was standing scowling with legs apart, hands on hips, at his kampung's celebration of Mother Kartini Day. Suddenly the most respected lady of the kampung addressed him in alus Javanese. Instantly, his countenance became a stylized smile, hands moved from hips to covering his pubes as legs moved closer together, and he bowed slightly, responding politely, "Yes?" in alus Javanese.

Political and educational activities mainly take place outside the kampung. A few kampung have elementary schools inside, but none have higher level schools. There are no large auditoriums for political meetings inside kampung. These, such as the Youth Hall, the Indonesian National Building, or the convention hall at the People's Amusement Park, are all outside the kampung.

It is clear, then, that a good proportion of the kampung dweller's activities take place outside the spatial bounds and organizational control of his kampung, and it appears that this proportion is increasing. The kampung dweller of today is less oriented toward the kampung than were his parents, or, if he is old, then he himself was, when he was young. Many of Surabaja's kampung dwellers have recently moved from rural kampung (the tripling of Surabaja's population since 1930 [2] is largely due to migration from rural areas to Surabaja kampung). As we have seen, a person living in a rural kampung or village is more fully controlled by that unit than is a man who lives in an urban kampung. Therefore,

[2] Karl J. Pelzer, "Physical and Human Resource Patterns," p. 19, says that Surabaja's population has increased from 341,675 in 1930 to 1,007,945 in 1961 — a 295 per cent increase.

migrants from rural to urban kampung have experienced a decline in the importance of their kampung for their lives. Furthermore, not only have persons moved from rural to urban kampung, but also rural kampung have become urban. Many Surabajans have lived since birth in kampung which thirty years ago were almost rural in character, with fields surrounding them. Now the fields have been turned into city lots, and those who tilled the fields have become factory workers. Consequently, these kampungs have lost their old rural functions. Finally, the amount of educational and political activity available to the kampung dweller has increased since colonial times. Since such activity is mainly carried on outside the kampung, intra-kampung life has decreased in significance.

Probably the shrinking role of the kampung in the urban kampung dweller's life is related to the decline of spirits and rituals signifying the sacred, autonomous, and corporate nature of the kampung. Informants from seven Surabaja kampung were questioned about the ḍanjang (place spirit) and bersih désa (place ritual) in their kampung. All informants described the ḍanjang in their kampung as "something in which only the old people believe," and several said, "newcomers to the kampung do not believe in it." A typical response: "The danjang? The old folks say there is one. But what's its form? Where's its grave? I don't know." All informants said that their kampung had an annual bersih désa ritual, but all stated that it had declined in importance since earlier years, and all but one said that nobody except the old folks took it seriously.

Geertz states that interest in the ḍanjang declines as one moves from village to town in East Java.[3] He also points out that in the town he studied, "where village [kampung] political structure has rather atrophied," the bersih désa "is also rather attenuated."[4] Geertz's observations support the notion that the decline of sacred-place symbolism and rites of the kampung is associated with urbanization and consequent shrinking of the kampung's role in the kampung dweller's life.

According to one informant, Marsaid, all generations care less about the slametan now than they did in his youth, and youths today believe in and practice the slametan less than do old folks today.[5] Said Marsaid:

[3] C. Geertz, *Religion of Java,* p. 27.

[4] *Ibid.,* p. 83.

[5] Clifford Geertz supports this view, remarking in several places that the kam-

The purpose of the slametan for those who believe is to honor the ancestors, to clarify a feeling of gratitude [to them], and to express magical hopes and gain good fortune. But I see a tendency nowadays to hold slametan only to maintain tradition and to harmonize social relationships, especially to pay attention to your neighbors' feelings. When I was a child, slametan were "heavier" in the qualities of expressing a feeling of respect, a feeling of gratitude, and magical hopes than they are nowadays.

Marsaid mentioned the demise of slametan for erecting houses and slametan for celebrating births. The first is seldom held now, he said, although it was held often when he was small, for "now there is no belief that the slametan honors the ancestors." The second was traditionally given on the day of birth, then five days after birth, three months after, and one year after, but now "modern families hold only the birthday- and one-year– slametans." Both of these slametan are of the type to which close neighbors are invited; in addition to celebrating births and house erections, these slametan serve to sanctify the bond among neighbors by drawing neighbors and spirits together as joint participants in a sacred feast. So the decline in attention to these slametan is correlated with the neighbor-to-neighbor bond's loss of sacred connotations. And this is related to a lessening of neighbors' practical obligations to one another. In rural villages neighbors apparently still help each other erect a house,[6] but in Surabaja kampung a man who wishes to build anything more than a shack must hire workers to do it. If no neighbors help build a house, the slametan among neighbors to celebrate a house-building loses meaning.

There is another reason for the decline of rituals and symbols that sacralize the kampung as a corporate unit. The kampung has become less and less an autonomous corporate unit, more and more a branch of the Indonesian Nation. The trend fully began when the Japanese established the Rukun Kampung system during the Second World War while they occupied Surabaja; then in 1950 the Indonesian Communist Party directed the establishment of RRKS (Surabaja City Kampung Association) as a functional extension of the municipal and national government to

---

pung dwellers in the East Javanese city where he lived performed the slametan less frequently than it had been performed in the past or found it less meaningful than in the past. See pp. 11 and 49 in *The Religion of Java*.

[6] But Donald Hindley, *The Communist Party of Indonesia 1951–1963*, p. 10, says that in the rural Javanese village itself a decline can be seen in "mutual cooperation" among fellow villagers in house building, farming, and ritual.

the kampung level. The various kampung became administrative subunits of the 27 lingkungan of Surabaja, which are subunits of *ketjamatan,* which are subunits of the municipal government (*kotapradja*) of Surabaja, which is a subunit, with some autonomy, of the national government. To symbolize the connection of kampung with city and nation, city and national rites are being substituted for the old rites which defined the kampung as an autonomus corporate unit.[7] The following is an example of such a national-municipal rite, superimposed on a slametan pattern:

On August 18, 1963, the day after Indonesian Independence Day, the R. K. of Kampung Tembok Lor organized a ceremony to celebrate the opening of a small road leading from the street to an elementary school inside the kampung. The R. K. explained that he had planned to organize an Independence Day celebration anyway, so opening the road (which had required moving some bricks and garbage) gave them "something concrete" to celebrate. The celebration began in the morning. Chairs were set up at the edge of the road, with a microphone for speakers, even though only about thirty people were present. First, the head of the road-opening committee spoke, explaining that formerly the children had had to go a round-about way to get from the street to the school, but now they could enter directly by the road. Next an R. K. from another kampung spoke. Then the R. K. from Kampung Tembok Lor spoke. Finally, a representative from the city government held forth congratulating the kampung (he had to be reminded of the kampung's name), expressing the city's pride in the new road; after his speech he cut a ribbon stretched across the road and kampung children dressed in white trod on the road, followed by the adults. All went to the house of the R. K. to celebrate what was called on the printed invitation to the event a *slametan umum* (general slametan). The "general slametan" opened with a speech by the head of the committee for opening the road, after which the R. K. said a few more words, and an Islamic official (*modin*) said a prayer, interrupted periodically by guests' chants of "Amen." Speeches and prayer were in Indonesian. Finally the guests ate (it was now midday). The food included yellow rice, molded into a cone, rice cakes wrapped in leaves with meat inside, and mush colored red and blue with grated coconut on top. I asked two men the meaning of the cone and colors; they replied that they did not know, but a newspaper reporter explained that in the past the red represented the father, blue the mother. Two other guests emphasized that this was true

[7] This observation parallels the argument of Clifford Geertz, "The Javanese Village," p. 38, that national celebrations are supplanting traditional rituals in Javanese villages.

"back then" but that these things don't carry meaning any more. Although this "general slametan" keeps some symbols of the traditional slametan, such as the opening speech by the host, the prayer, the chants of "Amen," and the colors and shape of the food, it differs in other respects — for instance, people sit on chairs instead of on the floor and they eat a full meal together instead of taking food home to eat in private. Even the traditional slametan symbols that remain have been given new (national-civic) meanings and have lost, in this particular context, their old meanings.

There are many kampung-affiliated ceremonies and symbols that signal the kampung's incorporation into the nation. On Independence Day, Labor Day, and Mother Kartini day, most kampung hold performances to which a large number of each kampung's inhabitants come. They stage ludruk shows with nationalist legends or variety shows with nationalist orations and skits by the youth. Almost every kampung in Surabaja has at its entrance a gate, built by contributions of the kampung's inhabitants, on which is painted a nationalist slogan, such as: "August 17, 1945 to August 17, 1962," "Now West New Guinea is returned," "Destroy the Communist Labor Union (*tjabut* SOBSI, *hapusnja* SOBSI,)" "Manipol-USDEK," "President Sukarno," "Nasakom," or "Wipe out Colonialism." Several have pictures of nationalist action; for example, one gate shows groups of soldiers and workers dashing toward Dutch-held West New Guinea, armed with rifles, grenades, and knives.

YOUTH

"Youth" plays a strong part in the imagery by which Indonesians depict their modern history. Speeches and books relate that the Indonesian nation began with a nationalist declaration by the Congress of Indonesian Youth in 1928 and that Sukarno declared Indonesia's independence in 1945 at the bayonet points of a gang of youths (who had kipnapped him to force him to make that declaration). The symbolic, perhaps actual, role of youth in early independent Indonesia is revealed by a story to the effect that in 1947 the government issued an order requiring all government officials less than fourteen years of age to return to school.

President Sukarno himself has resisted assuming the image of elder. He has often preferred to be called *bung* (comrade) rather than *bapak* (father), the term by which Javanese address most officials. Like Hitler[8] Sukarno has refused to become a father-

[8] Erik H. Erikson, "The Legend of Hitler's Childhood," pp. 284–315.

image, choosing instead to assume the image "youthful leader" of a "nation of youths," which (somewhat ambivalently) rejects the authority of elders, traditions, and paternalistic colonialists, and is now engaged in a kind of adolescent "search for our own identity." Much imagery of this kind appears in Sukarno's speeches.[9]

Youth symbolism is rife in Surabaja. As I have mentioned, the governor's mansion is on Youth Street, and Youth Hall, next to the mansion, is one of the largest and most popular conference halls of Surabaja, not only for youth but for adult political and cultural elite as well. Banners constantly announce youth congresses. Parades on national holidays such as Labor Day are almost totally composed of youths — marching, riding bicycles, wearing funny hats, and carrying posters.

People's Youth (Pemuda Rakjat) is the only mass organization in Indonesia with formal relations to the Communist party and is one of the most active of Communist-linked organizations. There are also active youth groups associated with Islamist and Nationalist parties. In the kampung youth groups, some affiliated with the People's Youth, spearhead collective action. The youth, under the supervision of the kampung headman, build stages, perform skits, sing songs, and set up chairs for kampung celebrations on national holidays, such as Mother Kartini Day or Independence Day. They also organize kampung cleanups on Independence Day. The striking thing is that these celebrations and cleanups which the youths command are the *major* kampung-wide activities in which adult kampung dwellers take part; youth dominate communal *adult* activities.

[9] See, for example, Sukarno's Independence Day Speech of August 17, 1960, "Like Angels that Strike from the Skies: The March of Our Revolution," p. 453, where he speaks of "Kepribadian Indonesia" (Indonesian Identity). This phrase "Indonesian Identity" is a key symbol in Indonesian ideology and is often seen in Sukarno's speeches as well as in those of his officials.

Sukarno's speeches sometimes identify Indonesia with youth. The references which I have on hand are unfortunately English translations; I do not have the Indonesian originals to check them against, but probably the English translates "youth" from the Indonesian "pemuda." In *Res Publica! Once More Res Publica!* p. 4, Sukarno speaks of the famous Oath of the Youth ("We are of one nation . . .") and says this idea "permeated the whole spirit of the Youth, and later of the whole Indonesian people." In "Youth Pledge," p. 4, Sukarno says that the "Youth Pledge" is the "absolute means" for accomplishing the revolution, and in the *Moluccas Speeches*, p. 5, Sukarno asks that the "entire Indonesian population" identify with the "Indonesian Youth" in remaking the pledge, "We are one nation . . ."

Friendship among male youths is very important. Boys go to movies together, sleep at each others' houses, study together, gamble together, and walk around holding hands, this custom having none of the connotations it would have in America. Friends sit and talk until early morning about girls or, if they are already married, household affairs. "I learned nothing from my mother and father," said one youth. "Everything I learned was from associating with my friends." Almost every youth to whom I asked the question, "If you feel sad and want to talk to somebody, who do you talk to first?" answered, "My friends."

Rock 'n' roll or mambo-samba-like music played on electric guitars and bongo drums is a pervasive and audible part of youth culture in Surabaja (dancing to rock 'n' roll is prohibited by the Central Government, but rock 'n' roll music is not). At a circumcision ceremony I was struck by the contrast between male elders sitting stiffly in starched white trousers and shirts and a rock 'n' roll ensemble on a raised platform in their midst composed of slouching slack-jawed Levi's- and leather-jacket– or figured-shirt–clad youths, strumming guitars, beating drums, or draping arms around one another and moaning, "I'm falling in l–o–o–o–o o–ve." Such music, which is increasingly part of Surabaja festivities, does seem to break down the formality of traditional etiquette.

The "youth" involved in most of the activities I have described are anywhere from teen-age to over thirty years old, and some are married. Thus some of the ludruk participants just starting to raise families are actively engaged in youth activities. Many ludruk participants are too old for that, but they cannot help but be caught up in the world of youth symbolism and activity. These adults walk on Youth Street, go to meetings at Youth Hall, and are exposed every day via banners, parades, and speeches to politically affiliated youth symbolism. At circumcision, wedding, and nationalist kampung celebrations, youths perform, and these adults watch. Adults express hope that their children will do what they could not (for instance, graduate from a university), and they characterize the youth as the hope of Indonesia: "It is the Youth who will build the bridge from Banjuwangi [on the East Coast of Java] to Gilimanuk [on the West Coast of Bali]!"

Clearly the prominence of youth symbolism in Indonesian culture has increased since colonial times, along with the Nationalist movement, the Indonesian Revolution, Sukarno's rise to power, the development of political youth organizations, and so on. Probably the extent to which youth organize and associate with one another has increased since colonial times too, partly because of stimulation by political groups, partly because so many more youths go to school nowadays and the schools foster youth activities and friendships, and partly because so many more people live in cities nowadays than thirty years ago.[10] Urban living frees the youth from involvement in the household as an agricultural-productive unit, so he has more time to seek extra-household companionship among his peers. It is said that friendship is not so strong among youth in rural Javanese villages as in cities.[11]

The ludruk prologue is pro-youth, pro-extra-kampung (street) society, and anti-elder, anti-kuna, anti-kampung society. Essentially, the prologue is a series of symbolic actions, rites (or anti-rites), that separate ludruk participants from their kampungs and denigrate elders and kuna, kampung-embedded traditions, while making anti-kuna, extra-kampung doings look like fun. This sort of action both mirrors and promotes the trends in Surabaja society that I have just depicted: the rising status of youth, increased salience of youth symbolism and organization, widening influence of youthful (anti-kuna) ways of viewing the world, coupled with a decline in the importance of the kampung community, a loss of sanctity of intra-kampung, kuna rites and symbols, and increasing involvement of kampung dwellers in extra-kampung activities.

These trends and themes are carried further, but in more positive and specific fashion, by parts of ludruk which follow the prologue, such as the melodrama.

[10] Pelzer, "Resource Patterns," p. 19.

[11] Robert Jay of the University of Hawaii remarked to me in an informal conversation during the summer of 1965 that, according to his impression, friendship among youth in the rural East Javanese villages where he had worked was less important than among urban Javanese youth, such as those of Surabaja.

8

Melodramatic Stories as Conceptions of Social Action

Ludruk participants distinguish several types of melodramatic stories: *tjerita rumahtangga* (domestic stories), *tjerita pahlawan* (stories about legendary heroes), and *tjerita revolusi* (stories about the Indonesian Revolution of 1945–50). Of the eighty-two stories that I saw performed, thirty-six were of the first type, twenty-five of the second, eight of the third, and the others were of various kinds not fitting any of these three categories.

The tales of legendary heroes are of two types, Javanese and Madurese. There are two popular tales of Javanese heroes, "Untung Surapati" and "Sawunggaling," which are allegedly influenced by the ancient Hikajat and Pandji epics of princes, seductions, and magic, and two popular legends of Madurese heroes, "Pak

Sakera" and "Sarip Tambakjasa" that apparently stem from Madurese folk sources. Sawunggaling and Untung Surapati are similar figures in that both drove the Dutch from Java during the eighteenth century and both connived with kings and nobles of that era. It is said that the tales of these heroes are a bit foreign to ludruk; they are borrowed from ketoprak. The Madurese tales are also outside the universe of Javanese ludruk stories since they feature Madurese heroes and are mainly presented in Madurese language. These stories are interesting in that they are almost the only ludruk stories which focus on the abangan-santri conflict. Both Pak Sakera and Sarip Tambakjasa are ferocious but good-hearted abangan roustabouts, who are slaughtered by pious but evil-natured santri in league with the Dutch (I have already mentioned, in chapter 5, Sarip's brother shooting him with silver bullets). In the light of statements by Geertz [1] and Koentjaraningrat [2] to the effect that the abangan-santri conflict in Java is more intense than class conflict, it is interesting that these Madurese tales show great violence and rather moving tragic qualities in contrast to the easy going comedy of manners, which is the prototype of the ludruk story focusing on class conflict. Of course, the violent and tragic quality of the Madurese tales may stem as much from their being Madurese (Madurese are noted for their violent way of life) as from the fact that their core conflict is santri-abangan.

The Revolution stories (several of which were summarized in chapter 4) are mainly presented at political meetings or at benefit performances attended by the political elite. They are rarely performed at commercial ludruk.

The unclassified group includes anything from folktales to fantasies such as "Njai Dasima," a tale allegedly written by an Englishman about an Englishman whose wife was taken from him by love-magic (in ludruk the "Englishman" is Dutch, and in Balinese performances of the same tale he is Chinese).[3]

The domestic stories are the Javanese stories most distinctive of

[1] C. Geertz, *Religion of Java*, p. 356.

[2] Koentjaraningrat, *The Javanese*, p. 92, says the santri group is more endogamous and closed to outsiders than is the aristocratic (prijaji) group. Presumably, there will tend to be more mutual suspicion and conflict between an exclusive group and excluded persons (santri/non-santri) than between a relatively open group (aristocratic class) and its potential members (lowborn persons). For detailed description of the santri/non-santri and also Dutch/Indonesian conflict in the Madurese plays, see Appendix D, and my article, "Anti-Dutch, Anti-Muslim Drama among Surabaja Proletarians: A Description of Performances and Responses."

[3] Beryl de Zoete and Walter Spies, *Dance and Drama in Bali*, pp. 321–22.

commercial ludruk. I shall treat these in detail, centering on those stories which take as their central theme the marriage or attempted marriage of a proletarian character to an elite character. There were about a dozen stories of this type popular around the Surabaja commercial ludruk circuit in 1963. I shall analyze ten of them.

THE PLOTS

A. River of Solo (Bengawan Solo)

1)[4] An elite man entices a servant girl with promises of marriage and impregnates her. (2) He cruelly rejects the girl and their child. (3) The girl leaps into a river and drowns, abandoning the child and another born to her previously. (4) As she leaps into the river it happens that two childless couples hear her screams and rush to the river — too late to save the girl but soon enough to find the children. One couple is elite, the other proletarian. The elite couple adopts the child fathered by the elite man. (5) Twenty-five years pass. (6) Now the elite man of the first scene is arranging a marriage between his son (by his elite wife) and an elite girl. Unbeknown to the father, this elite girl is the daughter spawned by him and the servant girl twenty-five years ago. She was raised by the elite family of scene four. (7) A long-lost brother of the servant girl appears at the wedding of the elite girl and boy and declares that they have the same father so cannot marry. The boy and his parents all smile chummily at the girl and say they accept her into their household as one of them.

B. Malay [Riau Island] Dance (Djogét Melaju)

1) A school principal becomes infatuated with a shameless actress of low birth and (2) leaves his wife to follow the actress to another city. (3) After the principal leaves, his wife, who was pregnant when he left, gives birth to a boy and is very sick. When she hears of the principal's affair, she dies from the shock. (4) Angered, the principal's parents trace him down and break his affair, forcing the principal to return home with them. (5) Twenty years pass. (6) The principal's son (by the principal's dead wife) is now grown. He meets a flirtatious and voluptuous girl who convinces him that he should marry her. (7) The boy's grandparents and the principal go to visit the girl. It turns out that she is the daughter of the principal (by his old actress mistress) so the girl and the principal's son cannot

---

[4] These numbers do not precisely refer to each scene (the division marked by lowering and raising a curtain) which I observed during the live performances.

marry. They happily reunite as half-siblings as the principal and his old actress mistress, who now works as a nurse in a hospital, also reunite.

C. *R.A. Murgiati* (*"Murgiati" is a name, and "R.A." is a girl's title signifying descent from nobility*)

1) A proletariat man is married to an elite girl but cannot support her; (2) so the girl goes home, taking their son but leaving their baby daughter with her husband. Once home, the girl's tyrannical father decrees that she must divorce her husband and stay home. The girl does so, regretfully. (3) The husband, stuck with a baby girl, (4) takes the baby to an elite family who agree to raise her. (5) Thirty years pass. (6) One evening the now-grown son of the elite daughter of the first scene meets a girl who invites him to spend the night at her house. Since it is late and the girl is charming, he accepts the invitation. (7) During the night a thief breaks in. The son chases him, catches him, fights him, beats him, and grabs his loot, just as the police appear. Seeing the boy with the loot, the police accuse him of robbery and take him to the police station. (8) The boy's mother and grandparents come to the station, as do the girl and her foster parents. The police inspector turns out to be the boy's father who in the first scene was jobless and penniless. The father recognizes that the boy's mother is his wife of long ago, and the girl turns out to be their daughter whom the father had given as a baby to the elite foster parents. They all cheerfully reunite.

D. *O Sarinten* (*Sarinten is a name signifying "peasant girl"*)

1) An elite boy, living away from home, (2) marries his maid, Sarinten, a girl of uncommon sweetness and beauty. She bears his child. (3) One day the boy's father comes to fetch the boy in order to marry him to an elite girl. The father finds that the boy is married to Sarinten. He insults Sarinten. He forces the boy to come back home. After the boy leaves, Sarinten, crushed by the father's insults and the loss of her husband, dies, leaving her baby daughter to be cared for by two male servants. (4) Years pass. (5) The elite "boy," now old, is having a wedding for his daughter (by the wife his father chose for him, who turned out to be spoiled and cold). Suddenly the daughter faints and dies. (6) The groom, rather distraught, wanders about. He spots a girl who looks just like the bride and tries to force her to come back with him. She takes him to her parents, the whole wedding party following. (7) The "parents" turn out to be Sarinten's old servants; the girl, Sarinah, is Sarinten's daughter, fathered by the elite "boy." Sarinah and her father joyfully unite.

E. Fried Bananas (Pisang Goréng)

1) An elite boy living away from home (2) marries a fried banana seller, Sumirah. She bears his son. (3) The boy's father appears. He forces the boy to come home with him and marry an elite woman. Sumirah returns to her village. (4) The elite woman turns out to be spoiled and the boy has to embezzle to satisfy her vanities. He is arrested and imprisoned. (5) Fifteen years pass. (6) The elite boy's now-teen-age daughter (by his elite wife) falls in love with a fried banana seller boy. Absorbed in their love the daughter and seller neglect the bananas, which are gobbled up by the elite boy — just released from fifteen years of prison and therefore hungry. (7) Angry, the banana seller chases the elite "boy" and banana thief to his house. (8) Meanwhile Sumirah comes to town to reclaim her rights as wife of the elite "boy." (9) Sumirah, her son (the banana seller boy), the elite "boy" (Sumirah's old husband, now middle-aged), his daughter, and his parents all have a reunion at the house of the elite family. The elite "boy" accepts Sumirah as his second wife and the banana seller boy as his legitimate son. Everybody, including the elite boy's parents, lives happily under the same roof as the story ends.[5]

F. Bandit of West Java (Bandit Djawa Barat)

1) A gang of bandits attack an elite youth, beat him, and steal his money. (2) He staggers bleeding to a house in town which happens to be that of the mistress of one of the bandits. While she heals his wounds the mistress falls in love with the youth. But he returns home after some sexual play with the mistress. (3) The

---

[5] Unlike all other plot summaries, which are my summaries of performances that I saw, the summary of "Fried Bananas" is taken from a scenario written in January, 1960, by a ludruk actor, Slamet Sardjono. Slamet said the play was performed before I came to Surabaja in 1962, but I do not know if this is true. Most ludruk plots are outlined roughly on a blackboard before a performance, but Slamet Sardjono typed this scenario because he happened to be working in an office with a typewriter. This text affords a check on my perception of live performances of plots.

When hero and heroine in plots B and C reunite, they simply tell each other, "I'm glad to see you after so long." No indication is given that hero and heroine will now remarry. Plot E, however, states explicitly that hero and heroine remarry. Thus, plot E includes the dominant element of plots A-D (breakup of hero-heroine marriage) and something similar to the dominant element of plots F-J (successful marriage of hero and heroine). Plot E is in a loose way a synthesis of all the other plots. Perhaps this synthetic quality of the E plot is related to the fact that, whereas all other plots cited here were performed live, plot E was written out — and may not have ever been performed.

mistress's bandit lover appears at the mistress's house soon after the youth has gone. The mistress and bandit quarrel. (4) The bandit, angry with his mistress, returns to his village through forests, pursued by police, to seek his daughter. (5) When he arrives, the daughter has already gone from the village to seek the bandit. (6) While wandering beside a river in the moonlight, the daughter comes upon the clothes of a harelipped man who is bathing. She dons his clothes, then (7) walks to an elite house and is hired as manservant. (8) The son of the elite family falls in love with the "manservant" after discovering that she is not really a man. It happens that this elite son is the youth who was beaten earlier by the girl's bandit father and loved by the father's mistress. (9) The mistress, jealous of the girl, arranges to have the bandit attack and beat her. (10) The bandit, after dragging the girl from her room and savagely beating her, realizes that she is his own daughter. He is sorry. (11) He gives himself up to the police, blesses the marriage of his daughter and the elite boy, and screams that the mistress was the cause of all his misdeeds.

A variant of "Bandit of West Java," called "Bandit of Minahasa" (Minahasa is the northern tip of the island of Celebes), copies "Bandit of West Java" to the point where the bandit father goes to seek his daughter. In "Bandit of Minahasa" the daughter is at home in a remote village when the father arrives. She has been raised and secluded by her mother and never told that she had a father, since her mother was afraid of the father's evil blood getting in her veins. The police, seeking the bandit, arrest the girl to question her about her father. The bandit father gives himself up to save his daughter but then she escapes and the father, learning of her escape, also escapes. The girl walks by a river, puts on clothes of a bathing man, gets a job as manservant with an elite family, where the elite son falls in love with her, while still under the impression that she is a manservant. Then at a birthday party, the bandit's mistress, jealous of the son's love for the manservant, has a fight with him and causes "his" long hair to tumble down, revealing that he is really a girl. Now the elite son obtains his father's permission to marry this girl. The girl's father gives himself up to the police, blesses the marriage of his daughter and the elite boy, and points a finger at the mistress, saying that she is the true bandit. The boy and girl chorus that she is indeed.

G. The Last Impression (*Kesan Terachir*)

1) An old proletariat man is dying in debt. His eldest daughter, skinny and mean, ignores him because she (2) is busy ruthlessly

trying to seduce an elite boy into marrying her. (3) The youngest daughter, gentle and beautiful, who loves the father, had money to pay the father's debt, but unfortunately she dropped it in the gutter. While searching in the gutter, she meets the elite boy whom her sister is pursuing. The boy wishes to give the younger daughter money, but each time he tries to do so the elder sister shoves him in the gutter and grabs the money. (4) The elder sister kills her father by roughly shoving him off his bed and becomes an Arab's mistress. (5) The younger daughter, homeless since her father's death, becomes the Arab's servant. The Arab takes a liking to the younger sister, but each time he tries to give her money, the elder sister grabs it and shoves the Arab against the wall. (6) The elder sister drives the younger one away; then the Arab drives the older sister away. (7) Again the younger daughter meets the elite boy, and (8) in the final scene the younger daughter and elite boy are shown happily married in a luxurious house as the evil sister, now a beggar, crawls to their door.

In another performance, this story was called "Slamet Trahaju" (a male name) but differed in no significant respect from the version above.

H. *The Robber's Nest of Djakarta (Sarang Rampok Djakarta)*

1) An old proletariat man is dying. His youngest son comes home from the sea bringing the old man a new watch. The father's eldest son, a hoodlum, who heads a gang of thieves, kills the father and steals the watch. (2) Since the father is now dead, his daughter leaves home. (3) She gets a job as servant in an elite house. (4) Meanwhile the younger son has returned again from the sea and is out for a stroll by the harbor. He meets an elite boy and shows him a picture of his sister. The elite boy becomes infatuated with the picture. (5) When he arrives at home, he discovers that his family has hired a new servant — the girl in the picture. After a brief flirtation, the boy and girl decide to marry. (6) The younger son from the sea happens to be standing on a street corner when he meets the sister of the elite boy. He flirts with her for a moment, moves close to her, puts his arm around her, and they decide to marry. (7) The elite boy and proletariat girl, now married, are visited by the elite girl (the elite boy's sister) and proletariat boy (the elite girl's brother — the "younger son"), who are also married now. As the two couples joyfully reunite inside a brightly lit house, the evil brother who killed the father is seen staggering down the street. He stabs himself with a knife, screaming, "My sin was that I killed my father."

In another performance essentially the same story was called "King of the Drunkards (Radja Pemabuk)."

I. *Revenge at Midnight* (*Pembalasan dilarut Malam*)

1) A poor village couple goes to town (2) where the wife, Inem, is corrupted by modern ways. She becomes flashy and likes to squander money on clothes and jewels. (3) An elite boy is, like Inem, leading a gay life until his father forces him to marry his cousin, whom the boy treats meanly. (4) The boy and Inem meet and run away together just as the police come to arrest Inem's husband because he embezzled to pay for Inem's wild spending. (5) The husband gets out of jail, marries the now-abandoned elite wife of the man who ran away with Inem, and the new couple is relaxing happily in their new house when two blind beggars are seen crawling along in the dust. They are the unfaithful former spouses of the couple.

J. *The Final Duty* (*Tugas Terachir*)

1) An army officer, fighting in the hills during the Revolution, meets a pretty village girl and carries on a romance with her. (2) At the same time the officer's ferocious comrade at arms, who also has a wartime sweetheart, murders a doctor because the doctor's cousin is a Dutch spy. (3) After the war the officer returns to Surabaja and a good job while (4) the murderous comrade enters prison. (5) The officer, out for a stroll one day, happens to run into his wartime sweetheart, who is selling fried bananas on the street. After buying all her bananas, he asks her to marry him. (6) One day the murderous comrade, having escaped from prison and under pursuit by the police, bursts into the officer's firm and accuses him of marrying his (the comrade's) old sweetheart. The officer protests. He calls and the comrade's old sweetheart appears and embraces him. At that moment the police enter and arrest the comrade. As the comrade is dragged away, the officer, flanked by his pretty wife (the former banana seller) and child, moralizes: "Yes, the murderous comrade must be punished for his wartime deed!"

In other performances this story was known as "Dust of the Revolution" (Debu Revolusi) or "Return to Society" (Kembali ke Massa).

ANALYSIS

The categories found necessary to analyze and compare the various plots as "conceptions of social action" were: *status* of main characters; *goal* of main characters; *outcome* of action; *agency* to bring about outcome; *setting;* and *time* to bring about the outcome.

Status of main characters refers to their class-status (for instance, elite). *Goal* denotes a future state of affairs anticipated by the actor. *Outcome* refers not to the anticipated state of affairs but to the state of affairs actually existing when the action ends. *Agency* denotes the main device leading to the outcome; if the agency is controlled by the central characters it is a means; if not, a condition. *Setting* denotes those conditions not classified as agencies, such as the social-cultural milieu in which the action is set. *Time* denotes the fictional duration of the action, the time characters claim has passed — they may claim years have passed although the story has only taken hours to perform.

The plots divide, according to the sort of social action they portray, into two types: "traditional" (plots *A* through *E*) and "modern" (plots *F* through *J*); I shall refer to the former type as "T" and the latter as "M." The crucial dimensions of similarity and contrast between the two types are as follows.

Status of Main Characters

In both plot types, one character (usually the hero) is elite and the other (usually the heroine) is proletariat.

Initial Goal of Main Characters

To explain what is meant by "initial" goal, I must first outline the time sequences of Type-T versus Type-M stories. Both Type-T and Type-M stories take objectively about the same amount of time to perform — two hours. But the time units within the fictional world of Type-T stories differ from those within the Type-M world. Type-T plots divide into three time-units: a first episode covering several weeks or months, an interlude during which an announcer states that fifteen to thirty years have passed, and a final episode lasting not more than a few days. Type-M plots comprise just one episode, which lasts a few weeks or months. Thus, in terms of fictional time, the first episode of T-plots and the first and only episode of M-plots are parallel. Now by "initial goal of main characters," I simply mean the institutional arrangement which these characters strive to create or maintain during the first episode of T-plots or during the first and only episode of

M-plots. In both episodes elite and proletariat characters strive to marry each other or to maintain their marriage. Marriage, its creation or maintenance, is the main characters' prime initial goal in all stories.

Consider the first episodes of T-plots. In "River of Solo" an elite man and girl dream of marriage (scene 1) but fail to marry (scene 2), and the rest of the episode is the direct aftermath of this failure. In "Malay Dance" a proletarian actress and (elite) school principal run away together (scene 1), hoping to marry, but are thwarted by the principal's parents (scene 4). In "R. A. Murgiati" a proletarian man succeeds in marrying an elite girl but cannot support her (scene 1); so the girl regretfully goes home to her parents (scene 2). In "O Sarinten" an elite youth marries his maid, Sarinten, (scene 2) but the youth's father breaks up the marriage (scene 3). A banana seller and an aristocrat marry in "Fried Bananas" (scene 2), but the aristocrat's father butchers their marriage.

Now consider M-plots: In "Bandit of West Java" various events cause a village girl and elite boy to meet, flirt, and wish to marry (scene 8). The story ends with the girl's father blessing the marriage. A proletarian girl and elite boy meet (scene 3) in "The Last Impression." As the curtain drops, the couple is happy in a luxurious house. In "Robber's Nest of Djakarta" a proletarian and an elite meet, court, and decide to marry (scene 5), while their siblings do the same (scene 6). The closing scene shows the two couples happily married. "Revenge at Midnight" ends with a proletarian-elite couple sitting happily in a nice house. In "The Final Duty" an aristocratic officer meets a village girl during the Revolution (scene 2) and again in peacetime (scene 5). The story ends with the officer and girl plus their child in a happy household.

The goal of proletarian and elite characters is the same in Type-T and Type-M plots: they want to marry each other or to stay married to each other. But as the first episode of Type-T plots ends, the characters have not achieved their goal. As the first and only episode of Type-M plots ends, they have done so.

Audience reactions and formal devices add a feeling of finality, durability, and release to the final scene M-plot attainment of the goal. Auditors and actors showed flashes of anxiety before the final scene, but, as the final curtain drops, characters say things like "this is just right" while auditors say of characters, "they are happy." The music builds to a clear climax of pitch, tempo, and volume as the story unfolds, but at the story's close it glides into a relaxed folk or child melody. Other formal devices show a parallel climax and release.

As the first episode of T-plots ends, characters' goals remain unfulfilled, and audience responses and formal devices continue building to a climax. That climax will be resolved in the second episode, to which we now turn.

Outcome of Story

The second and final episode of T-plots begins fifteen to thirty years after the first episode. The child born of the aborted first-episode union of proletarian and elite is now preparing to marry an elite. In "River of Solo" the parents of the elite and the foster parents of the child are in readiness, the guests have arrived, the wedding throne is decorated, but the marriage does not occur. It turns out, by some freak twist, that bride and groom are half-siblings. In "Malay Dance," "R. A. Murgiati," and "Fried Bananas" the child of the first-episode proletariat-elite union and an elite person indicate that they like each other and speak of marriage. But again the marriage cannot occur. Boyfriend and girlfriend discover that they share the same father. The closing scenes of T-plots do not witness the creation of a new household as in M-plots. They reveal the failure of a second try at creating such a household by marriage.[6]

After this second try at T-plot marriage fails, the elite father[7] of the child produced by him and his proletariat mate during the first episode proclaims his blood-tie to that child. The father and his family (all full-blooded elite) crowd around the microphone and chorus that they accept that mongrel child (born of elite father but proletariat mother) into their household. Then they shout the story's title and the curtain drops. Thus, said one ludruk watcher, "the daughter gets back into the father's family."

In the ending to "Malay Dance," "R. A. Murgiati," and "Fried Bananas," the father not only affirms his tie to his child. He also publicly acknowledges the mother of the child and his old liaison with her. As an aging, established man in a household occupied by his wife, children, and parents, he recognizes and has a reunion

---

[6] In "O Sarinten" this second failing marriage does not involve the child of the first failing interclass marriage, as it does in other *T* plots. But it does involve a (phenotypical) twin to that child. So "O Sarinten" is a neat permutation of the ending common to other *T* plots.

[7] In "R. A. Murgiati," the elite is a mother instead of a father.

with his old lover; the reunion is reminiscent of that in Romberg's "The Student Prince." In no case does the elite man repeat his youthful adventure, re-elope with his sweetheart of youth, and set up a new household. T-plots do not finish by creating new households. They end by incorporating a new (half-elite) member into an old household.

As new households *are* born in the final scene of M-plots, some bond between the proletariat wife and her old class is destroyed. Consider: At the moment the proletariat wife in "Bandit of West Java" announces her marriage to an elite person, the wife's father is arrested and he prepares to go to prison. Thus the father is removed from society. The wife's chances for interacting with him are lessened — conveniently so, at the precise time that the wife is moving out of the family and class represented by her father. At the moment "The Last Impression" reveals the proletariat wife happily in her new house with her elite husband, the wife's sister appears. She is an insane beggar (scene 8). The sister cannot even recognize the wife. "The sister is no more a member of society," informants said, "She is an animal." Again an old member of the proletarian newly wed's family and class is made incapable of normal relations with her right at the time she is marrying out of her family and class. At the moment the proletarians in "Robber's Nest of Djakarta" reveal that they have married elite, their brother appears — an insane beggar, incapable of recognizing or relating to his sane siblings — and kills himself. Once again "marrying up" is given a symbolic boost: the proletarian's sibling is rendered incapable of claiming the proletarian's old loyalties, exactly at the time that the proletarians form new loyalties to their elite spouses.

Endings to other M-plots differ slightly from those just cited, but the principle remains the same. In "Revenge in the Night" the proletarian's old spouse is shown begging exactly at the time the proletarian displays his marriage to an elite girl. In "The Murderous Comrade" a proletarian is sent to prison at the moment his friends, a proletariat wife and elite husband, publically affirm their marriage. Again, some person with whom the proletariat spouse, or both spouses, had a tie of solidarity is rendered incapable of claiming normal loyalties at the exact time the proletarian is shown married to an elite.

Some of the proletarian scapegoats of the final M-plot scene are prepared for sacrifice, as it were, by becoming increasingly villainous as the plot progresses. Spectators' jeers and yelling crescendo correspondingly until, when the villain is destroyed at plot's end, spectators scream that they are glad to see the villain meet a hideous end. Such screams seem to both accentuate and relieve tensions deriving from the proletariat protagonist's break with old class and family bonds.

In T-plots nobody is "destroyed" in the final scene. Yet T-plots do not lack a villain. In every T-plot the elite father who breaks up the proletariat-elite marriage is clearly defined as wicked. This is shown by onstage action and talk and by spectators' introspection reports. Regarding the elite father, spectators wrote comments like the following:

> Looking at the suffering of Jusuf [the proletariat husband in "R. A. Murgiati"] I join in his feelings. I watch the cruelty and extreme manner by which the elite father discriminates against poor persons — until I hate him.

Though stereotyped, the comment mirrors the onstage attitude toward the elite father.

Why then is this villain not destroyed at plot's end as is the M-plot villain? Several arguments present themselves. That which is relevant here is as follows: In M-plots, destroying the villain symbolically underlines the breaks involved in setting up a new household (this point is made above). The corollary of this relationship is that where no new household is set up — in T-plots — the villain is not destroyed. Indeed, destroying the villain at the end of T-plots would seem to go against the atmosphere pervading those endings. T-plots end in "an atmosphere of security and peace" (this phrase was used by an actor to describe the ending to "Fried Bananas"). T-plot endings show that the elite household which began the plot still stands, with its heavy furniture, old-fashioned culture objects, leisurely manners, with none of its members departed (for the elite son came home again), and with its founder and public symbol, the elite father, still in command. If this father — though a villain — were destroyed it would mar the tone of the elite establishment and hence the ending of the T-plots. T-plots allow the villainous father to stand because he happens to be the pillar of an establishment whose solidity the plot wishes to underline as the final curtain drops.

The above remarks partly add up to this: In the first and only episode of M-plots, elite-proletariat marriage is achieved, a new household is established, and the proletariat spouse's blood-bonds are violently negated, while in the first episode of T-plots, elite-

proletariat marriage is not achieved, no new household is established, and the old elite household is strengthened because the
elite spouse negates his or her marriage bond to affirm his or her
blood bond to that household. This contrast is diagrammatically
stated in Figure 1*a* and *b*.[8]

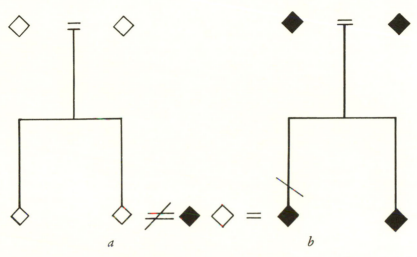

FIG. 1*a* and 1*b*. — Result of social action in "traditional" and
"modern" plot types (proletarian status, ◆; elite status, ◇; affinal
tie, =; consanguineal tie, |; negation of tie, /). *a:* T-plot, first
episode. *b:* M-plot, only episode.

Structurally, the outcome of the first episode of T-plots and the outcome of the only episode of M-plots are inversions of each other.

What of the last episode in T-plots? By affirming his or her
blood ties to the elite household, the elite spouse enhances that
household's appearance of solidarity — which is important since the
first-episode failure of the proletariat-elite marriage is compen-
sated by the ending where the half-proletariat child of the failing
union gains entry into the elite household. If this household were
fly-by-night rather than a bastion of solidity entry into it would not
be equally satisfying.

Table 2 shows in detail that the family group shown before last
scenes of T-plots (*A–E*) is still shown during the last scene of such
a plot: blood bonds which held before the last scene still hold

[8] I am indebted to Pierre Maranda of Harvard University for suggesting the
diagramatic summary of this point.

117

TABLE 2

DOMESTIC CYCLES IN MELODRAMATIC STORIES

Plot	Families Shown before Last Scene (in order of appearance onstage)	Families Shown in Last Scene
A	Elite family (husband, wife, child); elite family (husband, wife, adopted child); kampung family (husband, wife, adopted child)	All families that were shown earlier (except the kampung family)
B	Elite family (couple, child, husband's parents); village family (daughter, parents)	All families that were shown earlier
C	Elite wife, kampung husband, their children; elite parents; elite couple, adopted daughter	All families that were shown earlier
D	Elite son, his village wife, child; his parents; elite son, his elite wife, child	All families that were shown earlier (minus village wife and elite child)
E	Same as *D*	All families that were shown earlier
F	Village family (bandit father and his wife); elite parents and son	Village wife and elite husband (plus wife's father en route to prison)
G	Kampung family (father, son, two daughters)	Kampung wife and elite husband (plus wife's sister crawling away as a beggar)
H	Kampung family (father, daughter, her good and evil brothers); elite family (parents, son)	Kampung wife and elite husband; kampung husband and elite wife (plus kampung spouses' brother dying)
I	Village couple and husband's parents; elite couple and husband's parents	Village husband and elite wife (plus former spouses of each crawling away as beggars)
J	Village girl and her mother	Village wife and elite husband (plus former comrade of husband en route to prison)

during the last scene. In M-plots (*F–J*), however, family groups shown before the last scene are not shown during the last scene. They are replaced by a new family composed of newly wed husband and wife. Where a member of the proletarian spouse's family (which was depicted in earlier scenes) does appear in the last scene, the spouse's bond to that person is just about to be smashed. Thus, final scenes of M-plots replace blood bonds with marital bonds. It could be argued, of course, that creation of new marital bonds implies creation of new blood bonds, since those who marry tend to procreate. But in only one M-plot ("The Final Duty") do the spouses produce children before the curtain falls.

M-plot endings emphasize marriage. They de-emphasize the pro-creation that conceivably might stem from that marriage.

According to Geertz:

> The nuclear conflict of the *ludrug* seems to be the conflict of genera-tions, the conflict between the attachment to tradition of the older generation, particularly concerning arranged marriages, and the wishes of the younger. . . . In this conflict it is the younger generation which is always right. . . . All in all, the plays lend force to the common complaint of Modjokuto's chastened older generation. "We used to have a proverb, 'the buffalo's calf suckles the buffalo-calf,' but now we have to say, 'the buffalo's calf suckles the buffalo.' " [9]

Indeed, the conflict of generations is a major conflict in the T-plots where, as the story ends, the older generation still dominates (even though "the younger generation is . . . always right"), but in M-plots this conflict is hardly troublesome. The youth have thrown off the shackles of elders. As Table 2 shows, the M-plot ends with no elders in sight or else about to be sent off to prison.

From the standpoint of the individual life cycle and of the domestic cycle, type-T endings take a regressive turn. The child returns to the shelter of his parents (and sometimes his grand-parents, even more comforting figures in Javanese society) and the family fails to create new families since its offspring do not marry. There are, however, ambiguities about this ending. The child is not entering a totally comfortable environment. The household which she is entering contains her stepmother, and to live with a stepmother, Javanese say, is traumatic. Also, marital symbolism is not totally replaced by blood-bond symbolism. It is true that the lovers discover that they are brother and sister, but there is a Javanese tradition of husband and wife calling each other "older brother" and "younger sister." Further (if one wishes to push the point) both brother and sister are played by men, and there is apparently not, in Java or anywhere else, an explicit taboo against homosexual incest.[10] In spite of these ambiguities, however, the core imagery of the T-plot ending is of blood bonds overriding marital bonds. Said an informant, "The reason the hero and heroine in 'River of Solo' are happy to see that they are brother and sister, so cannot marry, is that one can easily break a bond to his wife [note remarks below on the high divorce rate among Javanese proletarians] but can never break a bond to his sister."

[9] C. Geertz, *Religion of Java*, pp. 294–95.
[10] Levy, *Modernization*, 2:419.

Agency Which Brings about Outcome

In "River of Solo" the girl to whom the father had arranged to marry his son suddenly turns out to be the son's half-sister. In "Malay Dance," "Fried Bananas," and "R. A. Murgiati" the girl and boy who had themselves expressed a desire to marry discover that they are half-siblings. In "O Sarinten" the father's plans for a wedding are suddenly wrecked by his daughter's death, and by some strange twist the daughter's twin by the father's old mistress pops up. All of these endings seem to be at pains to show that events' outcomes violate individuals' wishes and plans. People cannot plan and expect to have things work out that way. Fate — a quick and comic fate rather than a relentless force as in German movies or Hardy's novels — is the agency that determines outcomes.

M-plots do work out the way characters intend. Hero and heroine who decide to marry do not suddenly turn out to be half-siblings. They meet, flirt (in a peculiarly emotionless manner), decide to marry, and do so. Fate does not foil their intentions. Rather, insofar as fate does enter in, as when it "just happens" that hero and heroine get thrown together, fate supports individual efforts toward marriage; it simply helps those who help themselves. M-plots, unlike T-plots, depict a positive correlation between outcomes of events and individual choices or acts.

The heroine's entry into an elite household at the end of a T-plot depends on her blood tie to her elite father, and blood ties are independent of individual choice. The heroine did not choose her father. But M-plot heroines do choose their elite lovers who get them into a nice household.

The M-plot heroine achieves higher status by her own choices and ventures, but not through work at a job. She achieves by means of sex, which leads to marriage. We might contrast this agency with that of a current popular Hollywood success story, Youngblood Hawke. Youngblood, the hero, achieves his happy marriage and high status by driving a coal truck, writing novels all night, and opening a publishing business. Sex is not the main means for him. The M-plot heroine (or hero), however, is never seen working (or going to school). There are almost no M-plot scenes in a school, office, or factory, although significantly there are more such scenes in M-plots than in T-plots. The main place of action in M-plots is the parlor of elite households, or streets and pleasure spots outside the house. The proletarian in M-plots gets ahead not by doing productive labor but by being an object of consumption. She appeals to the elite male's sexual and romantic desires.

The fact that the M-plot heroine's mobility is by sexual, rather than occupational or educational, means may relate to another quality of her actions. She does not sit down and plan each step toward higher status.[11] She simply responds to opportunities (men) that present themselves. This kind of action would seem more likely in the sexual realm, whereas long-term planning would better fit the occupational or educational sphere.

This raises a broader question. Why is it that ludruk has chosen to depict sexual means toward mobility? Is it because ludruk participants find it easier to imagine the opportunistic quick-response way of getting ahead than the long-term-plan way, and sex is the best symbol of the "quick way?" (And women, in Javanese society, are more famous than men for exploiting sex to rise socially; therefore, ludruk, although an all-male troupe, makes virtually all its proletarians-who-get-ahead female.)

Settings

T-plots have many more scenes in traditional Javanese domiciles than do M-plots. T-plots have more characters with Javanese noble titles, more traditional Javanese culture objects, dress, and manners than do M-plots. Almost all characters in T-plots have Javanese names, but only half the characters in M-plots do. About ninety per cent of T-plot scenes are in Javanese language, and all begin in the Dutch colonial period.

Compared to T-plots, M-plots have more scenes in "open" areas of cities: streets, harbors, dens of iniquity, whorehouses, and business firms. There are almost no characters with Javanese titles but are many "asphalt jungle" characters: fat capitalists in flowered shirts, slinky prostitutes, ducktailed youths and hoodlums, Arab traders. M-plot characters more often wear Western clothes than do T-plot characters. About sixty per cent of M-plot dialogues are in Indonesian and less than forty per cent in Javanese language. All M-plots, to judge from settings and informants' comments, take place after the Dutch colonial era during the time of Indonesian Independence. Several M-plots, but no T-plots, take place outside

[11] Note that the ruthless elder sister in "The Last Impression," who *does* plan things, such as how to marry the elite boy, is punished in the end. All M-plot villains and villainesses are rational, ruthless planners to a fault, even to a greater degree than are M-plot heroes and heroines — and they finally are punished for it.

the Javanese culture area; the "Bandit" stories are in West Java (the Sundanese, not Javanese, culture area) or on the island of Celebes, and "The Robber's Nest of Djakarta" is in that city.

The difference of settings does not necessarily imply different origins in time or space for T- versus M-plots (there is evidence against this; for example, the T-plots "O Sarinten" and "Fried Bananas" were written after 1960, even though they are set in the colonial period). Rather, it seems that ludruk actors-authors (the two roles are often filled by a single person) place a story's action in a physical-cultural-social milieu that they feel is logically and emotionally appropriate for the action. M-plot action seems to them more possible in a modern "asphalt jungle" dominated by Indonesian culture, a setting likely to evoke fewer remembrances of "feudal" barriers to intermarriage, while T-plot action seems to suit stifling colonial, domicile-centered situations dominated by traditional Javanese culture.

Time to Achieve Outcome

It takes fifteen to thirty years for the T-plot outcome to come to pass, only weeks or months to reach the end of M-plots. (In some T-plots, such as "River of Solo," the long period gives the half-proletariat child time to master elite manners.)

Summary

If the stories can be said to express ludruk participants' fantasies and conceptions of social action, T-plots seem to be saying something like, "It would be nice to get incorporated, somehow, into a long-established elite household. But one's own efforts have little to do with it; trying to marry an elite person never works. Perhaps by fate the child of such a broken union will get back into elite society when the child's father recognizes his blood bond to the child. If so, it takes many years, and the mother may not be around to enjoy the fruits of her early union."

In M-plots ludruk participants seem to say, "It is possible to quickly achieve marriage with an elite person and set up a new household. Achieving such a thing depends on luck, on one's own actions, and on sexual attractiveness; it necessitates a rather violent break with one's old class and family."

See Table 3 for a schematic comparison of T- and M-plots.

TABLE 3

COMPARISON OF T- AND M-PLOTS IN MELODRAMATIC STORIES

	Type-M	Type-T
Status of main characters	proletariat and elite	proletariat and elite
Initial goal of main characters	proletariat-elite marriage	proletariat-elite marriage
Outcome of story	proletariat-elite marriage negated, elite blood bonds affirmed	proletariat-elite marriage affirmed, proletariat blood bonds negated
Agency which brings about story's outcome	blood bond between elite and half-elite plus fate, which opposes personal choices	personal responses (partly sexual) of proletariat and elite characters plus luck which furnishes opportunities
Setting	traditional Java	modern urban Indonesia
Time to bring about outcome	15–30 years	weeks or months

CHANGES IN CONCEPTIONS OF SOCIAL ACTION

During my stay in Surabaja, I tried to cover the repertoire of each of the major troupes. In so doing it became clear that some stories pass from one troupe to another (troupes send out scouts to watch other troupes and bring back their stories). It is striking that every one of the M-plots circulated between at least two troupes during my year in Surabaja, but I never saw a T-plot move from one troupe to another; in fact, I never saw a T-plot performed more than once.

It seems that M-plots are being imitated while T-plots are not. If this process continues, M-plots will become more and more frequently performed while T-plots will become more and more rarely performed relative to M-plots (unless each troupe invents many more T-plots than M-plots, which they are not doing now.) One may entertain the notion that the T-plot conception of class mobility is giving way to that of the M-plot among the ludruk participants.

There is some evidence that the present trend is an extension of one that has been going on for a long time. Ludruk Besut, performed until the late twenties, did not, according to various accounts,[12] even include extra-kampung elite characters in its stories. Besut had only kampung characters. Kampung proletarian and extra-kampung elite characters began appearing together in ludruk stories when ludruk began performing outside the kampung. The development of ludruk stories may have been along the following lines: first, elite and proletariat characters did not even appear in the same story (Besut era); then, elite and proletariat characters were included in the same story but did not successfully marry (post-Besut era extending into post-Indonesian Independence; stories of this sort are type-T, the only type mentioned in Geertz' summary [13] of ludruk stories performed in 1953–54); and finally, elite and proletarians not only are included in the same story, but they also successfully marry (present era; my 1963 sample includes twice as many type-M as type-T stories.)

Judging from place names, characters' names, and other elements, all of the T-plots are set in the Javanese culture area (Central or East Java), while at least five of the M-plots are set outside the

TABLE 4
SETTINGS OF MELODRAMATIC STORIES

Story	Setting	Performed by
River of Solo	Javanese	Mari Katon
Malay Dance*	Javanese	Enggal Tresno
Fried Bananas	Javanese	Mari Katon †
R. A. Murgiati	Javanese	Tresno Enggal
O Sarinten	Javanese	Tresno Enggal
Bandit of West Java	non-Javanese	Tresno Enggal
Bandit of Minahasa	non-Javanese	Irama Enggal
The Last Impression	non-Javanese	Irama Enggal
Slamet Trehaju	ambiguous	Sari Rukun
Revenge in the Night	Javanese	Tresno Enggal and Massa Rukun
Dust of the Revolution	Javanese	Tresno Enggal
The Final Duty	Javanese	Tresno Enggal
Return to Society	Javanese	Marhaen
Robber's Nest of Djakarta	non-Javanese	Mari Katon
King of Drunkards	non-Javanese	Enggal Tresno

* Although the title includes the term "Malay," all other elements in the story indicate that it is set in Java among Javanese.

† Written and reputedly performed by this company.

[12] Wongsosewojo, "Loedroek," pp. 204–07.

[13] C. Geertz, *Religion of Java,* pp. 291–95. The ludruk stories which Hildred Geertz reports seeing during 1953–54, are also type T (e.g., see p. 58, *The Javanese Family*).

Javanese culture area. We note further that the five ludruk troupes unanimously deemed the least madju and least accomplished of the troupes playing in commercial Surabaja theaters set four-fifths (4 of 5) of the M-plots which they performed in extra-Javanese locales while Tresno Enggal and Marhaen, universally considered the most madju and accomplished ludruk troupes, set only one-fifth (1 of 5) of the M-plots which they performed in extra-Javanese locales. Table 4 tabulates the facts supporting this last statement; what conclusions can be drawn from it? Perhaps the more madju, pace-setting troupes (and their audiences) have gone further toward incorporating type-M concepts into their Javanese lives than have the less madju troupes who still relate type-M concepts to some alien context. The more madju ludruk participants are able to imagine themselves as Javanese taking part in a type-M society while the less madju ones imagine Djakarta urbanites or Celebes islanders in a type-M society but do not feel at home in such a world themselves. Now, Tresno Enggal and Marhaen have led trends among ludruk troupes; they were the first to make transvestites get haircuts, they have spearheaded organization of a ludruk union, and so on. Perhaps they will lead a trend toward grafting M-plot spirit to Javanese flesh.

9

Melodramatic Form

TYPE-T PLOTS

The movement of type-T plots is cyclical, emphasizing that although things change, they really remain the same. Table 2 shows that in T-plots the same families shown before the final scene are shown during the final scene. The parents in control when the plot begins are still in control twenty years later when it ends. The same symbols of tradition and permanency that begin the T-plot are displayed at its close. Children separated from their fathers at the plot's beginning are returned to them at its conclusion. Youths who rebel against elders early in the plot have reembraced their values and authority by the last scene.

The movement of T-plots is institutional. Separation of child from parent leads to reunion of child and parents. Separation of child from parent at the plot's beginning throws the social machine out of kilter, and the rest of the story is concerned with putting it back into equilibrium. The movement in T-plots is toward institutional equilibrium, not toward fulfillment of an individual character's desires. There is no hero whose desires arouse tension at the beginning, whose strivings sustain excitement throughout, and whose fulfillment relaxes tension at the end. The hero and heroine who occupy most of the plot's time die or fall into insignificance by returning to their parents' fold before the plot closes; after their demise there is a twenty year interim during which no individual action is shown. During this period, time and fate place the heroine's child into position for reincorporation into the father's family. Attention is then centered on this child; yet the child is hardly an actor. She is only a cog of fate, and she appears onstage only long enough for fate to place her back in her proper position within the kinship network, and thus restore society to harmony.[1]

Every T-plot ends with at least three persons onstage and often with a crowd.[2] Directors and actors recognize that such group endings are an integral part of ludruk: "Ludruk is different from movies in that ludruk *must* have a crowd at the end; movies such as 'Black Beard' end with a lone figure." "The crowd ending is the symbol of ludruk." "The ending of ludruk *must* be noisy and crowded." Spectators, early in a performance, say, "A crowd will gather at the end." and when it does, they say they feel "relieved" or "contented": "*Lha,* thus it is done," sighs a woman after the crowd appears. "After all characters are reunited," writes Slamet Sardjono at the close of his "Fried Bananas" scenario, "there is again an atmosphere of security and peace."

[1] The ludruk play's treatment of incest gives further indication of its essentially institutional rather than psychological orientation. A Western play like Arthur Miller's "A View from the Bridge" sees incest as a problem of emotional attraction between daughter and step-father, which develops while they live together. But T-plot brother and sister, in cases where their parents arrange for them to marry, have no particular emotional attraction to each other. And they (like Oedipus) do not consciously move toward incestuous marriage — for they do not know that they are siblings. So their near-incest is not psychologically motivated, it is just a result of fate and the workings of the institution of arranged marriage.

[2] Interestingly, the one play by the entrepreneurial, individualistic santri that I saw ended with a lone figure in the desert praying to Allah. This was not a ludruk play, but a modern drama staged by a santri youth group.

The endings of T-plots stress harmony of the group rather than judgment of individuals' bad deeds. The aristocratic father, although all agree that he did wrong, is never punished in the end because to do so would impair the final harmony of the group. The question of motives and punishment of individual guilt is not explored. The rather philosophical-minded Mr. Karjono, drama inspector at the Regional Office of Culture, said of the T-plot ending:

> Such togetherness is the most important thing to a Javanese. The goodness or badness of the individuals with whom one comes together does not count. A criminal is thought to be criminal only when he's not himself — an evil soul entered him for a moment. Now it's gone, so he can be together with us. This is a Buddhist-animist concept, and although the ludruk players may not be consciously aware of it, it is a structure imbedded in their minds which they express whenever they get onto the stage.

Comic Catharsis: Master-Servant Jokes

Many more master-servant jokes, such as those to be discussed in the eleventh chapter, appear in T-plots than in M-plots; 70 per cent of T-plot scenes (30 of 43) include master-servant jokes, whereas only 23 per cent of all M-plot scenes (18 of 76) have master-servant jokes. Thus, master-servant jokes are a distinctive trait of T-plots. What function do they serve for T-plots? The jokes can be viewed as attempts to instantly bridge the gap between aristocrat and proletarian, either by rephrasing alus aristocratic symbols (e.g., coffee drinking ritual) in proletarian terms or by putting aristocratic roles on proletarian bodies (as when the servant imitates his master). Such "joking" bridging of the aristocrat-proletarian gap would seem more necessary in T-plots, where the gap is very wide and attempts at marriage do not succeed in uniting aristocrat and proletarian, than in M-plots where the gap is not so wide, and high and low classes do succeed in marrying. Tension deriving from the class gap is not resolved by T-plot narrative, so it must be resolved by T-plot joking.[3]

---

[3] Although the number of master-servant jokes in T-plots versus M-plots is only one index of the amount of interclass tension-release in the two types of plots, it is a good index because jokes of this type deal more purely and explicitly with difference of rank per se than do most actions in ludruk, although other jokes (such as bureaucrat-rustic) mix this theme with others.

Maudlin Catharsis: Sad Submission and the Abandoned Child

Whereas M-plots violently kill a villain, T-plot characters submit sadly and passively to a villain, the aristocratic father. A scene that is always found in T-plots, never in M-plots, is staged at the time the aristocratic father foils the attempted marriage of his child to a proletarian; his child and the proletarian submit passively to the evil fathers' will. In "O Sarinten," the heroine, Sarinten, kneels before her husband's aristocratic father and begs his forgiveness for her rash act of marrying his son. The father coldly asks Sarinten what her family background is. She admits that her father is a peasant. The aristocratic father says everybody will laugh at her. Sarinten tells the father all that she does for his son — cooks, washes, nurses him when he is sick. The father asks, "When I go to a restaurant, do I love the person who brings me food? When I take my clothes to a washwoman, do I love her because she cleans them?" Sarinten begins weeping gently and begs forgiveness again. The father scorns her and leaves after commanding his son to abandon Sarinten and return home. Sarinten encourages her husband to follow his father's wishes, to leave her and marry his arranged bride. She blames herself for the marriage's failure and wills to sacrifice herself so her husband can set up a new household with a calm heart. (At this point a woman spectator says, "I truly feel pity for Sarinten.") The husband does leave Sarinten (who is a beautiful girl), after which she dies of a broken heart, leaving her child motherless.

In "Malay Dance," "R. A. Murgiati," and "Fried Bananas," a similar pattern is seen. "River of Solo" is a slightly variant case; there it is the aristocratic husband himself (instead of his father) who breaks up his liaison to a proletarian. When he tells his mistress that he will leave her, she whines, grovels on the ground, pulls at his pants leg, and begs him not to go, while he sits calmly in a chair (after dusting it with his handkerchief). The girl then kills herself, abandoning two children — one fathered by the aristocrat. (The imagery of the ill-used proletarian is enhanced by showing her as impregnated, "made heavy with child," "burdened" by the aristocrat.)

Thus, the aristocratic father (or, in the last case, the aristocratic husband) is depicted as a tyrant who ruins lives and drives women to their death, causing them to leave their children motherless. Yet the characters never protest; they do not, like a Heathcliff, defy the gentry. They just kneel and beg forgiveness.

I asked the actor who played the kampung husband in "R. A. Murgiati" why he did not protest when the aristocratic father decreed he must divorce his wife. The actor replied:

> Yes, I experienced great suffering because of the father. The father was to blame. But I felt very ashamed and embarrassed in the presence of the aristocratic father. Around the father I wondered, "Do I disappoint you?"

In the story when the actor heard of the aristocratic father's decree that he must divorce his wife, he did not even inquire why. He just began lamenting his child's fate. Nor did audiences score the aristocratic father in this or other T-plots the way they do villains in M-plots. Yet they felt secret hatred toward the aristocratic father, as introspection reports (like the one cited in chapter 8) testify.

Right after the proletarian's passive submission to the aristocratic tyrant, there appears, in most T-plots, a scene showing an abandoned child — the fruit of the proletarian's now-broken marriage. This abandoned child is apparently more touching to Javanese than the breakup of spouses itself. When it becomes clear that the child will be left motherless, spectators respond as follows:

> A woman says, "What a pity for the child."
> A female worker at a bread factory sighs, "My goodness, the baby is abandoned. If it cries, what will the father do?"
> A servant, in his introspection report, says, "It is as if I join in the feeling of suffering. Tears appear."
> A bricklayer says in his introspection report, "This reminds me of the time I was disowned by my parents. The trouble was that I was supposed to be married according to their choice. Finally I was disowned. Then I left their house. I roamed without purpose until I finally got work. Did the same work for two years. But for two years I thought of my father, as I was in that faraway place. Then I returned. Finally I was conscious [of what was right]."
> A clerk says in his introspection report, "This reminds me of the time when I had just married, having been forced by parents to do so. I stole for the sake of the household. Then I roamed, seeking understanding. I always faced the trials and suffering of roaming with patience, always remembered my family. My mother died; I was forced to return to the kampung yard. Everybody was very moved by my sad situation. I felt ruined, with my own father and mother separated. The result of the forced marriage was a son. I

continued my roaming to help the fate of my son, leaving him at the home of his mother."

The abandoned child image calls to the minds of the clerk and bricklayer a chain of gloomy memories — separation from one's mother and father, lonely wandering, yearning for home, and forced marriage.

I asked Toebi, a ludruk clown, what scenes in ludruk, if any, "touched his heart." He answered:

> Whenever a child is abandoned. For instance, in the story "Meet and Return," Sudiardi is a highschool student, becomes pregnant, walks by the river into the forest alone, gives birth, abandons the child. I feel pity, for I have my own child. How would its fate be? Also, in "R. A. Murgiati," when the child is left by its mother, I feel sad. For other scenes I feel nothing.

I asked him about the closing scene of "Pak Sakera," when the hero is mobbed and killed while dancing. He repeats, "I feel nothing." Each of nine kampung men who were asked, "What in ludruk touches you most?" replied, "The abandoned child." I asked them about other scenes such as one showing a pregnant girl dying in the woods. One man said that when he saw that he just laughed for it meant her lover had left her, and it was her own fault anyway.

Another sign of the poignancy surrounding the abandoned child is the music accompanying its appearance. In ludruk, music is truly a response of musicians to what they see onstage, for musicians sit watching the stage and improvise what they feel is appropriate for each action. For the abandoned child scene, siter and gendèr improvise softly, producing a soft, flowing figuration. Occasionally the *gambang kaju* (a wood xylophone) improvises. It has a soft, muted, flowing quality, unlike the loud iron or bronze saron; whereas the saron is brassy like a trumpet, the gambang kaju's tone is mellow and covered like the sound of a French horn. The whole effect is sweet and sad.

Pathetic children (such as Little Annie Rooney and Little Nell) have appeared in English literature. Probably there are pan-human features of a child — helplessness, inarticulateness, innocence [4] — that make people feel sorry for it. But the abandoned child may have special poignancy for Javanese kampung dwellers because of an experience which they share as a result of their

---

[4] Northrop Frye, *Anatomy of Criticism*, pp. 38–39.

society. Many kampung dwellers have experienced separation from one or both of their parents owing to the extremely high divorce rate among Javanese kampung dwellers and the custom of parents "lending" their children to other parents who lack them. Many kampung dwellers have been separated from one or both parents and forced to live with one or more step-parents. Their life stories are filled with tales of unhappy times at step-parents' homes. A clerk explicitly related the ludruk "abandoned child forced to live with step-mother" theme to such an experience, saying that he feels pity for the step-child in "Red Onion and White Onion" (a folk-tale performed by ludruk). He then said "white onion" was like him when he was "lent" to his aunt. He just stayed one month: "She had a son who was naughty. That child was regarded by her as right even when he was wrong. I had trouble eating. I ran after my mother. . . ."

Many younger ludruk participants reveal in their life stories that they have experienced even more separation from their parents than they would have normally because their childhood occurred during the 1945–50 Revolution; when the Dutch occupied Surabaja, many Surabajans fled inland and families were broken up.

Why should the abandoned child scene always appear immediately after the scene in which a proletarian character submits to the aristocratic father's command that the proletarian break his or her relation with an aristocrat? We might see a psychological link between the two scenes as follows: To make the aristocratic society into which the proletarian is incorporated in the final scene appear as solid and secure as possible, it is helpful to depict the prime symbol of that society, the aristocratic father, as all-powerful. To aid in this imagery, the proletarian character submits unquestioningly to the father. He does not rebel and smash the father's appearance of control over society. But the father's tyranny evokes hostility from ludruk participants (introspection reports reveal this). How can this hostility be expressed without overtly invalidating the father's control? One way is to weep tears of pity. Maudlin pity for the child is a way of indirectly painting the father blacker. By making the child's plight seem more pitiful, the man who caused that plight is made to appear more wicked (note that Dickens linked the terrible villain with the pitiful child). This indirect way of censuring the aristocratic father and releasing tensions which he evokes does not directly challenge his organizational control of society, so the assumptions on which the stasis of T-plot society is based are left secure.

TYPE-M PLOTS

Type-T movement is institutional and cyclical, punctuated by comic or maudlin catharsis. Type-M movement is more individual and innovative (resulting in the creation of new households) and less punctuated by periodic comic or maudlin catharsis of interclass tensions. The main catharsis in M-plots is postponed until the final scene when the heroine achieves her goal (marriage to an elite man) and the villain gets his just deserts (violent punishment).

The Buildup to Violent Punishment

From the beginning of "Bandit of West Java," the bandit father is sadistic. He and his cronies beat an aristocratic boy whose money they want. They slap the boy's face again and again with a rolled up newspaper, perhaps twenty times (more exaggeratedly vicious, less efficient, than the beatings administered by the icy, ruthless criminals of American movies). The boy tries to stand. They smash him down with a stick. The boy masochistically revels in the beating, writhing about the floor, flopping his head back, arms out limply. In the final scene the bandit father himself becomes unresisting, submitting with hanging head to arrest and imprisonment. Then suddenly he shifts the blame to a whore, pointing his finger at her and screaming, "She's the one who received the stolen goods!" Apparently spectators accept the sudden, last-minute scapegoating of the whore; a male onlooker, Sanjoto, wrote in his introspection report: "The whole story shows that the behavior of Arifin [the bandit] is evil, and caused by the evil prostitute. Prostitutes cause all the evil in this world. Why is a sinful woman born into this world?"

The evil elder brother in "King of the Drunkards" is a big-city, loud, Indonesian-talking, cigarette-smoking, swaggering, black-shirted hoodlum with ducktail and sideburns haircut. He kills his feeble and aged father, stealing a gift given that father by the good younger brother. Even the callous sensibilities of the evil brother's criminal pal are offended by the vile killing of an aged father, so the evil brother kills his protesting pal. Finally the brother is arrested, released, then seen in rags, ranting insanely that he is the toughest hood in Djakarta. In this state he appears at the place where his good younger brother and sister are happily married to elite spouses. In one version, the evil brother shouts curses at his siblings, then stabs himself on a dark stage screaming

"I know who killed my father. I am sinful!" In another version, the siblings — both newlyweds — follow the ranting brother to a graveyard where his father is buried. There the evil one asks forgiveness; the siblings try to speak with him, he threatens them with a knife. Finally he screams, "Look up! The birds are singing!" As the newlyweds look up, he stabs himself crying "The birds witness my deed! Forgive me father! Aiiiiiiiiii!" After the killer is dead, the good son turns to the group and says, "We need not be sad about his happening. You knew my father's wish. This is the consequence for a son who did not obey." They all turn and walk away, showing no emotion, as in some existentialist satire.

The evil sister in "The Last Impression" is tagged from the first as a shameless hussy. She wears sweater, pony tail, skirt above the knees, has a hard face, rasping voice. She tries to snare an elite boy, who is more attracted to her gentle sister than to her. When he tries to give the gentle sister money, the evil sister rudely shoves him aside. He submits, then suddenly becomes aroused, spits on her, and shouts, "I will not marry you!" at which point the audience cheers. The evil sister then becomes the mistress of an old Arab who hires the gentle sister as a maid. When the Arab tries to give the gentle sister money, the evil one snatches it from the younger's hand, shoving the feeble old man against the wall. Finally the old man commands the evil sister to get out of his house. She grovels, begging forgiveness, but he is adamant. The clown sweeps her on out with his broom. In the final scene she appears in rags, crawling down the street to beg at the door of her gentle sister, and a male's introspection report summarizes with satisfaction that, "Rujiati [the evil one] is mean and jealous; this shows what happens to mean and jealous women."

The villainess, Inem, of "Revenge in the Night" is branded with every possible repulsive symbol of "modern" or "new rich" stereotypes. She eats Dutch food rather than proletarian food, calls herself "Lilik" rather than "Inem," her village name, and asks to be called *djeng* (a term of address for aristocratic girls). She wears tight slacks and a pony tail to her thighs. She will not speak Javanese.[5] These modern affectations cause a spectator to scream at her, "Fuck! Hak! [expletive]. Your destiny is to be a villager!"

Later Inem's girl friend appears, who is ridiculed by the clown

[5] Every one of the M-plot villains or villainesses speaks Indonesian rather than Javanese throughout most of the plot, whereas M-plot heroes or heroines usually speak Javanese at least part of the time.

as she dances around singing her modern song. Then Bijantoro appears, announcing, "I am Mister Mbitje." Piet, the servant, wriggles his body, clasps his fingers over his pubes, and smiling shyly, says, "I'm Pietje." (making fun of Bijantoro's precious Dutch-style nickname). The audience has words for Bijantoro and the girl friend, calling the first a liar and the latter a "girl-pimp." Finally, when Inem is about to leave her husband and child, to run away with Bijantoro, her servant reprimands her with a hint: "If a child cries, drink is given. If it is sick, it is doctored. That's what parents are for." At this, a spectator screams: "True! If you abandon the child, you are a whore! Remember your child and husband! The child is not considered! Whore! You want to become a beggar!"

Inem leaves, not before showing the police her husband's room so they can arrest him for embezzling money to pay for her philandering and vanities. She flits out, covered with spectators' ridicule and abuse, waving her hand and yelling a Dutch goodbye.

In the end, when Inem and Bijantoro crawl in the gutter, begging at the door of the spouses they spurned, the audience is happy. Spectators say:

> Good, that makes me feel good. That person takes another's spouse, forgets prayers to her parents, forgets her relatives, forgets her child. Now she's rejected!
>
> Great! This is revenge. Just silent [the spurned spouses don't speak to the beggars]. Not even a sneeze!
>
> Wonderful! *Lha* [a sigh of satisfaction]. That's the consequence of being a delinquent person.

This is enough to give a flavor of the M-plot buildup of aggression, which culminates in violent or wretched suffering of villain or villainess. In contrast to the fairly calm imagery that pervades most of each T-plot, the M-plot moves through scenes of beating, destroying, grabbing, spitting, and killing, toward a savage victimization.

The villain's eventual punishment is not explicitly linked to a cosmic machine that rewards evil with suffering. Javanese do vaguely believe that bad action today will some day cause the actor to be "struck by" ill fortune, but they do not define any agent or agency that does the striking. As in Buddhism, there is no god to do it; unlike Buddhism, there is no karma or other cosmic mechanism. In the M-plot itself, no allusions at all are made to a cosmic cause of the plot's outcome.[6]

---

[6] In general, one sees very few supernatural objects or spirits in ludruk. One interesting quasi-supernatural figure who appears is a masked man who is in reality

Nor is the villains' punishment the result of some simple social device such as revenge. It never happens that a villain hurts his brother early in a story and so is killed by him at the end. The person whom a villain has harmed never harms the villain.

The chain of events leading to the villain's punishment is in large part psychological in most M-plots. The evil sister in "The Last Impression" is ambitious; her ambitions are frustrated, so she goes insane, finally becoming a beggar. The evil brother in "King of the Drunkards" kills his father, develops feelings of guilt, compensates by wandering around ranting about how tough he is, and then stabs himself screaming that he is guilty because he killed his father. The brother's final suffering stems largely from his own emotional reactions to his crime.

The Quest

In "The Bandit of West Java," there occurs the following sequence:

> The bandit father's daughter has left her village hut. She is wandering beside a river in the moonlight. It is cloudy; dreamy music is playing. A harelipped man is bathing. The daughter picks up his clothes, and muses, "Whose clothes are these? So big. . . ." She puts them on. Then she continues wandering, comes to an aristocratic house and goes in. Inside, a servant, Amat, looks around, sees her, and exclaims, "A visitor just winked at me!" She flops her old sleeping mat onto the table, collapses into a big chair and falls asleep. Amat sneaks around with painful grimaces expressing tensions arising from the presence of this foreign object: "Why did you come here?" She: "This house looked so big and quiet." Amat: "You're beautiful but uncivilized." She casually picks up the table cloth and starts to walk off. Amat, scandalized, races after, grabs the table cloth, walks back muttering angrily. She casually mutters, "A thousand pardons."
>
> A master and mistress appear and see the girl. "Are you looking for a job?" asks the mistress sweetly, "Fine, for everything is Amat here. Cleaning is Amat, Eating is Amat. . . ." The girl says, "I'll just eat. No need for a salary." Amat screams, "Wah! You kill me

---

of the elite class, but who dedicates his life to helping the "little people" cope with villains of the big city. This figure, with the help of magical capes and swords, beats up city gangsters who victimize peasants-come-to-town. It seems that this "Batman" serves as a city substitute for traditional rural magical protectors (guardian spirits, etc.). He is a more personal protector than the police, whom, as we shall see, the kampung dweller fears.

when you say that! Just eat and not get pay! Are you a cow? You'll ruin the servant's racket!" He strikes the girl (audience laughs). The master steps in, "Now you sleep in the chicken house, Amat. Take her mat." (Amat angrily grabs it.) The master places his fingers, stiff, under Amat's nose and pushes, laughing. Amat stomps out holding his nose and gripping the mat with the tip of his fingers, holding it away from his body as if it is a polluted and foul-smelling thing.

The bandit daughter's passage from village hut to elite household is accompanied by bathing imagery, sex change (the daughter dons male clothes), and a surrealistic confrontation with the household's servant. This is followed by another weird scene:

> The prijaji master tells the girl, hired as manservant, to guard the door and not admit anybody. The son of the master enters. The girl chases him with a sickle. He finally convinces her to put the sickle away and asks her to give him a massage. She refuses. He lies down to sleep. So does she. He hops onto a chair, squatting. So does she. He throws a shoe at her. She throws it back.

Note the tentative communication: massage, imitation, throwing shoes. Then the boy discovers that the "manservant" is a girl. An extra strangeness is added to this sequence by the fact that the "girl" playing a "manservant" is a male transvestite who seems to get a special thrill out of acting like a girl who is trying to masquerade as a man but is not very good at it because "her" hands are soft, her hair is long, and her hips wiggle. After this sequence the girl marries the elite boy: She has completed her quest.

In no other M-plots is there such grotesque passage imagery underlining a character's shift from low to high status. In almost every M-plot, however, a proletariat character marries an elite character only after wandering homeless. In "The Final Duty," the heroine leaves her inland village and wanders to Surabaja; in "The Last Impression," the heroine leaves home after her father dies; in "King of the Drunkards" the proletarian hero marries an elite girl after he has been at sea. Such imagery of wandering [7] serves to underline the M-plot heroine's or hero's sustained quest toward a goal — higher status. In T-plots, where no such sustained quest appears, no comparable "passage" imagery is seen either.

[7] The image of lovers (usually brother and sister) spending a period of solitary wandering before happily marrying is also found in Javanese folk tales. See W. H. Rassers, *Panji, the Culture Hero: a Structural Study of Religion in Java*, p. 4.

We are now in position to summarize the contrasts between T-plot and M-plot form:

The M-plot heroine or hero sustains a quest until she or he reaches her or his reward in the last scene. Meanwhile, villainess or villain has sustained a movement toward her or his last-scene punishment. The audience experiences its main catharsis during the last scene, when rewards and punishments emerge. The last scene is "innovative," resulting in a new state of affairs.

No single hero or heroine sustains a quest from the T-plot's start to its finish. No T-plot villain sustains a movement toward a final-scene punishment. The T-plot moves more toward harmonizing the group than toward punishing an individual or fulfilling an individual's aim. The T-plot does not postpone catharsis until the end to the degree that the M-plot does; the T-plot lets participants release their tensions periodically through laughter or pity. The last scene completes a cycle, returning society to its beginning state.

The M-plot, then, comes closer than the T-plot to giving the ludruk participant a chance to identify with an individual protagonist who moves through a sustained sequence toward a goal and new creation.

But a final twist: several traits of the M-plot protagonist might keep the participant from fully identifying with that protagonist. First, the M-plot heroine or hero is usually under thirty and single during most of the plot, whereas most ludruk participants are over thirty and married. Therefore, the participant can only identify with the hero or heroine by remembering past times. Second, the protagonist is almost always a heroine, and the heroine of M-plots is always played by a male actor. This might allow both men and women (who are approximately equally present in ludruk audiences) to identify with the heroine, for "she" has both male and female attributes. Yet because "she" is neither sex totally, either sex's identification with her is ambiguous. Nor, one suspects, is this the only ambiguity associated with the playing of the proletarian protagonist by a transvestite.

10

Mobility, Romance, and Melodrama

MOBILITY

Kampung dwellers say the elite "live in the *kota* [city]." The elite are "orang kota" or "downtown people." Usually when I asked a kampung dweller about the "elite who dwell in the city," he would contrast the social disadvantages of their lives with the social advantages of dwelling in a kampung. Elite kota people do not enjoy associating with one another "just for the sake of associating; they only associate when they want to get information" while the kampung person "doesn't even notice the time passing," when he associates with his neighbors. In the kampung "social concerns are magnified," and neighbors *rukun* (cooperate). The

R. K. might even take up money for a kampung person in need; this could never happen in a kota neighborhood. The kota has no unity. In this respect the kampung is stronger. In the kota there are boundaries between neighbors, not in the kampung. In the kota, there are not strong associations to help with funerals as in the kampung. In the kampung where everybody knows everybody else personally, a man's personality counts. In the kota what counts is not soul but status.

In spite of these opinions, which are almost classic contrasts of *gemeinschaft* and *gesellschaft* modes of social life, kampung dwellers are fascinated and awed by the wealth, luxury, power, and sheer rank of the elite. As we have seen, a favorite ludruk fantasy depicts a kampung person becoming an elite kota person. It is worth noting that the urban kampung dwellers have plenty of opportunity to see elite houses and personages because the elite *are* in the kota. There has never been a Javanese equivalent of the European feudal lord and country squire, or even American suburbanite.[1] Javanese elite have their houses in cities. And these houses are not set back in wooded lots, shielded from the public gaze. They are close to the street and have no walls around the front yard. When Surabaja elite hold wedding celebrations, kampung dwellers gather at the edge of the lawn and watch the wajang and aristocratic guests all night long (kampung children are permitted to crouch right on the steps of the porch, where the wajang screen and the guests are). This kind of access to elite lives coupled with steep class barriers of other kinds would seem to stimulate the proletarian's fantasies about elite life (it is not just on the ludruk stage that elite characters parade before proletarian audiences) and perhaps his aspirations toward higher status.

Probably the most popular path upward for the kampung dweller is education. Since the beginning of the twentieth century, education has increasingly become a path along which Indonesians move toward government posts. The trend was accelerated during World War II when the Japanese gave the Indonesian intellectuals many government posts previously occupied by Europeans and nobles.[2] By 1953 there were 570,000 posts in the Indonesian bureaucracy,[3] more than four times as many as had existed under the Dutch, and all were open to Indonesians, mainly through the channels of

[1] C. Geertz, *Religion of Java,* p. 229.

[2] W. F. Wertheim, "Changes in Indonesia's Social Stratification," p. 43.

[3] Hindley, *Communist Party,* p. 14.

education. Today, several million Indonesians have government positions.[4] It is fairly easy for educated Indonesians to get government posts. There are not many literate unemployed in Indonesia as in some emerging nations, although there are many underpaid literate.

The population of students has grown, as have government opportunities for the educated. The number of pupils in elementary schools has tripled since pre-war times and there are fifteen times as many junior secondary school pupils, ten times as many senior high school pupils, and over ten times as many university students now as there were in pre-war times.[5] Inceases in the student population above the elementary school level are the most significant, since it is above this level that education begins to qualify a person for a white-collar government position.

Growth of the student population is paralleled by florescence of schools. In Surabaja there are elementary schools, junior secondary schools, and senior secondary schools, of government, Christian, and non-Christian private varieties (for instance, Taman Siswa, the "Garden of Students"). There is a government university, Airlangga, which has faculties of medicine, dentistry, and law (and education, in Malang, a nearby town in the highlands). There are kindergarten, technical high schools, training schools for teachers of physical education, midwife and nursing courses at the hospitals, and the Indonesian equivalent to the United States Naval Academy. Elsewhere in Java there are schools for fish culture, communication, navigation, chemical technology, agriculture, police administration, fine arts, journalism, foreign service, and so on.

I met a number of kampung youths who were taking advantage of these educational opportunities. A school teacher who lived in my kampung estimated that in this kampung of about 400 households there were thirty boys in SMA, a highschool more like a German gymnasium than an American high school in its training and in the status of its graduates (an SMA graduate can go straight into university, medical, or law training). I knew two boys from that kampung who were in a university. Every kampung with which I gained some acquaintance had a few youths in high school or university. The one ludruk actor whom I interviewed fully who was old enough to have a son in a university did in

---

[4] Seymour Topping, "A 'New' Indonesia Faces Huge Tasks," p. 4, estimates that there are between one-and-a-half– and five-million civilian government employees and over half-a-million military personnel in Indonesia today.

[5] Stephen W. Reed (ed.), *Indonesia*, 2:437.

fact have a son studying at a college for physical education teachers. This actor had only finished the third grade. One gathers an impression that the tremendous growth in Indonesian education has not been without impact on kampung society.

But what about the education of the ludruk participants (who are mostly above thirty years old)? As I have said, almost none of these had gone further than elementary school. Several expressed dissatisfaction with the low status to which they felt consigned by their lack of education:

> A ludruk actor who only got through the third grade said, "A diploma determines one's rank. I may be able to make this spoon [he holds up a spoon] and a man with a university degree may not be able to. But if there is a high position open [in a spoon-factory?] he can have it, and I cannot. Only one of our troupe [Tresno Enggal] got as far as junior highschool, and the lack of opportunity for those who do not have diplomas is a constant subject of talk among the "children" [members] of Tresno Enggal. . . .
>
> A pedicab driver who got through the sixth grade during the Japanese period and had once worked as a garage mechanic said, "I feel that many of the high people of Surabaja just study the theory of making things. A high person may have a 'recipe' that tells him how to make this plate [he holds up a plate]. But what use is his education if he can never put it into practice? I would like to rise in status but I don't have a diploma. Still in practice I feel that I'm cleverer than a man with a doctorate."

Military service is another channel toward higher status. Several ludruk actors and spectators between thirty-five and forty-five years of age had been soldiers of some kind during World War II or the Indonesian Revolution. Some had been members of HEIHO (Indonesian soldiers under Japanese command during World War II). Others had been in the guerilla "people's forces" of the Revolution, which in 1950 had become the nucleus of the present Indonesian army. Several of these former soldiers complained that, had they stayed in, they would now be officers (one said his brother had stayed and was now an officer). As in the case of education, the ludruk participant expresses a sense of missing an opportunity which others of his class seized.

By rising in political parties, especially the Communist party, the kampung dweller can rise in rank, although it is said that most of the proletarian leaders of the Communist party still live in kampung. Many of the ludruk participants with whom I talked said they were disillusioned with politics and not much interested anymore, although they had once been members of "People's Youth" or some other Communist-affiliated group. Now they only cared about "making a living." I have mentioned, however, two ludruk troupe managers who seem to be successfully moving up in status by taking part in Communist or Nationalist politics.

Since ludruk participants are mostly abangan, they are not eligible for moving up the Islamic religio-bureaucratic hierarchy which flows from the Ministry of Religion of the central government.

Among abangan Javanese there is traditionally ambivalence regarding traders, that job being classed lower in moral terms than farming, and certainly lower in spiritual refinement (alusness) than poorly paid jobs such as schoolteacher or clerk. I am not sure to what extent these sentiments discourage abangan proletarians from entering trade, since many do. But most of the petty traders with whom I talked seemed to see their trade not as planned, cumulative steps toward wealth and higher status, but as disconnected transactions to make ends meet. Nevertheless, I did see at ludruk performances some tradespeople who appeared to be lowborn but prosperous: they drank beer, ate big suppers, and one man sported a battery-operated electric fan.

Many ludruk participants have risen slightly in status simply by moving to town. Their fathers had kasar jobs (farmer), but they have relatively alus jobs such as petty clerk in a government office, messenger in a bank, or clerk in a Chinese bookkeeping firm.

Social contacts furnish a general path upward. The great flowering of education has increased the chances for kampung youth to mingle with elite children. For example, I knew a daughter of a princess from Djokjakarta, now living in Surabaja, who was in a government senior highschool along with a number of kampung boys, one of whom was her boyfriend. Several kampung boys told me about some mild affair they had had with an elite girl during school; although none had married such a girl, such experiences must make the possibility of elite-proletariat marriage seem more real. (Interestingly, none of these boys talked about elite friends of their own sex.) Certainly school widens the range of contacts which a kampung boy can make with elite. In the past his main contacts seem to have been mediated by kin ties (a father working for a firm headed by an elite man brings his son to that man to see if his son can get a job with the firm) or neighbor ties (a man in my kampung helped several of his neighbors' sons get jobs in an office where he had been employed before he retired).[6]

ROMANCE

Among Surabaja Javanese proletarians, parents usually arrange children's marriages. Sometimes the parents choose the child's mate. Sometimes the child gets acquainted on his own with someone and tells his parents that he would like to marry that person, after which his parents visit the person's parents and propose marriage. If the two sets of parents agree that their children will marry, they set the date, and the wedding follows in due course.

A number of male ludruk participants in their late twenties or early thirties told of having a romantic love affair during early youth with some‚ girl whom they almost married, but they always married a girl whom their parents had chosen for them. For instance, Supii, who got as far as junior high school, relates that when he was twenty-three he met a high school girl and lived with her in a student compound. His parents were angry when they discovered what he had been doing, for they wanted to choose his wife. They were kuna, said Supii. He himself held the opinion that he must be acquainted with a girl before he decided to marry her. But his parents scolded him, "Look at that girl. She is better educated than you." One night his father got drunk, came to the girl's compound, and insulted the landlord about the affair between Supii and the girl. The girl packed up and left the compound, leaving word for Supii to meet her at Red Bridge (a bus departure point). She proposed that Supii and she go together to her parents' home. Supii did not "even ask permission from my parents . . . I just went." Once at the girl's house, Supii says he and the girl were not even "respectful" to her parents; he would sit in a chair and the girl would perch on the chair's arm. Also, Supii was shy around the girl's parents and could not think of anything to say. The girl's stepmother would not agree to the marriage. Finally, Supii went back to Surabaja, saying to the girl that he would return to her shortly, but he never did. Then one day a letter came to him in Surabaja informing him that the girl was married to somebody else. After that, his mother told him he would have

---

[6] As a general comment on this section, it should be said that virtually all writers on Java express the view that opportunities for upward mobility have generally increased in Java since pre-war times. As Clifford Geertz puts it (*Religion of Java*, p. 360), mobility is "a normal, expectable occurrence" in Java today.

to marry another girl. His mother and father picked a girl and arranged a wedding for him without his knowledge. His fifteen-year-old bride was in the third grade of elementary school. Now she and Supii have two children. "I have no feeling for my wife," says Supii, "only *kasihan* (sympathy). She is not very clever, and does not respond to anything I do, whether it is good or bad."

Supii appears to get a certain sad pleasure from pitying himself as a victim of parents and the social order. Yet he seems genuinely sorry that his marriage falls so short of his earlier romantic experience. His peers feel the same way. Almost every young married man whom I interviewed contrasted "youthful romance" with his passionless relationship to the woman he had finally married: "I feel kasihan (sympathy), not *tjinta* (love)." "I don't believe in tjinta." "Tjinta" is an Indonesian word meaning "love" in the sense of romantic love of man for woman. It is interesting that Supii and his peers judge their marriages against the standard of romantic love, for this ideal does not quite fit the main traditional Javanese ideal of marriage, which several informants described as "man and wife being like brother and sister." [7] (In idealized traditional elite marriages portrayed on the Ludruk stage, husband and wife follow the Javanese custom of calling each other "older brother" and "younger sister" and treat each other rather formally, never touching one another physically in public.)

There is a high divorce rate among kampung Javanese. I have heard of people who had been divorced over a dozen times, and one man listed eleven women whom he had married, in sequence. Excluding the man divorced eleven times and another who said he had been divorced seven times, seventeen of thirty marriages which occurred two years or more before my fieldwork had ended in divorce by the time my fieldwork began. This supports H. Geertz's finding that half the Javanese marriages end in divorce.[8] Casual separations were not regarded as particularly unusual. A wife would stay home at her village with her children, looking after family fields in that village, while the husband worked in town as a pedicab driver or factory hand, visiting his wife once a month.

Javanese often seem to value marriage more for the parent-child tie that it can produce than for the husband-wife tie that is (in romantic ideology) its substance. At weddings bananas are hung

---

[7] See also H. Geertz, *The Javanese Family*, pp. 134–37.
[8] *Ibid.*, p. 69.

outside the house to symbolize the couple's fertility, thus shifting the emphasis immediately toward the parent-child relation. There is great interest in procreation. No woman whom my wife met failed to ask her when she would have a child, and Javanese women constantly perceived in her face or torso signs of pregnancy. Another sign of great emphasis on the parent-child bond appears in ludruk scenes like the following:

> A father tells his daughter she must divorce her husband. The mother exclaims, "Oh No, do not say that! Think of the children!" The daughter moans, "Oh my child, my child, I weep for my child." Nobody speaks of the husband. Later, when the husband is told by a messenger that his wife will be staying with her parents rather than returning to him, his first words are, "What will be the fate of our child?" He does not mention his wife.

I have heard tales of a strange marriage pattern which seems to combine husband-wife and parent-child relations into one: a young boy marries an old woman who is rather motherly toward him. For instance, a story is told of an eighteen-year-old boy who liked to "play" at the house of a rich divorcee who would give him money and trinkets. She came to like him, persuaded him to marry her, and then pacified his parents — who were angry about the marriage because they had arranged for the boy to marry a young girl — by giving them gifts.

Another marriage pattern which is often mentioned pairs a domineering, fussy wife and submissive husband. This pattern would seem to mesh with the matrifocal household pattern, where the wife has great power.

MOBILITY, ROMANCE, MELODRAMA, AND MODERNIZATION

At an obvious level there are parallels between ludruk melodrama and actual society. As we shift from T- to M-plots, proletarian characters are increasingly successful at moving to higher status, and in reality in the years since Dutch rule kampung dwellers (especially the youth) have been increasingly successful at moving to higher status, principally through channels such as education. Changes in melodramatic content parallel changes in Javanese society.

When we look closely at proletarian mobility — onstage and in reality — the parallels are more subtle.

Both story characters and real Javanese are increasingly acting in terms of a universalistic ethic — a trend toward "being modern" according to modernization theory.[9] An ethic is "universalistic" to the degree that it tells those who follow it to judge people according to what they can do; it is "particularistic" to the degree that it leads its adherents to judge people according to "who they are," according to qualities which they can *do* nothing about, such as their sex, age, family, race, or ethnic membership. Obviously, then, a capable man born into a lower class family is more likely to rise to higher status in a society with a universalistic ethic than in a society with a particularistic ethic, for in the former society a man's status depends on what he can do rather than on his birth. The increasing popularity of M-plots indicates that ludruk is increasingly expressing a universalistic ethic, for M-plots depict a society in which proletarians climb socially by their own actions, in spite of their low origins, whereas the T-plot heroine gets into an aristocratic household because of "who" she is — daughter of the household head.

The form of M-plots also expresses increasing universalism. In T-plots what matters is who you are (where you fit in a kinship network); so the whole movement is toward getting the illegitimate child back into her proper position in that network (as in "River of Solo"). The child herself does not *do* anything. Fate does. By contrast, in M-plots the outcome depends more upon the heroine's own action, and focuses on the heroine achieving her goal. The T-plot gives the spectator the feeling that what he does makes no difference and encourages him to let his tensions out during comic and maudlin scenes unrelated to his goal. By contrast, the M-plot lets the spectator vicariously experience achieving by his own doing and release his tensions when he has achieved.

Not only does the M-plot give the participant the feeling that rewards depend on action; it also lets him experience punishment as a consequence of action. The villain is punished in M-plots because of what he does (kill his father). The villain in T-plots is exempt from punishment in spite of what he does because of who he is (highborn), while the gentle heroine in T-plots is often punished in spite of what she does because of who she is (lowborn).

Ludruk has come to shorten the actual time of its performances (from all-night to four hours) and the fictional time of its melodrama (from thirty years in T-plots to weeks in M-plots). The shorter time span of ludruk action, and the drive to compactness

---

[9] See Levy, *Modernization* 1:52.

by directors like Soetjipto, probably help the ludruk participant grasp more clearly the relation between the chain of events composing the play and the reward or punishment that is a consequence of that chain.

In sum, it seems that the M-type melodrama is allowing its participants to experience a society which rewards them universalistically.

This type-M experience jibes with trends in daily life: society increasingly does reward ability and industry. Ludruk participants see that their neighbors and kin do succeed in climbing socially by getting an education, by making political contacts, or by serving in the army.

Yet at a more specific level what the melodrama depicts and what happens in daily life differ. In the M-plot mobility is largely by sexual means — quick response to a sexually-socially opportune situation. In real life it seems to be rare for a person to rise socially by a sexual liaison which leads to marriage. Typically, education is the path upward. Education requires more planning than does the M-plot heroine's landing in a situation where she can sexually attract an elite male and marry him.

Since, as we have seen, ludruk participants' age or bad decisions have nearly excluded them from channels that many of their young neighbors or kin (or even their own children) are taking advantage of, we could view the M-plot as symbolic compensation: ludruk participants are excluded from "rational" mobility channels (education, etc.), so they enjoy empathizing with a fictitious character who moves upward via an irrational channel — sex. But if we ask the question, "How does participation in the M-plot encourage modernization?" we interpret this pattern differently.

We ask, "How might ludruk best stimulate its participants to feel that social mobility is something one can do oneself and that it is not totally in the hands of the fate depicted in T-plots?" The answer is perhaps not by presenting a harsh portrait of a self-made man who achieves by totally rational planning and industry. The leap from T-plot fatalism to such a conception may be too great, but by depicting the heroine who gets ahead by proper sexual response, ludruk mixes romantic and colorful imagery with a certain amount of universalism; it gets across the idea that mobility can be do-it-yourself while concealing from view some of the planning and sacrifice that are involved.

Consider the following: Ludruk participants are not in position to move upward via education and similar paths, but their children and young neighbors or kinfolk are. Therefore, it may be that the best way ludruk can encourage proletarian mobility is by inciting ludruk participants to stimulate the efforts of the younger proletarians to get ahead by their own efforts. The M-plot, by imbuing the notion of do-it-yourself mobility with a nice romantic flavor, may encourage ludruk participants to do this. The M-plot experience gives the proletarian parent a vaguely romantic feeling about universalism and do-it-yourself mobility so that he encourages youth's efforts to act and plan in these terms. Since Javanese kampung elders traditionally voice sentiments such as "yearning and trying will make you sick," this new parental attitude may be very important for Javanese modernization.

It is said that as a society becomes more modernized, it tends to accentuate husband-wife bonds and to de-emphasize parent-child bonds.[10] With the shift from T- to M-plots, ludruk melodrama has shifted its emphasis from parent-child to husband-wife relations. M-plots end with only husband and wife in the household. These have arranged their marriage with little or no help from parents, have violently negated their bonds to parents or kin (siblings) related to them through descent from parents, and they live apart from parents. Furthermore, they themselves are not parents and give no sign of planning to be. They are just husband and wife.

Note that they are situated in an elite household, not in a kampung. Ludruk adds extra glamour to conjugality by giving it a luxurious setting.

Romance seems to catch the imagination of ludruk goers. They clap and cheer when stage characters praise romantic, as opposed to parent-arranged, marriage (this is almost the only onstage action which evokes handclapping). These positive sentiments regarding romance and marriage parallel fantasies expressed by young men like Supii, but oppose traditional Javanese ideals, where parents arrange marriage, and the husband-wife relation is phrased in terms of blood-relation metaphors (husband and wife call each other "brother" and "sister" as if they were related by descent from common parents, rather than conjugally).

Since Ludruk participants are mainly parents — not youths and maidens — it is tempting to see the M-plot romance as a fantasy fulfillment of the participants' romantic yearnings not fulfilled by real-life marriage; note the case of Supii. But if we ask, "How does

[10] *Ibid.*, 1:75.

participation in the M-plot encourage modernization?" we arrive at a different interpretation. If the M-plot sparks and keeps aflame romantic fantasies of parents, it may help stimulate these parents to encourage their children to "marry for love" rather than insisting that they follow their parents' wishes and plans with regard to marriage. If this happens, the romantic marital notions expressed by ludruk will find institutional expression in the next generation. As with the case of mobility, there may be a generational lag between ludruk's symbolic display of modernizing ideologies and the enactment of such ideologies in real society.

11

Jokes in Melodrama as Symbolic Classifiers

ALUS-KASAR JOKES

Distinctive qualities of aristocratic etiquette are summed up (and satirized) in a stereotyped T-plot scene that we may call "the visit":

> The scene opens with a middle-aged aristocratic couple sitting alone, awaiting their guests. Then the guests, another middle-aged aristocratic couple, arrive at the door crooning "Kula nuw–u–u–u u–un," a plea to enter. Host and hostess answer in the same tone and rhythm, "Mangga–a–a–a–a–a," an invitation to enter. This exchange may be accompanied by a constant tinny laugh (heh–heh–heh) and fixed smile on both sides. The language used is refined Javanese. The guests are invited to sit in chairs around a low table on which coffee or tea is set.

After an interval of small talk, during which the drinks stay untouched, the hostess purrs, "Please go ahead and drink," and the guests get around to asking host and hostess to let their daughter marry the guests' son. After the request is made, the date is set, and a few more polite remarks exchanged, the guests ask permission to leave. Formalized responses flow back and forth, permission is given, and the guests coast out, bowing and crooning "Sampu–u–u–u–u–un" ("All is finished") in the same smooth tone they used to begin the visit.

In terms of a metaphor which Javanese themselves use, guests and hosts are building a wall around each others' feelings by covering each other with politeness.[1] Affect remains low. The rhythm of interaction is smooth with crooned utterances melting into each other.

By contrast, observe the following "visit":

In a run-down shack sits a proletarian father in his old black clothes jabbering away in a coarse voice. His son wanders in, mouth agape, stupid expression on his face, and barefoot like the father. He flops down on the floor. The father rails at him because he's so lazy: a grown man, the son has never had any kind of job. The son listens, mouth agape, and finally whines, "Pak [which here could be translated into the stereotyped comic hillbilly "paw"], I got some work and I got some money." He gets up, falls on the bench beside his paw. "A hundred-and-twenty-five," he says, "Eeeee!" exclaims the paw grinning and beside himself with eagerness, "Give it here." "Well, Paw," says the son, "twenty-five went for a pedicab to ride here in; I was scared I'd faint if I walked." "All right," says the paw impatiently, "that leaves a hundred." "Well, Paw, then I saw some of the boys and gambled a little on the birds. Lost forty." The paw rasps a curse. The son continues, "Paw, then I stopped at a food stand. I ate my dinner, but here's the leather the money was in. There isn't any money."

The paw flies into a coarse rage which is interrupted by his blind daughter staggering in, beating her stick on the floor. The son ambles over, takes the end of her stick, and leads her in. She sits down and begins telling them about some aristocratic man she met on the street who wants to cure her eyes. The father says, "Nono-nonononononononononononono!" in his crude voice, shaking his head so vigorously that the audience laughs. "Not right. Not right. Not

[1] Many Javanese gestures can be seen as attempts to remove the "rough" or "sharp" edges of interaction. For example, rather than pointing the sharp index finger, the Javanese point blunt thumbs. Also, men who assume a polite standing position cover their "sharp" genitals with their hands.

right . . . [he says it again and again]. Your eyes will be brushed with a wire brush!"

Somebody is heard asking permission to enter. It is the aristocrat who desires to cure the girl's eyes. He enters, offers everybody cigarettes. Father and son bump into each other in their eagerness to grab them. The son puts his behind his ear. Now the aristocrat sits and begins to talk in a refined way, constantly smiling. The father gets up, goes off to the side, pulls the son up beside him, and says in a loud singsong voice, "Two coffees!" The idiot son repeats wrongly, then says, "Can't hear Paw." This exchange continues as the father's coarse whisper gets louder and louder. He keeps pinching the son's rump to stimulate his senses; the son jumps each time and then settles like a hound dog. Finally he catches on, prepares to get the coffees for guest and host. The rich man steps forward to pay. "Nononononononononono," the father says, waving the money away with one hand, while pulling it in with the other. The idiot son leaves.

They wait and wait. The son does not appear. Finally the aristocrat goes away. The son ambles in. The father, furious, screams, "Where's the coffees?" The son whines, "Awwww. I just ate up the money myself at the food stand." Now the father glimpses a pack of cigarettes the guest left on the table. Grinning he grabs them and slaps them in his pocket. The guest reenters. "Ah . . . I left my cigarettes." "Cigarettes?" asks the father innocently. Guest: "Yes, I am certain I left them here." Father, "Well, I don't know . . . [suddenly] these?" He whips the cigarettes out of his pocket, grinning, white teeth shining in his dirty face, bowing to the man and crooning "Yes, yes, yes," in polite Javanese. The guest just leaves with no comment.

The father comes to the microphone and rasps, "My son is unbearable. When I see my daughter, she's unbearable too — and me too!" (Audience response: a little girl urinates on the floor in front of seats reserved for dignitaries, while other spectators laugh raucously.)

The aristocratic visit eliminated abrupt climaxes by its smooth, muted rhythm of interaction, but the proletariat visit is punctuated by vulgar outbursts and bellowed *faux pas*. The language of the proletarian "visit" is mainly ngoko (crude) Javanese, rather than the refined krama of the aristocratic visit. The melody is singsong and twangy (*kopi loro* ["two coffees"] with pitch rising and accent falling on the last syllable of each word) or hoarsely muttered with raucous explosions.

Proletarian settings contrast with aristocratic settings. Proletarian households are always dark, often lit with only one electric bulb on the stage. The stage depicts a hut with rough, dark walls

(Note the response of a proletarian highschool boy to such a scene: "The humble hut of Rukijati shows persons who are suffering and poor. So the darkness, shadows, and black screen with a dull shine fit.") No art objects are shown.

Aristocratic families, by contrast, are shown in a brightly lit parlor. The room has a rattan or upholstered sofa and chairs and a low table in the center on which coffee and tea can be placed. There are often refined art objects about, such as shadow-play puppet designs on the tablecloth (some scenes also feature modernistic decor). Audiences adjudge such rooms to be "show-off," but "nice".

Public, outward orientation toward high society rather than inward orientation toward domestic affairs is signaled by the setting of the aristocratic visit in a reception room rather then a bedroom or kitchen. By contrast, ludruk proletarians usually focus on domestic affairs rather than guests, although in real life proletarians place great stress on their public face. (Proletarian Javanese mental patients who were asked to sketch their house plans drew only the parlor. They did not draw kitchen or bedroom. Apparently they symbolized "house" by "parlor" rather than by some more private room.)

Aristocratic fathers dress in fine sarong, jacket, and headdress or in more modern fashion, with tie and trousers (but still with headdress). Aristocratic mothers wear a fine sarong and jacket. Aristocrats have more frills — spectacles, canes, shoes — than proletarians. No proletarian ever has these extras.

Because of their formalized etiquette, there is less body contact among aristocratic characters than among proletarians. Proletarians nudge and shove each other a lot, especially when they sit together on a bench. A proletarian wife jumps into her husband's lap; he dumps her on the floor; she crawls back in his lap, and so on.

Aristocratic culture seems to deny physical ills. No ludruk aristocrat ever speaks of his sicknesses. But proletarian men constantly talk about their bad teeth, sexual impotence, and stomach trouble. Sometimes they just die, emitting strangled, rattling sounds from their throats. Proletarian men are plagued by wives whose mouths move at fantastic speeds causing them to resemble meat grinders. Sometimes as the wife's mouth movements speed faster and faster, she explodes into a rump-shaking dance accompanied by slaps on a drum. The point is that proletarian bodies often run away from their owners, breaking through cultural controls.

What, then, are the main features that distinguish aristocratic from proletarian families and characters in ludruk? Aristocratic genealogies are not stressed. Though many aristocratic characters possess titles such as "R." or "R.M." which theoretically show their descent from pre-colonial nobility, in no case are an aristocrat's ancestors mentioned; ludruk aristocrats are not given a literary family tree as are Faulkner's Compsons or Mann's Buddenbrooks. Nor is the aristocrat's position within a hierarchy of wealth or jobs made clear. In almost no plot is an aristocratic family head's job or wealth mentioned (although the house in which the aristocrat lives indicates a certain level of wealth). The crucial feature distinguishing aristocrats from proletarians is their *alus* life-style. It is contrasted with the *kasar* style of life of the proletarian. This distinction is made clearest by presence versus absence of social graces and refined trappings.

I now wish to cite a few jokes which turn on the contrast — alus-kasar — of aristocrats and proletarians in T-plots. Most such jokes in T-plots are made by clown-servants who work for aristocratic families and mock them. Some of the jokes explicitly apply the terms "alus" and "kasar" as when a clown teasingly states that his master, being Central Javanese, is alus — while he, being Surabajan, is kasar. In other jokes, the terms "alus" and "kasar" themselves are not used, but the contrast which the joke expresses is clearly between alus and kasar attributes. Most of the jokes I shall cite are of this type.

A servant mocks the way his master offers guests coffee; the servant pretends to offer guests coffee, then says, "Go on, slurp it up!" The audience laughs. To understand why, we must understand real-life proletarian Javanese visit etiquette: After a crooning ritual surrounding their entrance, the Javanese proletarians' guests are invited to sit at a low table on which drinks, such as coffee, are set. Guests do not straightway drink as Americans would. They must wait perhaps fifteen minutes (a long time on a tropical day) after which host or hostess finally croons, "Manga– a–a–a–a–a" (Go ahead). Only then do host and guest drink. Now, this custom of waiting to drink seems a clear instance of refined culture, embodied in rules of etiquette, restraining a biologically based kasar impulse — to quench one's thirst. But in the joke the servant in kasar language invites guests to immediately express that impulse: "Go on, slurp it up! ("Slurp [*disruput*]" is a kasar word substituted for the expected one, "dipon undjuk," which is an alus word for "drink"). The servant pops the bubble of manners and lays bare the animal desire lurking beneath polite facades. He substitutes kasar elements (impulse-expression, crude speech) for the expected alus elements (polite restraint, refined speech).

There is yet another dimension to the joke. The servant-clown represents in ludruk (and other Javanese drama) an *ur*-proletarian. In the joke, this *ur*-proletarian makes fun of etiquette that is customarily (in ludruk) carried out by aristocrats. The servant mocks his master's haughty ways. As Marxist sociology would predict, the proletarian audience laughs.

But note other audience responses to the joke. A man yells at the clown, "That's your way; when there's food and drink — you just eat and drink!" A woman says, "Huh, indeed this fellow asks for a rock to be thrown at him." People mutter that the clown is *kurang adjar* ("uncouth" or "unschooled in refined Javanese ways"). Why should a proletariat audience be irritated by an *ur*-proletarian mocking an aristocrat? Because, I suggest, the servant is not just mocking aristocratic ideals. He is mocking alus manners idealized by all Javanese, including the ludruk audience. He is mocking ideas embodied in the pan-Javanese alus-kasar cosmology — and that is kurang adjar. To comprehend the audience's reaction, the joke must be interpreted cosmologically as well as sociologically.[2]

In ludruk aristocratic receptions feature a dance (*tajuban*) in which a female dancer dances with guests in the order of their social rank, high ranking ones before low ranking ones. A master of ceremonies points out to the dancer which guest should be danced with when. In the following scene a clown-servant is present at a tajuban. He is, of course, of too low rank to be invited to dance. The inspector of police is dancing. While the inspector dances, the servant off in a corner goes through the motions of dancing, smiling in ecstasy. The master of ceremonies glares at him, walks over and kicks him. The servant looks hurt and stops. The music starts again. The servant wanders over behind the MC's back and begins dancing again. Slowly the MC grows aware of what is happening behind his back. He swivels his head around until he spots the culprit, then he shoves him. Again the clown stops dancing. Several times the clown tries to dance and is stopped. Finally, the clown pokes his hands up under his shirt

---

[2] The analyses of Indonesian clowns cited by W. F. Wertheim, *East-West Parallels*, pp. 28–30, generally interpret the clown as a proletariat symbol rebelling against aristocrats and aristocratic values. My example suggests that these sociological interpretations could be supplemented by cosmological ones.

(which hangs down to his crotch) and begins doing the dance motions under his shirt, in front of his genitals, smiling dreamily. The master of ceremonies angrily slaps his hand. Might the hand motions about the genitals allude to masturbation — which evokes a slap on the hand from authority? At any rate, it is clear that the servant's actions contrast private, body-oriented pleasures (accompanied by a dreamy smile of the sort Gregory Bateson photographed and described as a "simpering narcissistic expression commonly adopted by male [Balinese] dancers")[3] with public social-oriented protocol. The servant ignores the larger aristocratic cultural framework within which the dance has the meaning, "a way of symbolizing one's status." He treats it as a chance for bodily pleasure.

On another tajuban occasion a clown-servant, Amat, wanders in. He shuffles around the room shaking hands with the guests, who respond rather unenthusiastically. The host now begins to make a speech: "Comrades, fathers, mothers. . . ." When the host is finished, Amat stands up and begins to speak in his whining gutter dialect: "Comrades, fathers, and *mbok-mbok*. . . ." For "mothers" (*ibu-ibu*) Amat substitutes a Javanese word which means something like "old kampung mammas." Then he tries to sell patent medicine in the manner of the medicine seller in the market. The landlord drives Amat away. Amat goes off in a corner and begins singing loudly a vulgar song about Surabaja (pronounced "Su–ra–baw–yaw") while the master of ceremonies attempts to start the dance. Failing to treat the speech in terms of aristocratic culture (and also madju culture — this joke is ambiguous in that it contrasts alus with kasar but also madju with kuna), Amat inserts elements of his own lowly culture which superficially resemble elements in his master's speech. He substitutes a crude word for "mother," a patent medicine spiel for "speech," an uncouth song for "music."

Some of the favorite jokes link figures of alus wajang kulit mythology to kasar elements:

> An elite master asks his servant, "What does Semar come from?" "God," replies the servant. [Sang Hjang Tunggal, the One God, is Semar's father.] "And what does Bagong come from?" "Cowhide," the servant replies.

Instead of viewing Bagong in terms of the mythical wajang framework and naming his mythical father, Semar, as the aristocratic

---

[3] Bateson and Mead, *Balinese Character,* p. 172.

master expects him to, the servant gives Bagong's literal, material ancestry — his animal origins: literally it is true that the puppet who represents Bagong is made of cowhide. The joke goes genealogically from the totally alus, God, to the half-man, half-god, Semar, to Semar's son, down to the totally kasar — animal material. Said a female hawker of cloth, "This joke is a good example of the *nglètèk* form of humor: reducing high to low. It makes me feel let-down."

> An aristocrat asks his servant, "Do you know who the five brothers are?" "Pandawa," replies the servant, naming the five brothers of the Mahabharata myth. "Who do they come from?" "Pandu." [King Pandu of Amarta is the father of the Pandawa.] "And who did Pandu come from?" "Old man Mangun," says the servant.

The servant ignores the mythical universe which links alus culture with the whole Hindu culture area of Southeast Asia. Instead he thinks of a local kampung man who makes puppets. (I am told that "Mangun" is a typical kampung name.) He brings out the kasar human origin (and low-grade human at that) of the mythical figure, Pandu. He links alus mythology with a kampung man who made the material object, the puppet, which symbolizes Pandu, who symbolizes aristocratic values.

A master asks his servant, "Do you know about Buta?" "Yeah, Bu To," replies the servant. Buta is a giant who guards entrances to temples in the wajang. The clown pun is that "Bu" means "Ibu" (Mother or Mrs.) and "To" is the last syllable of a name such as "Sutarto." "Bu To" is a familiar way of referring to a woman such as "Mrs. Sutarto." By a superficial resemblance of sound the servant links a mythical figure to the image "local woman" or "old lady so-and-so." Again a symbol from alus art and myth is joined to kasar everyday reality.

A number of jokes involve kasar servants taking on alus roles; servants dress up in alus clothes, mock alus manners, pretend to be of high rank. In the following often staged scene, master imitates servant and servant imitates master:

> The servant is dusting to the sound of the gamelan tinkling like a music box. The servant slaps a chair with his dust rag; the high pitched instruments crash. He slaps at the table; the drum beats. He dusts very fast; the whole orchestra bursts into tune. He yells at it to stop; the gamelan plays on. He then smiles dreamily and begins to dance; the gamelan accelerates, then shifts into a dirty-sounding upward rolling melody with each phrase climaxed by a

whomp of the drum. The servant begins wiggling his buttocks from side to side, smiling. "I'm crazy," says he, "This may have no rules, but it's sheer pleasure."

The audience finds the moment pleasant too; a man says, "Well, every cow gets to rest. Men, too. I only wish I didn't have to work all the time." The servant, helplessly drawn in the gamelan rhythm, can not stop himself from dancing. Now he gets caught up further:

> The drum is hit thrice on the wood, "Clack, clack, CLACK!" With each "clack" the servant's head jerks back.
> The master enters. The servant is unaware that the master is there. The drum goes, "Clack, clack, CLACK!" Both master and servant jerk their heads back in rhythm with each "clack."

Master and servant have been seduced into jerking to the same rhythm.

> Then the master begins rearranging furniture which the servant had earlier arranged. The servant lounges back in a chair as if he were the master; he orders the master to bring him coffee and cigarettes just the way the master customarily orders him about. The master chases the servant away. The master's hatchet-faced wife bustles in. She protests that the master is letting the servant make sport of him. "Why, he's no servant," protests the master, "I consider him a member of the family. Sometimes *I* imitate *him*."

First the servant was seduced by the music and rhythm. Then the master was sucked into going through the same motions to the same rhythm. Next the master began enacting the servant's social role and the servant started performing the master's. Music and body rhythm led to the role switch.

As the master started jerking his head along with the servant, one spectator screamed, "Why, it's *latah!*" Latah is a mental disease where a person who is confused by a loud noise begins imitating another's motions. According to a Surabaja psychiatrist, Professor Soejoenoes, many latah sufferers in Surabaja are lowly workers or servants; sometimes these persons imitate their bosses. In the example cited here the reverse is true as well.[4]

---

[4] Note the resemblance between latah and the prologue swindle, where the victim cannot resist imitating the dancer, and so gives the dancer money. Latah is widespread in the Indonesian-Malay culture area. Latah in Java may relate to the fact that Javanese are trained so much through bodily imitation (as opposed to verbal instruction). Javanese children's hands are repeatedly prodded into position by parents until they learn how to gesture properly. Javanese students are taught to play the gamelan by having their hands manipulated by the teacher

MADJU-KUNA JOKES

"Revenge in the Night" contains a series of joking contrasts between madju and kuna attitudes and symbols:

Scene four: As the scene opens, Piet, a clown-servant, is talking about his mistress, Inem. Inem, reared as a villager, is now a *wanita madju* [progressive woman]. Inem eats bread [Dutch food] instead of *témpé* [traditional village food], wears a yard-long pony-tail hairdo, lipstick, and tight slacks instead of traditional clothes, insists on speaking Indonesian, refuses to speak Javanese to her own parents, claims she is a person in her own right and "won't *have* parents who are like buffaloes [i.e., stupid]." (A spectator screams, "Her parents are called buffaloes! Is that fitting, by the one who was given birth to, nurtured till grown? That's gratitude to parents!")

Inem swishes in, wearing her flashy modern clothes. Her husband urges her to be more conservative. She retorts that he ought to be glad he's got a wife who keeps up with the times. He whines that women try to be madju while he's kuna. (Audience laughs throughout this dialogue.) After more talk, Inem exits.

A girl, Mientje (this is a Dutch name), shimmies up to the door, clad like Inem. She keeps trying to ask in jazzed-up Indonesian slang if this is Inem's house. Piet, the servant, finally grasps the question and verifies that it is Inem's house. At that the girl enters, dancing and whirling and singing a wild Indonesian "modern" song. Piet curses in Surabaja Javanese. The girl asks again if this is Inem's house. Piet says it is and again the girl begins to whirl and sing while Piet curses and the audience laughs. Piet mocks the girl in a coarse voice. Spectators scream that the girl is a whore.

Inem enters. She and the girl arrange for Inem to rendezvous with a youth, Bijantoro, at a movie theater (a central outlet for madju culture).

Scene five: Inem and Bijantoro meet at the movie, carry on a schematic romantic dialogue until Bijantoro says in English, imitating movie dialogue, "I shall marry you."

Scene six: The police arrive to arrest Rusman, Inem's husband, because he embezzled to pay for Inem's modern ways. Piet receives

---

until complex compositions have been learned. Almost no verbal explanations are given.

A Javanese, W. S. Rendra, who read these comments on the latah complex among the Javanese, agreed that this is, indeed, a salient feature of Javanese national character; Javanese, said Rendra, have an unusual love for imitating rhythms and sounds. Latah is the "national neurosis," and it is this neurosis that Sukarno exploited (presumably by his manufacture of floods of rhythmic slogans, which the Javanese could imitate).

the policeman, who says, "I am here in my official capacity." Piet replies, "I am here in my unofficial capacity." (This contrasts Piet's *kuna* rustic orientation with *madju* bureaucratic realms.) The policeman asks Piet his name; Piet asks him his (further contrasting Piet's homey ways with official procedure). Finally the policeman asks if Rusman is present. Piet, using Javanese language, denies that he is. (Piet supports a friend against officialdom.) But Inem pipes up in Indonesian language that Rusman is home. (She acts as a traitor to her household.) The policeman carts Rusman off to jail. Inem then flits out to have an affair with Bijantoro, waving her hand and yelling, *"Dag, dag, dag. . . ."* (a Dutch "good day" adopted by Indonesians who imitate Western ways). That wave and cry of *"dag"* is entirely repulsive to auditors. A man screams, "Like she has an itch!" and insulting laughter follows as Inem prances on out.

Another kind of madju-kuna joke that appears frequently in M-plots features a provincial who mixes the Javanese (provincial) and Indonesian (national) languages. For instance, the provincial inserts Javanese words into an Indonesian sentence to produce what some spectators called a *gadogado* (potpourri) sentence: "Now I feel *sekétja*," or "*Saiki* I would like to say." "Sekétja" means "comfortable" and "saiki" means "now" in Javanese. The rest of the sentence is in Indonesian. The total affect is much like reading these English sentences with the Javanese stuck in. Another favorite of this genre is pronouncing Indonesian words in Javanese fashion: *situ* (there) is pronounced *sinu* because *sini* (Indonesian for "here") has an "n" in the middle, and in Javanese ngoko, an "n" in the middle of "here" (*ngéné*) implies one for "there" (*ngono*) too. Thus, Indonesian nouns are declined according to rules of Javanese grammar. Modern-national categories are reduced to traditional-regional ones. A similar joke is to respond to Indonesian words as to their Surabaja homonyms; *kasihtahu* (inform) in Indonesian is taken as *kasih tahu* (market Malay *kasih* means "give" and *tahu* is soybean cake), so that the provincial hears the question, "Can you inform me?" as "Can you give me soybean cake" He asks, "With salt?" The provincial seizes on a superficial homonym between "kasihtahu" and "kasih tahu." He hears the former in terms of the latter and thus perceives madju culture in terms of provincial market culture.

A number of jokes depict rustics who deal in kuna fashion with madju agencies, such as the government; for instance:

At the police station, an official is questioning a peasant who acts a bit stupid. "Bisa Bahasa Indonesia?" ("Can you speak Indonesian?") asks the official briskly. "Bisaaaa," singsongs the peasant, pronouncing the last syllable "aw" as if he were speaking Javanese. The official asks the man's name. He receives a grotesque answer, and asks again. A strange sound again passes the peasant's lips. "I thought you could speak Indonesian," says the official. "Bisaaaa boss, but only sekeḍik," replies the peasant, using the Javanese word "sekeḍik" ("a little") instead of the Indonesian word "sedikit." The official hits the peasant in the face. "Hahahahahaha," giggles the peasant stupidly. To all questions he drawls, "No" in Javanese until the official raises his hand to slap him, at which point he screams, "Yesyesyesyesyesyes!"

Amat and Slamet are being questioned by the police about their involvement in a murder. Amat tries to lie, but repeatedly fouls up the story. Then the police question Slamet. Slamet leans over and asks Amat in a loud whisper, "Uh what time did you say we left the house, *mas* [older brother]?" Finally the policeman tells Amat he can leave, but Amat just keeps sitting there. "I hate to leave because you look so sad," he says to the policeman (phrasing an official relationship as if it were a personal one).

Two servants enter a police station, crooning, "Nuwuuuun" (they follow traditional custom for entering a domicile rather than appropriately entering an office). They start jabbering away to the police, inserting Javanese into Indonesian sentences: "Yes it is *njamang* (delightful)!" After awhile the policeman gets things clear: "So it was a bribe. Where is the money?" "Right here, Sir," replies the clown. "Only nine hundred?" replies the policeman, "You said one thousand." After an awkward moment, the servant grabs another one hundred from his cap and slaps it on the desk. Then servants and police go to confront the briber (a murderer who bribed the servants not to tell). The servant who had been bribed is requested to step forward and accuse the murderer. He steps forward, looks the murderer in the eye, then says severely, "All right you . . . give me some more money!" (laughter).

Piet, who often plays the role of the provincial who confronts the police, had this to say:

Fear can become laughter in ludruk. For example, I am at the police station being questioned. Because since childhood I have had little experience with the police, I fear them. So I make mistakes. And these become jokes. For example, in response to the question, "Can you inform me?" I ask, "With salt?" [the kasih tahu pun]. Just like talking to you, sir. I feel fear so I make mistakes [he laughs].

There are many ludruk scenes showing a rube newly inducted into the army; for example:

A harsh soldier enters. A female soldier announces, "Two enlisted men are ready for action as spies!" Piet and Toebi stagger in. The harsh soldier screams, "ATTENTION!" in Indonesian. Piet and Toebi try to draw themselves to attention, but one gets his elbow facing right, the other left. "ABOUT FACE!" yells the soldier. Piet and Toebi whirl around, but when they stop one is facing one way, one the other. "All right," says the soldier, "count CADENCE . . . COUNT!" Piet and Toebi scream out hideous sounds: "Eeet, Nee, Sang, see. . . ." "Excuse me, sir," says the harsh soldier, turning subdued to his superior, "They learned to count from the Japanese." "FORWARD . . . MARCH!" screams the soldier. Piet and Toebi begin goose-stepping away. The soldier hits them in the mouth. Then he gives them their weapons — a gun to Toebi, who salutes with a snap. Piet also salutes with a snap, and is given an old piece of paper.

"Piet and Toebi are idiot soldiers," says a pedicab driver, "really funny!"

Other examples of jokes making madju-kuna contrasts: A servant mixes a modern Indonesian song "My Heart is Flying," with a classical Javanese song. An office clerk mocks his boss's Indonesian language telephone conversation, since Indonesian language sounds over-serious and mechanical to traditional Javanese. A clerk says, "I have a *gambar* (picture)." "Blueprint (gambar of a building)?" asks his fellow clerk. "No, gambar of Bagong (wajang clown)," replies the first. For the expected modern technological symbol, the clerk substitutes a traditional mythical one.

RELATIONS BETWEEN JOKE TYPES AND PLOT TYPES

A rough count of jokes recorded in my fieldnotes [5] reveals that alus-kasar jokes are much more frequent in T-plots than are madju-kuna jokes, and madju-kuna jokes are much more frequent in M-plots than are alus-kasar jokes (see Table 5).

---

[5] Jokes were recorded in my fieldnotes before I had decided that "alus-kasar" and "madju-kuna" were good categories for classifying jokes and before I had any notion that plots fell into T- and M- types. Undoubtedly many jokes in each performance were not recorded in my notes, either because I missed them, had already recorded them before, or did not have time to write them down. But the omissions were, as far as I can see, random with respect to the above classification.

TABLE 5
JOKE TYPES IN RELATION TO PLOT TYPES

Jokes	T-Plots	M-Plots
madju-kuna	4	80
alus-kasar	36	16

NOTE: This table shows the total number of alus-kasar or madju-kuna jokes that were recorded during performances of those stories analyzed in chapter 8.

To judge from jokes, then, the alus-kasar symbolism is more relevant to T-plots, while madju-kuna symbolism is more relevant to M-plots.

This statistical relationship seems to reflect a logical relationship between the type of symbolism and the type of conception of social action dominant in each plot type.

Thus, in terms of alus-kasar symbolism, proletarians are ascribed to the kasar pole and aristocrats to the alus pole of the universe. That is, the proletariat class is bound to one set of categories and symbols (stages of evolution, colors, fabrics, substance, mythology, art, regions, groups, manners, odors, physiques, and emotions) while the aristocrats are bound to another such complex; alus-kasar cosmology symbolizes, concretizes, monumentalizes, and sacralizes the split between the classes. To put it metaphorically: alus-kasar cosmology chains each class to a separate side of the cosmos and weights each down with symbolic baggage so that either has to struggle to cross to the other side. Can it be fortuitous that such a cosmology should be associated with the T-plot image of society — a society composed of classes that cannot intermarry?

Furthermore, the two poles of madju-juna ideology are not so securely bound to the two classes. Neither madju (progressive) nor kuna (conservative) attributes or symbols are rigidly bound to either proletariat or elite. There may be both kuna and madju elite, as is vividly demonstrated by the two most elite (in traditional terms) of Javanese — the emperors of Djokdja and Solo. The former is considered extremely madju and the other quite kuna. There may also be both madju and kuna proletarians. Many proletarian youth of Surabaja consider themselves madju while they think of their parents as kuna. Madju and kuna cut across class lines. Some proletarians and elite are joined together by being madju, while others are joined together by being kuna. It seems logical that such a cosmology is associated with the M-plot conception of society — a society composed of classes that can intermarry.

The joke-plot relationship can also be phrased another way. In

T-plots a great many alus symbols and values are displayed — titles, elevated language, and so on. The main people who display such symbols are those who control the fictional society of T-plots — the aristocratic parents. The clown-servant, whose job is to poke fun at the dominant values and ruling notables in whatever situation he is placed, pokes fun at the aristocrats and their alus values or symbols. This he does by contrasting the alus elements with kasar ones. Consequently, there are many jokes in T-plots based on the contrast between alus and kasar.

In M-plots the aristocratic parent is a forgotten figure. Youth appear more frequently than parents, and youths' decisions guide most of the story's action. These youth, and also government officials who appear frequently in M-plots, exhibit madju values and symbols (e.g., tight slacks, Indonesian language, government uniforms, desks, ambition, idealism). The clown, whose role, again, is to ridicule the dominant values, symbols, and persons, makes fun of these madju values and symbols. He does so by contrasting the madju elements with kuna ones. So there are many jokes in M-plots based on the madju-kuna contrast.

No matter how we look at it, it is clear that alus-kasar or madju-kuna jokes — and the symbols which evoke the jokes — express assumptions about the way society is constituted. Alus-kasar jokes project the idea that society is composed of fixed strata, each linked with a particular level of refinement. Madju-kuna jokes and symbols say that the most significant division is not between upper and lower classes or refined and crude qualities, but between traditional and modern ways.

Since M-plots are becoming increasingly popular relative to T-plots, and madju-kuna jokes are associated with M-plots while alus-kasar jokes are associated with T-plots, there appears to be a trend toward seeing the world in *madju* vs. *kuna* terms. How to explain this trend? Perhaps by the fact that the madju-kuna worldview does better than the alus-kasar worldview at classifying (i.e., making meaningful) social change in Java today.

THE CLOWN'S ROLE AND THOUGHTS

The clown is a suitable character to grasp the categories underlying Type-T and Type-M societies. "Clowns," said a Javanese intellectual,[6] "are the intellectuals of ludruk. They view things

---

[6] I am indebted to Mr. Karyono of the Inspectorate of Culture for this as well as other insightful comments.

more abstractly than do other characters. They stand outside the trees to see the forest."

The "slurp" joke shows how clowns "view things more abstractly than do other characters." In that joke the clown substituted a crude word "slurp" for the expected refined word. The joke explores the relationship between alus and kasar categories. Such a joke requires a more abstract perspective than that of ordinary ludruk characters who, instead of exploring the relation between alus and kasar categories, simply try to fit themselves into one or the other; for instance, they try to act alus. Clowns grasp the dominant categories of a story, then widen the audience's perceptual field by bringing in — via instant aphorisms and puns — categories which contrast with the dominant ones.

As befits one who would "see the forest," the clown stands "outside the trees." The clown is an outsider to the story-society whose categories¹ he lays bare. In type-T stories the clown plays a celibate, infantile, orally focused, ageless servant in a society whose citizens marry, form families, act adult, are genitally focused, and age. In type-M stories the clown is a rustic amid youths and progressives. The clown's apartness from action integral to the type-T and type-M stories is recognized by serious actors, who complain that clowns hurt the story-length climax by "bursting the balloon" with jokes; by spectators who omit clowns when they retell stories they have seen; and by gamelan musicians who quit playing the "story-climax" music when clowns appear. The clown's spatial domain is the stage's edge, where he is onlooker to the story characters living their lives in the center. A marginal citizen in fictional story-society, the clown is apt to suddenly bring in foreigners: A story-citizen is stealing. "Somebody's watching!" exclaims the clown, "Who?" asks the citizen, startled. "They are!" replies the clown, indicating, with a sweep of his arm, the audience.

The clown need not be regarded as intellectual. He can be seen as a superficial thinker, one who gives little thought to plot structure or underlying values but instinctively reacts to whatever symbols appear before his eyes. When a symbol appears, the clown just blurts out something that contrasts in surface ways with it. If a plot-character says a few words in Indonesian, the clown utters something in Javanese. If a plot-character says something polite, the clown says something uncouth. Ludruk clowns are comic geniuses, splendid actors. But it is hard to say how much of the clown's wit derives from insight into underlying patterns and how much is simply skill at mocking alus or madju motions and sounds.

12

Singers as Symbolic Classifiers

The main singers in ludruk are clowns and female impersonators. The clown singer sings the song at the beginning of the dagelan. The transvestite singer sings all between-scene songs (*selingan*) and alternates with a man dressed in male clothes in singing the song that is part of the opening dance (ngremo).[1] The object of this chapter is to show how costumes, settings, lyrics, motions,

---

[1] This male ngremo singer has many features in common with the female transvestite, but he is more dynamic in his dance. Since he does less than 10 per cent of the ludruk dancing and singing, I omit him, as well as some transvestite choirs and dancing groups, from this chapter. The clowns and individual transvestite singers, whom I discuss in this chapter, do about ninety per cent of ludruk's singing and dancing.

and other qualities of clown and transvestite singers contrast along alus-kasar and madju-kuna dimensions, with the latter contrast tending to replace the former.

ALUS VS. KASAR QUALITIES OF TRANSVESTITE AND CLOWN SINGERS

Alus Transvestites

Sometimes ludruk spectators use the term "alus" in reference to transvestite singers. For instance, a woman, speaking of a transvestite singer's clothes, says, "A jacket like that is too alus to be worn by a kasar woman like me!" Spectators occasionally compare transvestite singers to the nobles and aristocrats whom they deem the most perfect personifications of alusness. Spectators remark that a singer's face, figure, or manner is "like that of a prijaji" or that a singer's voice and clothes are "like those of a princess of Solo." (Solo is the home of Javanese court culture and is regarded by Surabaja Javanese as the model city of alusness, the place where dance, clothes, etiquette have reached the highest earthly level of refinement).

The transvestite singer tries hard to look like an alus female. He dawdles meticulously for perhaps two hours backstage before a performance, covering his face with a fine white rice powder or with Max Factor powder (which cost 1,000 rupiah per compact in 1963, a month's salary for many ludruk participants) plus eye shadow, rouge, lipstick (and perfume, although the audience cannot smell him). He wears a jacket of fine quality lace and a fancy sarong of alus *batik* fabric; both jacket and sarong are far finer than those kampung women ordinarily wear (the material for such a jacket cost 1,200 rupiah in 1963, and such a sarong cost 10,000 rupiah, a year's salary for many proletariat). He frames his face with a chignon that is heavy, perfectly smooth, and regarded as aristocratic in style by contrast to the skimpy, straggly twist worn by ordinary kampung women.

Transvestites who sing between scenes strive for a *lemes* (smooth, soft, graceful) motion by walking in stylized fashion as they sing, one hand raising the sarong while the other is lowered, then lowering the sarong while the other is raised; the free hand is flipped limply from the wrist as it goes down and some fingers are flexed more than others as it comes up (Plate 21). This "walk" resembles certain movements of the srimpi court dances (see chapter 4 regarding historical connections between the transvestite ludruk singer and *talèdèk* who danced srimpi style in the courts). When done awkwardly, the motion elicits the contemptuous cry "Kaku!" (stiff). Singers recounting their first try at the "walk" invariably mention the struggle not to be kaku.

The transvestite's opening dance (ngremo) involves three parts: dancing in the center of the stage, walking around the stage's rim, and gracefully sembahing as the curtain drops. During the first part, the singer's feet stamp the beat, so that a bell-studded anklet rings a rhythm; graceful movements are concentrated in his hands. The singer reaches out to the audience, palms down, then gracefully rotates his hands to palms up, arms pulling back toward the body. He floats his cape out, lets it settle gently over a shoulder, twirls it slowly in front of him so that it inscribes a circle. During the second part, the dancer often rests an elbow on his hip, flipping his lower arm, limp-wristed, from side-to-side as he saunters in a circle. He may float his cape and rotate his hands as he goes. During the third part, the dancer sinks smoothly to a crossed-leg sitting position; his head bows, hands are raised, fingers extended, and thumbs touch his nose — a sembah.[2]

Note the graceful hands of both opening and between-scenes dancers (Plates 20–22). These gestures do not denote specific meanings as do gestures of classical Indian dance. They just express softness and grace. It is interesting that, whereas the ludruk transvestite dancers emphasize the palm-up gesture and employ fingers or fingerjoints as separate units (Plate 21), Surabaja manual workers lay stress on palm-down grasping with fingers and joints coordinated. Carpenters and mechanics tend to point all fingers in the same direction when grasping a tool, rather than limply rotating to palm up with fingers positioned individually. The transvestite's gestures express an alus aesthetic rather than kasar task ideal.[3]

Transvestite singers carry refined and aesthetic motions into task contexts, as witness the following notes on a transvestite singer

---

[2] C. Geertz, *Religion of Java*, p. 289, labels the opening dance of ludruk and ketoprak "alus."

[3] Margaret Mead and Frances Cooke MacGregor, *Growth and Culture: A Photographic Study of Balinese Childhood*, and Bateson and Mead, *Balinese Character*, pp. 18, 96–102, emphasize that in general the Balinese tend to use the hand in a palm-up position, to center on the finger tips, and to use fingers as separate units. This is true of Javanese as well, but the extent to which they exercise this tendency depends on the context — task versus aesthetic — in which they find themselves.

observed at work as a messenger in the Chartered Bank of Surabaja:

> While other workers (especially the Chinese, but to a degree the Javanese) moved rather abruptly from one task to another, jumping up from a desk to get something, reaching out quickly to pick an object up, the singer moved fluidly from one desk to another to pick up documents. His hands were kept at his sides, neck straight, chin up, head balanced as if on a straight line cutting through the s-shaped vertebral column. Little tonus. Never missed a stride as he approached a desk. Without leaning and changing rhythm he limply extended his arm, picked up a document from a desk, and stapled it. He seemed more intent on balance and fluidity of body than on performing his task. His face was expressionless, poised like a fashion model's.

Ngremo transvestite dancer-singers copy steps from the wajang wong, a dance-drama which Surabaja proletarians deem alus. Javanese observers point to many ngremo steps that resemble wajang wong steps, such as walking, primping motions, and a stylized courting motion that involves moving forward, then suddenly rocking back with cape held gracefully at the side. Sometimes the ngremo setting is a mural showing a palace with walled garden and fountains, a setting that resembles murals in wajang wong and gives an aura (slightly tawdry) of courtly life. It is interesting that Javanese scholars [4] claim, without much evidence, that the ngremo was first danced in a palace by a nobleman, Djajèngrana III, who bore the titles Pangeran (prince), Adipati (king), and Tumenggung (regent) in the day when kings vied with the United East Indies Company for rule of Java. The scholars' speculation may reflect their perception that present day ngremo dance has a slightly courtly and classical aura.

The singing style of the transvestite resembles that of female singers of classical Javanese songs. The voice is in the soprano range, with a rather nasal sound. There seems to be little diaphragmatic support of the voice. Teeth are set in a smile (Plate 22); both upper and lower teeth can be seen during singing (except when a kerchief is held over the face, since showing teeth is somewhat unrefined). As a result, vowels are moved forward in the mouth. Back vowels, where the dorsum approaches the soft palate, are turned into front vowels, where the front of the tongue approaches

[4] Hadiwidjojo, *Fungsi Semi Ludruk,* p. 20 and Ki Soemadji Adj., "Penjanggah Umum Ki Soemadji Adj. Untuk Prasaran Sdr. Lesmonodewa Poerbokoesoemo," p. 6.

the hard palate. "A" as in "father" becomes "è" (a sound between "e" of "set" and "a" of "sat"). "Mriksani" becomes "mriksèni," "sandiwara massa" becomes 'sendiwère mèsse." This style can produce a bright, almost childlike tone.

There is much ornamentation in transvestite songs (see line H Appendix A). The songs are full of embellishments, such as flattings of notes — a device used in classical Javanese singing to produce a sad feeling.[5] Singers also ornament their songs with sad, chanted refrains, such as "Rama, rama, rama" (a very alus way of saying "Father, father, father").

During the transvestite's song the *gendèr, suling,* and *siter* are the main accompanying instruments. These are all instruments which the Javanese classify as "soft." The gendèr is made of thin metal keys hung over bamboo resonators; its tones are high and flow into one another. The suling is a flute, which is soft and not shrill like a piccolo; it plays a high descant during the transvestite's song. The siter or zither plays "runs" very softly all during the song. All of this gives a dreamy quality to the transvestite's song, which contrasts to the raucous clang of the clown's song's accompaniment, as we shall see.

In addition to incorporating bits of alus culture into his performance, the transvestite singer expresses alus qualities through his total mien. The singer's expressionless face and chant manifests the flatness of affect and the formal control, which Javanese consider alus. The transvestite's dance and song is stylized, a feature of alus art (since natural reality is kasar). The transvestite's seesaw walk and distorted vowels are, like their classical models, unlike any woman's walk. They are stylized expressions of qualities which in terms of Javanese aesthetic conventions express womanliness. The ludruk transvestite singer, says Mr. Soenarto, "is an artifact of the feudal era when people did not want to look at genuine women but at those who create an illusion of women's qualities." [6]

Perhaps partly because he is stylized, the transvestite is ritually secluded from more naturalistic parts of ludruk, such as the prologue and melodrama, which, actors say, "copy behavior of day-to-day." The transvestite singer is always separated from prologue or melodrama by a curtain that falls and rises before and after his song. By contrast, the clown singer — who is a sort of everyday

[5] Kunst, *Music,* 1:328.

[6] Soenarto, Comment during "Sidang Komisi D" (Session of Committee D), Seminar Ludruk, Balai Pemuda in Surabaja, December 25–28, 1960.

fellow — is never secluded in this way. After singing his song, the clown begins his monologue, then plays a role in the prologue. No curtain separates him from the prologue.

Further proof that the transvestite expresses alus qualities is offered by the fact that those who wish to parody him do so by acting kasar. The alus singer of whom we have spoken so far is Javanese. The kasar parody of this singer is by a Madurese. (The Madurese, who live on an island off the coast of East Java, and also in East Java, contrast strikingly in their ecology, demography, and culture with the Javanese: they live on barren land, in widely scattered settlements, and are thought by Javanese to be kasar in character, appearance, etiquette, and art.) After two or three Javanese transvestites have performed between scenes, there appears in the same between-scenes position a Madurese transvestite singer who acts extremely kasar. Instead of white powder, the Madurese paints red stripes on her face (the stripes are said to serve as a headache cure for Madurese, but for Javanese red symbolizes kasar impulses). The Madurese singer wears a cheap jacket and sarong, and a straggly bun. In place of the "soft" walking-in-place motion of the Javanese, she exhibits a gawky striding gait with arms swinging widely back and forth, pausing occasionally to scratch lice on her belly. Her song is a wild Madurese melody, like that heard at Madurese bull races, sung in a raucous voice. When she finishes, instead of curtesying gracefully, the Madurese yells, "Let's go home!" then hoists her skirt and dashes off the stage while spectators roar with laughter and remark that she looks like a seller in the market (the market is generally regarded as a kasar place in contrast to the household where alus manners more nearly prevail — the palace is, of course, one type of household).

In sum, the transvestite manifests many alus traits, more than do other ludruk characters. (On the other hand, by comparison with truly alus Javanese characters, the ludruk transvestite is rather crude; a genuine Javanese queen, for instance, compares to the ludruk transvestite as would Queen Elizabeth in her robes to a Royal Drive-in carhop wearing a paper crown.)

Kasar Clowns

The transvestite wears fine clothes, but the clown dons a plain sarong or long khaki pants, or both, a cotton shirt (colored, open necked) or a servant's white coat. He wears a black cap. Usually he is barefoot.

The transvestite's motions are smooth, but the clown punctuates his dance or song with kasar gestures: scratching his buttocks or nudging an imaginary person with his elbow. The transvestite has a palace courtyard as his setting; the clown stands in front of a mural depicting downtown Surabaja.

The clown's image is that of a Surabaja proletarian, and he is so regarded by the proletarian ludruk goers, who say the clown reminds them of themselves. Intelligentsia see the clown similarly; the same Javanese scholars who imagine that the ngremo dancer had an aristocratic ancestor regard the ancestor of the clown singer as a kind of *ur*-proletarian. Poerbokoesomo calls the ancestor of the clown singer, Besut, a "symbol of the baby of the child-masses",[7] and claims (somewhat wildly) that Besut's

> unclothed body is a symbol of the poverty of the masses in an exposed situation. His short black trousers express the misfortune of the masses with regard to clothes. His white sash expresses the holiness which is contained in the masses' hearts. . . . The four torches in the corners [of the stage], which are at first unlit, then lit by running back and forth, are a metaphor representing the consciousness of the masses. . . .[8]

The clown singer does not manifest the flatness of affect or formal control of the transvestite. He grins, jerks his head forward on lewd words. The gamelan accompaniment to his song gives an impression of being more raucous than that accompanying the transvestite's song. Whereas the transvestite's song was accompanied prominently by instruments Javanese call "soft"; the clown's accompaniment features *saron* (heavy bronze or iron keys) and *kendang* (drum beaten with the hands), instruments Javanese classify as "loud." The clamorous, jazzy quality of the accompaniment is mirrored in the song, especially in the second part when the clown improvises on the melody he set forth during the first part (see lines F and G, Appendix A, for sample improvisations). A Westerner, humming the improvisations in lines F and G might be reminded of a Dixieland jazz man "taking a ride" on a trumpet or trombone. In a typical clown's song, forty-five per cent of the vocal progressions were repeated tones, thirty per cent were steps up and down the scale, and twenty-five per cent were skips up and down. There are more steps and skips than in the transvestite

[7] Poerbokoesoemo, "Ludruk," p. 6.
[8] *Ibid.*

song; this may be an objective correlate of the "lively" (*hidup*) quality some informants perceived in the clown song.

The clown retards and sings an exaggeratedly straight tone on some words, to give an affect not unlike that "dirty" sound which Dixieland sometimes achieves by retards and straight tones (whereas classical Western singers, say of *lieder*, sometimes achieve pathos by the straight tone). Occasionally, the drummer, who always accents the last note of a phrase, gets a dirty "dropping the bottom out" effect by hitting a low note (slapping the drum's large end) on the last rhyming syllable of a phrase, wherein usually lies the satirical climax of a verse. For example, in

> *Beras, gula, lenga diantri*
> *Sebab metu koperasi.*
> *Olèhé antri sampek djam sidji,*
> *Nanging djalané métu mburi!*
> [Rice, sugar, oil must be stood in line for
> Because it comes from the cooperative.
> One can stand in line till one o'clock,
> But everything goes out the back!]

the satirical crux is *mburi* (back), which also means "black market." On this word, the clown jerked his head forward as the drum was slapped, and the audience burst into laughter. If "a" (pronounced "aw" as in hee-haw) occurs as the final syllable of a final word in a song, the clown indulges in an orgy of rolling the "aw" around inside his mouth, slurring it up and down the scale, as the audience laughs. This back-vowel orgy contrasts nicely with the transvestite's pushed-to-the-front vowels; perhaps a contrast "visceral versus sublimated" is involved here.

Three informants were asked what images the clown song evoked in their minds. One said, "Life in the village." An aristocrat described the *djula-djuli* melody, which is heard in purest form in the clown's song, as kasar, and said hearing it made him feel like a villager, not an aristocrat. A kampung headman gave an extraordinary response: "It makes me feel like a man who has impregnated a girl, given her some money, and is running away." So the tune evokes feelings ranging from countrified to immoral.

No listener ever describes the clown singer as alus or "like a prince from Solo." The typical response to the clown is raucous laughter of the kind one spectator characterized as *"terbahak-hahak* ('guffawing,' as opposed to *terkekek-kekek* 'giggling') to the point where I have to urinate."

MADJU VS. KUNA QUALITIES OF TRANSVESTITE AND CLOWN SONGS

Madju Transvestite Songs

Transvestite songs often ask that Indonesians be "progressive" (madju) or that they act in line with this time of "progress" (*kemadjuan*). One frequently sung song goes

> Indonesia, all my folk,
> Islam, Christian, Buddhist, and Hindu,
> Come be together, do not quarrel and argue.
> Remember, it is time to progress [madju]!

Another:

> Red, white, yellow, blue:
> Colors like a morning star.
> Do not just sleep!
> Rember that your nation is not yet unified and madju.

Many other transvestite lyrics, although they do not use the word madju, call for action that Surabaja proletarians commonly regard as madju. For example, transvestite songs exhort their listeners to "Come work for Guided Democracy," "Reach the National Goal," "Get in tune with the ideological stream of the present era," "Move upward," and "Get up!" A verse of this inspirational type:

> Do not wait for the surfacing of stone,
> Nor wait for the sinking of cork.
> Do not anticipate that which is still doubtful.
> Come let us make a better effort!

A very large number of verses ask for national unity — a state of affairs which Indonesians identify very strongly as part of "progress." For instance, verses plead for unity of what Sukarno calls "functional groups":

> Workers, peasants, youths, students, women's movements,
> and managers of national businesses!
> Come let us stand side by side,
> To defend our rightful destiny for this era!

Other verses ask for unity of political factions: "Nationalists, Communists, Religionists" or "Army and Labor." The first three factions are represented by PNI, PKI, and NU parties and the second two by the army and PKI.

Still other verses call for unity of religious groups (Islam,

Christian, Buddhist, Hindu), ethnic groups (*bangsa-bangsa*), regional groups ("from Sabang to Merauke,") and social classes. Some verses just assert that all Indonesians are one:

> Our president, Bung Karno, is clever and wise.
> We are united, a sign of his goodness.

Verses exhort listeners to be loyal to national symbols such as "The Constitution of '45," a document drawn up at the beginning of the Indonesian Revolution, which Sukarno says should be re-invoked: "Indonesians should return" to the Constitution as to a "lap," [9] for it is "magically-sentimentally-nationally-loaded." [10] Mother Kartini is another charismatic symbol:

> Kartini, heroine of Java
> Let us celebrate her birthday.
> She's our mother,
> Who will defend her "immature" folk.

Mother Kartini, daughter of a regent, was a feminist involved in nationalism of the early nineteen-hundreds; Mother Kartini Day is a major national holiday (The role of mother symbols in Indonesian nationalism would be an interesting subject for study: for instance, why did the Indonesian pavilion at New York's 1964 World's Fair have as its centerpiece a huge portrait of Sukarno's mother?)

Kuna Clown Songs

Whereas transvestites plead with Indonesians to be madju, clowns lament that with progress and the break with old customs, evils and excesses have emerged. Clowns sing that in this "era of progress" women's fashions have gone to extremes:

> Era of Progress [*djaman kemadjuan*].
> Women dare wear pants.
> To the point they dare wear tight pants!
> (But there's not yet a man who dares wear a skirt.)

Similar verses castigate women of the "modern era" for wearing dresses, pony tails, shorts, cutting their hair, imitating movies, following the fads.

---

[9] "Penemuan Kembali Revolusi Kita," p. 426.
[10] "Res Publica!" p. 13.

Clowns contrast present and past and imply that past is best:

> There is a difference between girls of present and past.
> In the past if a girl fell, she uttered a goddess's name.
> In the present if she falls, she shouts, "Oh horse!"
> In the past while cooking, a girl sang of the rice goddess.
> In the present she sings of a picnic.

Similar verses lament that in the past parents chose their children's mates, but now the children choose freely; in the past, people married neighbors, now they marry anybody, even foreigners; in the past maidens did housework and read the Koran, now they go to movies.

The clown always assumes that breaking with tradition causes young girls to become sexually loose, and promiscuity yields a sad fate:

> Young men and women, if you mingle freely with one another,
> Do not go past the limits,
> If girls are not able to guard their honor,
> Finally they will be pregnant without being married.
> If a girl is pregnant, her parents do not want to live with her.
> Straightaway she is ejected.
> Then she is roaming the streets.
> Her aim is to find a job, but she is ashamed of her pregnancy.
> Because she is depressed and her feelings run away with her,
> Eventually she settles in the west area there [Potter's field].

Most of the clown's ire is directed at girls, but he has words for male youth too:

> Hair cut like a cock's crest,
> He wears tight breeches.
> If he sees a girl he whistles,
> But he doesn't look after his own pockets!

Older listeners mumble or yell that they agree with the clown. Youths heckle him. An older person says, in response to a verse about sexually loose girls, "Children are naughty." Others mutter, "True, Man (nickname for Parman)," or "Agreed, brother Parman." Another says, "That song is very critical of this era." When the clown sings of the youth with "hair like a cock's crest," an older person says, "Yes, that's the way it is," while a youth rasps sarcastically, "Bah, he tells a secret."

In verse after verse clowns lament that the modern age is fraught with economic misery:

> These are terrible days in Surabaja.
> Many of my people complain.
> Because many cannot make a living.

Present and future are seen as worse than the past:

> Once there was only a little lack of food;
> Now there is much lack!
> What will the fate of the poor people be?

Everything economic is miserable, as revealed by a kind of synthesis lamentation, incorporating into one song complaints heard again and again:

> The people defended the country when there was a revolution;
> The people all worked together.
> The government should remember this.
> Let us remember the people's suffering now!
> They need rice, sugar and oil . . .
> The price of food is increasing.
> Women are depressed.
> The price of cigarettes is rising; many men roll their own now.
> This is only a stopgap method. The prices are not fixed . . .
> People who make profits feel happy — but neglect their relatives.
> Relatives may suffer, but the new rich don't care . . .
> Crops are good when they come from the soil, but
>   when they reach the people, they have changed. . . .

The clown moves from describing economic problems to pinning the blame for them on somebody. Corruption is the scapegoat. The cooperative store, which is supposed to distribute food rations, is the main agency blamed. In many verses (such as the one about rice "flowing out the back") the clown paints a picture of a kampung person standing in line at a cooperative store, being told that his ration of sugar or rice weighs X amount, reweighing at home, and realizing that it weighs less than X amount. Where did the rest go? Or the clown observes that

> They say rice is in the sheds
> But all of it does not appear at market

Where did the rest go? The clown sings that he "does not comprehend and does not hint" at where the rest goes but (he implies) just describes what he sees. Nevertheless, to explain the vanishing rice, the clown conjures up a scapegoat: "The rest goes to the cooperative committee!"

or

A thief is a witness.

There is a chairman; he does not inspect.
This is an era of putting in your pocket, in order to fill needs of today.

The clown forecasts a dire end for those who prosper by corruption:

A person is rich.
Does not want to help others.
Does not think about our troubles.
Associates only with the rich.
Just likes to go to parties.
May go to a national meeting but just dances there.
Continues to be corrupt.
Fills his house with furniture.
Goes to a cafe with wife and child.
A neighbor dies, does not visit his family.
Becomes more and more corrupt.
The government loses.
He is arrested.
Thrown into prison.
Cannot have intercourse with women,
So he just . . . well you know [the clown grins; I am told that
he implies that the corrupt one now has homosexual relations].

A verse with similar intent:

Corrupt officials will die and hang like *djambu mété!*
[a fruit whose seed bursts out when it is hung upside down;
the singer smiles evilly when he forecasts this fate.]

Other diatribes are directed at "leaders" or "those who lead."
Just who those leaders are is left ambiguous, but it appears that
they are below the level of President; I heard only one verse that
could be interpreted as a criticism of Sukarno.

To criticism of corrupt officials or leaders the clown frequently
appends a sly remark like the following:

I am not criticizing, just talking.
But if somebody feels something because of my talk —
that's all right too.

How do people respond to the clown's protest songs? When
the clown wails about economic miseries, people agree: "True,"
"That fits," or "Yes." They remark, "True — much is expensive,
that's true," or "Yes! Prices of objects and clothes are not controlled carefully."

When the clown criticized corruption, a man said, "This is the
era of corrupt people." (To which his companion replied, "Not
just this era.") Others said, "That certainly fits the facts of this

era." "True, this era is indeed that way." A woman said, when the clown sang about goods being sold out the back door, "That's true, all of it. They come from the back, like Brantas [a neighborhood of Surabaja where there is a co-op and also a river into which people defecate; corruption is linked to defecation]."

The clown inveighs, Amos-like, against the corrupt rich, and someone says, "He hints at the rich." A woman just utters the word "corruption." The line about the official hanging like djambu méte evokes loud laughter and the remark, "He stiffens my belly if he jokes. I am really happy when he criticizes somebody!" A man says, "The leaders ask to be killed — just like that!" "He is really clever at hinting," says somebody else.

According to my labels, the clown is anti-modernization, whereas the transvestite is pro-modernization. The clown is kuna, the transvestite madju. But the clown's criticism of today's misery, corruption, and moral looseness need not imply that he wishes for the past. Such criticism could also reflect the clown's hopes that society will create a good future to replace the evil present. Still, the clown never recommends a future, and the only state of affairs which he describes positively is a past one — when prices were lower, girls paid homage to goddesses, and Surabajans married each other instead of foreigners. By contrast, the transvestite is explicit about the new way of life Indonesians should adopt; they should adopt Guided Democracy and achieve national unity. The clown is more explicitly kuna than he is madju, and less explicitly madju in his stance than the transvestite is.

A related contrast: the clown talks almost totally about local affairs, the transvesite about national matters. Clowns complain about Surabaja prices, youth, women, and fashions. Transvestites preach national goals, national unity, ideologies. Clowns describe local situations that a man can see with his own eyes. Transvestites dream of abstractions and situations (such as national unity) that do not exist in local space and cannot be viewed with the naked eye. There is a striking symptom of this difference in orientation. In 1963, the Balinese volcano, Gunung Agung erupted, covering Surabaja with dust. All clowns sang about the eruption and the economic miseries it caused. Not a single transvestite mentioned it in song. Transvestites ignored this extraordinary local event, clowns dwelt upon it.

The clown verses, then, report local suffering and evil that has come with social change. The transvestite verses imagine potential national progress. A count and classification, in these terms, of all relevant clown and transvestite verses that I recorded appears in Table 6.

TABLE 6
TRANSVESTITE AND CLOWN SONG TOPICS

	Transvestite	Clown
National progress	196	41
Local problems	24	198

It is clear that transvestites sing an overwhelming majority of the "national progress' (madju) verses while clowns sing most of the "local problems" (kuna) verses.[11]

TREND FROM ALUS-KASAR TOWARD MADJU-KUNA CLASSIFICATION

I have argued that the main ludruk singers — transvestites and clowns — distinguish their roles, divide their labor, along alus-kasar and madju-kuna dimensions. Transvestites specialize in expressing alus and madju orientations. Clowns specialize in expressing kasar and kuna orientations.

To what extent do clowns and transvestite singers exhibit a trend toward distinguishing their roles along madju-kuna rather than alus-kasar lines?

At least since the nineteen-twenties, many transvestite lyrics of a non-political nature have been about unrequited love. About one-third of the lyrics sung by transvestites in the late twenties, judging from verses collected by H. Overbeck,[12] focused on this theme. In the early thirties, Gondo Durasim took ludruk downtown; subsequently transvestites began doing alus dances, acquired alus gamelan (up to that time the gamelan accompanying ludruk songs had been modeled after Madurese rather than Javanese gamelan), and the songs of unrequited love took on much alus imagery. For example, names of mythical heroes, kings, queens, and princes were added to the songs. Transvestites began to sing of Gatutkatja, Ardjuna, Kresna, Bima, Djoko Tingkir, or Tjakraningrat. Such mythical figures appeared in verses like the following:

> Tjakraningrat is regent of Sampang.
> Radén Pandji is prince of Djenggala.
> I know you pass by but don't want to see me;
> One's heart becomes sick.

[11] A computer analysis of these verses pointed up a similar contrast. See my doctoral thesis, "Javanese Folkdrama and Social Change," pp. 170–80.
[12] Overbeck, "Pantoens," pp. 212–30.

Forget, forget, try to forget,
But the image becomes clearer and clearer.
Triple love, as if loving one who resembles the goddess Ratih.
Queen Ratih is queen of the people of Tjokrokembang.
O widjokokusuma flower, please have pity on me!

Djoko Tingkir sails on a crocodile;
Will visit the king in his palace.
Don't think about her.
It will just lead to sadness and no results.

Nowadays, though the *non-verbal* alus apparatus of transvestites
— dress, dance, palace murals, hairstyles — hardly seems to be
declining in importance, transvestites say that they sing fewer alus
lyrics about lost love than they "used to." (It is not clear exactly
when such lyrics reached their fullest flowering among the transvestites.) This, the singers say, is because they sing so many
political verses nowadays. Indeed, most transvestite singers today
sing many more madju political verses than alus love songs. It
appears that madju lyrics are replacing alus lyrics among the
transvestites. Yet almost no transvestites wear madju clothes
(slacks, dresses) when they sing, dance madju dances (samba,
rumba), or sing madju tunes. Although verbal aspects of the
transvestite's performance have become in great part madju, non-
verbal aspects have remained largely alus.

We know that the government introduced madju political verses
and encouraged singers to sing them. The shift from alus to madju
symbolism hardly took place in non-verbal realms, and this is a
realm the government apparently ignored. Therefore, it appears
that the shift from alus to madju symbolism is, in this case, a
direct result of government stimulation rather than a spontaneous
expression of changes in ludruk participants' world view. Nevertheless, we can expect the shift to affect the world view of ludruk
participants. Participants' minds are flooded with symbols that
divide the world in a new way — the madju-kuna way — rather
than the old way — the alus-kasar way. Just how much these new
verbal symbols affect participants' thoughts, when the old non-
verbal symbols are left intact and displayed along with the new
verbal ones, is one of the questions which gives rise to later
discussion.

Social Correlates of the Jokes and Songs

Having shown that ludruk jokes and songs are increasingly replacing alus-kasar symbolism with madju-kuna symbolism I wish
now to explore in some detail the social and psychological meaning which these symbols or categories have in the daily existence
of the kampung dweller. This should give us a stronger sense of
what the shift in ludruk symbolism means.

I shall approach this question by attempting to define the major
dimensions along which Javanese kampung dwellers contrast the
ideals of "being madju" and "being alus."

RESPECT VERSUS INFORMALITY

Javanese social relations are almost always hierarchical, and the
forms for showing respect (*urmat*) toward a person of higher

status than oneself are markedly elaborated. The most striking way of showing respect is linguistic.[1] Hundreds of basic Javanese words have several forms, ranging from kasar to alus. For example, to say "eat" a speaker of Javanese can say "mangan," "neda," or "dahar" and to say "house" he can say "omah," "grija," or "dalem," depending on how alus a word he wishes to use. All the words for "eat" denote the same act. All the words for "house" denote the same object. But the different forms have different "connotative meanings." By using one form rather than another, the speaker reveals how much status distance (and familiarity) exists between himself and the person he is addressing. As the addressee's status becomes higher relative to the speaker's, the speaker uses increasingly alus words to show greater respect to the addressee. Affixes also change in this fashion; as the addressee's status becomes higher relative to the speaker's, the speaker changes to more alus affixes (for instance, from "di" to "dipun" prefixes for passive verbs). Such a large number of words change as the Javanese speaker shifts from kasar to alus levels of speaking that it sounds as if a Javanese speaks one language to a superior and a totally different language to an equal or an inferior. For example, to an equal with whom he is on familiar terms, the Javanese might ask, *"Iki bukumu?"* (Is this your book?) but to a superior the same question would be *"Menika buku pandjenengan?"* The Javanese themselves label the different Javanese "languages"; from most kasar to most alus, these languages are labelled *ngoko, ngoko saé, krama madya, krama,* and *krama inggil.*

As Geertz demonstrates, the Javanese, by increasing the level of alusness of the language with which he addresses a person, increases the thickness of the wall of formality around that person's inner feelings, thus protecting and stabilizing those feelings. A speaker talking to a superior will "in deference to the other's great spiritual refinement, build him a wall without any demand or expectation that the other reciprocate." [2] For instance, an ordinary urbanite, by speaking krama inggil, highest of the four Javanese vocabularies, builds four walls around a district officer to whom he is speaking; while the district officer, speaking ngoko, lowest of the four vocabularies, to the urbanite, builds only one wall around

[1] Much of this and the next paragraph were suggested by observations reported by C. Geertz, *Religion of Java*, pp. 248–60, which correspond to my own experiences with linguistic etiquette among Javanese of Surabaja.

[2] C. Geertz, *Religion of Java*, p. 255.

him. As one of my informants put it, "Prijaji can always talk straight to us, but we can never talk straight to them."

Behaviorally a Javanese expresses respect for a superior in many ways, often following the metaphor of lowering himself spatially before the superior. In the house of a princess from Djokdja who lived in Surabaja, servants served guests on their knees. One day, upon being greeted by the princess's husband, a psychiatrist, an old servant who had returned for a visit performed a sembah. ("Take a picture," the psychiatrist said to me, "you'll not see this kind of thing much longer.") But even modern Javanese feel uncomfortable when their heads are higher than a superior's; I have seen Javanese hop out of a chair and squat because a superior squats. In ludruk plays depicting olden times, low people always squat or sit on the floor in the presence of elite.

There appears to be a connection between the Javanese father-child relationship and the strong emphasis Javanese place on alus respect etiquette. I did not make a special study of child training but would like to summarize some observations by H. Geertz [3] on this matter and then present evidence I have which supports her views. Geertz says that before age five, as the child is learning to walk and is being weaned, he and the father enjoy great intimacy. After age five, child and father become very distant. The child must act respectful to the father and address him in krama. As the child learns these alus ways, and loses his intimacy with his father, he learns to "know *isin*," to feel crippling shame in the presence of a superior. The child's behavior in general changes; the spontaneous and laughing child becomes restrained and controlled like his elders.

Several pieces of evidence suggest that this picture holds for Surabaja Javanese: Javanese fathers in Surabaja can often be seen cuddling their young children — which gives quite a bit of body contact since the children are usually half-naked and the fathers often are clad only in short pants. According to some informants, such cuddling (and the habit of father and son lying together on a mat) stopped when they were four or five years old. Halting such intimacy when the child is about five-years-old seems to be an explicit ideal. Said one father:

> At about five years, the child and I must separate even though at that time if it loses something it runs to me [for comfort], not to the mother. If we don't separate and become distant to one another

[3] H. Geertz, *The Javanese Family*, pp. 105–18.

at that time, the child will wither and not mature to take up for itself.

The father-child relationship after age five is one of alus respect.

Various adult fantasies contain themes that might reflect an early father-child relationship of the kind Geertz describes. Adults have fantasies about *losing* the father. (One man said he often dreamed that he got on a streetcar, looked across the aisle, and saw his father sitting there; after father and son rode together awhile the father said, "Well son, I have to get off here," and did, while the boy rode on alone.) Adults also have fantasies about *finding* the father. (Mangkunegara, a Javanese prince, divides the classical puppet plays into four types according to the goal of the action portrayed in each. The goal of one of the four types of action is knowledge of origin, gained by traveling through a strange forest, fighting off sirens, but finally arriving at a capital city and discovering one's lost father.) [4] Finally, there are fantasies which explicitly connect losing the father, searching for him, and finding him, with mastery of alus respect etiquette. "Sawunggaling" is a story taken from keṭoprak, but often performed by ludruk:

> In a sorry country shack there lives a boy named Djoko Berèk ("Berèk" means "the odor of putrid fish"). Djoko's mother was once the mistress of a king, but when she became pregant she had to leave the palace and now she and her son — the king's son — Djoko live with her parents. Djoko Berèk has not learned alus Javanese etiquette. He cannot speak krama at all, which causes his rustic grandfather to keep laughing at him, shoving his head down, and rasping, "He's like a girl, not a real male." Djoko says the reason he cannot speak krama is because he has no father. "Show me my father," he commands his mother. "I'm your father," says the grandfather. Djoko denies this, saying he will go and search for his father. As he prepares to go, his mother gives him a piece of alus (batik) cloth which the king gave her so that if Djoko finds the king, he can show him the cloth and thus the king will know that Djoko is his son. When he departs, Djoko changes his name to Sawunggaling ("Sawung" meaning "cock" and "galing" signifying "a powerful element"). On his way to the city to search for his father, Sawunggaling encounters the sons of the king. They make fun of him because he cannot speak krama. Sawunggaling challenges them to a cockfight. His cock wins. They run back to the palace in shame, he pursuing. At the gate he encounters the king and begins

[4] K.G.P.A.A. Mangkunegara VII of Surakarta, *On the Wajang Kulit* (*Purwa*) *and Its Symbolic and Mystical Elements.*

to speak to him in ngoko. The king mutters something about Sawunggaling being a stupid villager and shoves his head. Sawunggaling draws forth the cloth his mother gave him. The king, upon seeing the cloth, stands perfectly still, remembering his past love and realizing that this boy is his own son. Sad and sweet music plays as Sawunggaling kneels at his father's feet, performing a sembah. (At this point, a Javanese school teacher watching the performance said the scene reminded him of his asking his father's pardon on Ramadan, when all Javanese children must kneel and beg their parents' pardon for their ill deeds during the year. He would approach his father, who was an assistant *wedana* [a fairly high position in the civil service], and, unable to speak, silently sembah before him.) The king receives Sawunggaling into his palace. Sawunggaling, having found his father, immediately begins dressing like a prince, carrying a *kris* (sword with explicit phallic connotations), and speaking krama. Then he becomes King by shooting an arrow into a distant field, and he drives the Dutch from Java.

"Sawunggaling" reveals clearly the relationship between fathers and alusness. There is one more evidence of this relationship that should be cited: Javanese explicitly state that alus respect relationships are patterned on the father-child relationship. "Father" (bapak) is a word by which superiors are often addressed, and a paternalistic relation between an official and his subordinates is called "bapakism."

What evidence is there that, with the current emphasis on madju symbols and values, alus respect etiquette is declining? The sembah is rarely seen now (remember the psychiatrist's remark). Servants in most houses do not serve guests on their knees anymore. Some Surabaja youth speak Indonesian to people of high status so they do not have to worry about alus respect language (Indonesian is not divided into discrete alus-kasar levels the way Javanese is). One also sees other interesting signs of informality: a son of the princess from Djokja used to slip through a small green door leading from the walled inner backyard of his house to the street outside where there was a concession stand which pedicab drivers and other lowly types frequented so as to entertain himself at the stand joking in sign language (for which there are no status-classifiers) with a deafmute yardman.

The increased stress on "youth" activities would seem to promote informality. Youths usually speak ngoko Javanese or Indonesian to one another. So the more time a boy spends with his peers rather than his parents, the more time he spends not following alus respect etiquette. Also, since elders are frequently the audiences of the youths, what youths do may influence the elders' thoughts and thus affect the way they raise their children.

In connection with the link between respect of the father and alus etiquette: as mobility increases, the father's authority should tend to decrease, for sons will be surpassing their fathers; also as respect for tradition declines (madju values flourish), respect for the main vehicle of tradition, the father, should decline. It is said that in Surabaja, sons have virtually quit sembahing to their fathers when they ask them forgiveness at Ramadan, though they still sembah in Central Java (as I have said, Surabaja is always deemed more madju and kasar than Central Java, which is considered more alus).[5]

Many politically minded Javanese who profess madju ideology explicitly classify alus respect etiquette as kuna and "feudal." Such persons speak in favor of more informal and egalitarian relations. Sukarno is an interesting symbol in this regard. He musters some of the imagery of the ancient Hindu-Javanese king, who was considered as a different order of being from ordinary man. As the king lived in his kraton, so does Sukarno live in his Freedom Palace, with his own variety of harem and entourage. Yet Sukarno likes to be called *bung* (brother), and ludruk actors who have played in his palace say he insisted that they speak ngoko Surabaja Javanese with him. It is interesting that Bima, the shadow play character under whose name Sukarno once wrote, is the least alus of the Pandawa brothers, despising pomp, and speaking ngoko even to the gods.[6]

AESTHETIC RITUAL HARMONY VERSUS INSTRUMENTALITY

Alus etiquette serves not only to keep harmonious and respectful relations between inferior and superior; it also maintains harmony between equals among whom there is tension and social distance. Strangers who are equals speak and act more alus to one another than do friends who are equals. In-laws act alus to one another. Parties who have quarreled treat each other in alus fashion.

[5] Robert Jay of the University of Hawaii remarked informally to me in the summer of 1965 that he had noted a trend toward the father-child relationship becoming less distant among the East Javanese. Jay also thinks there is a relation between the fact that Javanese children suddenly become distant from their fathers at age five and the fact that Javanese adults place so much stress on alus art and symbolism. He has comparative evidence to support this correlation.

[6] Anderson, *Mythology*, p. 28.

The notion that alus etiquette sustains harmony between equals links alus to another important Javanese concept, *rukun*. I have heard Javanese use the term "rukun" to refer to: active cooperation toward completing some specific task, such as repairing a roadway to a kampung; a group's members feeling as "one" with each other and cooperating in all spheres of life; just getting along in relaxed and harmonious fashion with whomever one is thrown.

Javanese place great value on this last type of rukun and are good at it. They are adept at quickly and smoothly adapting to situations in such a way as to maintain social harmony. A bus passenger just relaxes when the conductor suddenly sits on his lap to count his tickets. Passengers on streetcar, train, or truck remain at ease as bodies press against them, and many more people per square foot crowd into Javanese than into Western vehicles. A hostess keeps smiling while a guest visits for two months in a crowded house.

Often it seems that personal integrity is sacrificed to keep a harmonious relationship with whomever one rubs shoulders. A woman bragged about becoming santri — even teaching the Koran, she said — when she lived in a santri kampung; but now that all her neighbors are abangan, so is she, she said. A man working in a factory joined all the labor unions who approached him because he did not wish to offend any.

Some Javanese said the desire to keep harmony in face-to-face relations made them vulnerable to exploitation. A cook said salesmen could always talk her into trading her gold things for cheap things. A man said the Dutch talked the Javanese into giving away Java because Javanese just melt when talked nicely to.

Javanese seem to consider it more important that people who are thrown together keep harmony than that they stay together. People say it is better to divorce a quarrelsome spouse than to stay with him or her and disturb one's soul. It is important to get along with a spouse, said an informant, but also important to let go without caring (with *iklas*) when the time comes to part.

In many situations more primacy is placed on face-to-face harmony than on goals or obligations separate from oneself in space and time. If a person has an appointment when a guest comes, he should forget the appointment and be nice to the guest. One ought not to embarrass an incompetent worker by firing him even though his incompetence threatens the goals of the organization. It is wise to avoid directly refusing a request that one has no intention of fulfilling, even though a direct refusal might let the person making the request know where he stands and thus achieve his aims more efficiently.

Finally, there is the custom of asking persons forgiveness in order to harmonize one's relations with them. Before singers start to sing, they ask their listeners to forgive their mistakes. Before borrowers request money from creditors, they ask their forgiveness. During the week before my wife and I left Surabaja, several Javanese came by to ask our forgiveness for all the ways they had wronged us during our visit. "Javanese cannot lose the need to ask forgiveness," said a ludruk actor, "they are more alus than other people, such as Balinese or Madurese."

This last remark links again alus action and face-to-face harmony. Alus behavior is only one way to rukun, and to be alus is not necessarily to rukun; a man can quarrel in alus as well as in kasar fashion. Nevertheless, in most cases, it seems that the terms "alus" and "rukun" describe actions oriented toward keeping social relations harmonious.

Alus behavior has aesthetic value. The surface appearance of alus etiquette is beautiful, therefore good in itself. The form and style of alus behavior often means more than any practical end it serves. Javanese care about manners for manners' sake. They strive to speak beautifully, to move with controlled balance and grace. Alus art is an extension of alus manners.

Alus behavior has ritual value. Alus values and symbols are part of Agama Djawa (Javanese Religion), a complex of philosophies, sacred objects, and art forms which Javanese regard as a transcendental system of almost metaphysical reality. Therefore, every alus action is a ritual action in the sense that it expresses this transcendental system. Alus action is also ritual action in a humbler sense: certain alus performances, such as shadow plays, are regarded as rites with power to keep evil spirits away.

Madju action tends to be more instrumental than alus action. That is, madju action tends to be seen as a means towards future goals, whereas alus action is oriented toward maintaining harmony with persons present, aesthetic appreciation of present actions, and ritual expression of a timeless, everpresent set of transcendental values.

To be madju does not necessarily mean channeling one's action toward a future goal, but it does imply rejecting tradition, and it often happens that actions labeled "madju" are oriented toward some future goal rather than guided by tradition. Nationalist ideology is full of instrumental imagery. The word "retool" which is a key part of Sukarno's current ideology signifies a view of present actions as instruments toward future goals ("Retool the bureaucracy in order to achieve national prosperity!") as does the term "functional groups" ("All functional groups of Indonesia are to be coordinated toward a single set of goals, the goals of the Revolution!"). We see much instrumental imagery of this kind in transvestite songs.

Surabaja Javanese youth who talk about madju attitudes often use imagery with instrumental connotations. "The kuna way was to be patient," says a youth, "but the younger generation is less patient." Adds his friend, "We seek a more dynamic way. In the past, it was said, 'It does not matter if you eat, the important thing is to be together harmoniously' but we say, 'It does not matter if you are together harmoniously, the important thing is to earn a living.' " "We youth work hard at the office," says a youth who heads a kampung youth group, "for we want a raise. The older generation just accepts what is given them." An old Javanese woman warns that those who "yearn" will disturb the peace of their hearts and get sick in their bodies, but the young ludruk director who seeks a "dynamic way" writes:

> Peace without freedom
> Is like a hot coal in a husk

> Peace is eternal;
> Freedom loves and yearns.

> A white dove flies in the blue sky;
> I choose death rather than challenge yearning.

There are other signs of instrumental tendencies among Surabaja youth. Modern paintings by youth show grasping fists rather than the delicate, curved finger gesture which represents beauty in classical alus art. "What is the direction of steps toward fastening tight the fists of today's age?" asks the young ludruk director in a poem. This same man told me that he had been trying to train his child to be dynamic in the Western tradition. Kuna Javanese, he said, are unable to bear hearing a baby cry, so they pick the baby up immediately and suckle him or cradle him in their shawls. But he, Basman, has been trying to avoid picking up his son every time he cries for he wants his son to grow up knowing that he must strive for what he gets — it will not be handed to him. Unfortunately, added Basman, the child's grandmother, Basman's mother, lives with Basman and his wife, and she is kuna. She cannot bear to hear the child cry so she immediately puts it in her shawl when it does. (One wonders if Basman would be so madju without the knowledge that his mother is there to temper his radicalism.)

Madju action is not always opposed to aesthetic, ritual, or harmonious action. The following remarks by an insane pedicab driver mix madju goals with images of social harmony and personal regression that normal Javanese might not find unappealing:

> Now my aim is to become one and becoming one is pleasant — the pleasure of being collected together — pleasant being one, a real pleasure. . . . The person who works in the field should give his fields to the government, then he will be paid. Rice will be given to the government, then everybody will share in it equally. There will be no corruption. . . . Sukarno promises no corruption. . . . I dream of plucking a milk banana [*pisang susu,* so called because its end looks like a woman's breast and its contents are the color of milk]. I go to the field. Just pluck the banana. Very soft when I ate it . . . very sweet. How delicious. . . .very soft. . . .tasted very sweet and rich [he laughs]. . . . I'm just wondering why President Sukarno has a connection with me. *Susu* Sukarno. . . . *Susu* Sukarno. Before I go to sleep I think about what I'll do in the future. Corruption will be solved. I will go directly to Djombang [his home town] and make peace. I hope my thoughts can become stable. . . .

UNIVERSALISM VERSUS PARTICULARISM

Being alus is integrally associated with being highborn, whereas being madju is not so tightly linked to one's class origin. This is partly so because alus manners and ways (such as the ability to speak good krama) are learned at home from birth, whereas madju behavior and trappings (such as fluency in Indonesian, a jazzy mien, and modern clothes) are mainly learned, or bought, by persons past elementary school age in places outside the home — school, political meetings, stores. Since the person from a lowly home has a chance to acquire a madju surface away from home, his origins do not show as much when he is acting madju as they do when he must act alus. Now, if it becomes harder to judge a person's class origin, some other way of judging him is required, and one way to judge him is by what he can do. Therefore, insofar as madju ideals become dominant in Javanese society, and alus ideals peripheral, the likelihood that people will judge each other on a universalistic basis increases. Thus, madju ideals are associated with universalism, alus ideals with particularism.

This is the situation that some of the ambitious young proletarians, such as Shamsudin and Basman, are taking advantage of
when they try to move in circles where madju symbols count and
alus values are relatively peripheral.

NATIONALISM VERSUS REGIONALISM

Obviously, madju symbols are part of being national-minded,
Indonesian, cosmopolitan, whereas alus symbolism is intimately
bound up with being a good Javanese (regionalist). To be madju
is to speak Indonesian, wear Western-style clothes, use nationalist
jargon; to be alus is to speak Javanese, wear Javanese-style clothes,
comprehend the intricacies of Javanese mythology, and be attuned
to the beauties of Javanese dance and culture.

PROGRESSIVISM VERSUS CONSERVATISM

Finally, we reach the most direct meaning of "being madju."
To be madju is to reject the old, simply because it is old, and
to accept the new, simply because it is new. To worry about being
alus is to think in kuna terms; alusness is one of the old traditions, so acting alus is one way of being kuna.

JOKES, SONGS, ALUS-MADJU VALUES, AND MODERNIZATION

Having defined five major dimensions along which the ideal
of "being madju" contrasts with that of "being alus," I wish
now to sketch quickly how the shift from alus to madju symbolism
exhibited by ludruk's songs and jokes is a shift along these dimensions; the symbolic shift of song and joke expresses an increasing
emphasis on progressivism rather than convervatism, nationalism
rather than regionalism, universalism rather than particularism,
instrumentality rather than aesthetic ritual harmony, and informality rather than respect.

We need not elaborate on the way madju transvestite lyrics
emphasize progressive-nationalist orientations. What of the clown's
madju-kuna jokes? Freud saw puns as, among other things, veiled
expressions of sexual impulses that were stifled by Victorian Europe;
we might see ludruk clowns' madju-kuna puns as expressions of
conservative-regionalist sentiments that are suspect in revolutionary
and nationalistic Indonesia. Yet the puns and other jokes do not
necessarily undermine the movement toward centralization. By

building bridges — even phonetic ones — between Javanese and Indonesian languages and symbols, the puns help ludruk goers step from local to national culture, and laugh away tensions aroused by conflicts between the two cultures. Thus, the clown as well as the transvestite can be seen as contributing to the centralization of Indonesia, a movement in the direction of modernization.[7]

We have already shown, in our analysis of the link between joke types and story types, that the shift from alus to madju jokes is associated (statistically and logically) with a shift toward a more universalistic way of thinking about social action and social classes.

Many of the anti-alus jokes of the T-plot clowns parody harmonious, ritualized, aesthetic social behavior. Madju lyrics of the transvestites have many instrumental connotations. The transvestite asks that "parliament, ministers, doctrine, people, professors, and youth" unify *in order* to achieve Guided Democracy and sings that Guided Democracy must be achieved *in order* that "we can get cheap food and clothes" as well as achieve other national ends. The action requested is justified by claiming that it is an efficient means toward a stated goal. The *form* of argument is instrumental, or, in terms of modernization theory, "rational," and therefore tending toward "modern" style.[8]

Finally, it is clear that ludruk's jokes and songs are increasingly ignoring the trappings of respect — alus language, obsequious postures — while increasingly calling attention to the symbols of informal relations — Indonesian language, casual and egalitarian manners.

We have by no means tapped all the dimensions involved in the categories "alus" and "madju." For example, when alus is contrasted with kasar, dimensions such as "otherwordly-thiswordly" or "restrained-impulsive" are involved. But I have tried to define the major dimensions along which madju and alus contrast with each other. Apparently, although the particular symbols displayed by ludruk differ from some of the symbols associated in daily life with the categories "alus" and "madju," the shift from alus thinking to madju thinking that is expressed by ludruk occurs along the same dimensions as does the parallel shift in thinking by Javanese proletarians away from the ludruk stage.

What does this shift mean to the ludruk participant? Imagine, first, what the alus-kasar categories mean to him. These categories

[7] Levy, *Modernization*, 1:55.
[8] *Ibid*, 1:139.

serve what Durkheim and Mauss call a "purely speculative function." [9] By classifying acts, objects, statuses, qualities, evolutionary levels, regional cultures, and ethnic groups in terms of the alus-kasar distinction, the Javanese cognitively orders many of the elements that compose his universe. Just as the Christian views work, war, and death in terms of a superordinate framework, so the Javanese fits a cosmic design to Madurese whom he meets on the street, manners to which he must conform, and his own impulses. In terms of the design, discrete chunks of existence assume meaning; they make sense, and the Javanese responds to them differently from the way he would if they did not. He is more apt to be polite if he sees the place of etiquette in a cosmic design, more likely to restrain his appetite when fat men occupy a low position in his cosmology, less likely to display his lust when continence has cosmic meaning.

The alus-kasar scheme also has behavioral consequences in other ways. As Durkheim says, in discussing cosmologies of the Australians, if a man is classified with another person or group, he feels in sympathy with that person or group.[10] In similar fashion, the Javanese proletarian who is classed with another person (e.g., a peasant) by virtue of sharing kasar qualities with that person will feel differently toward that person than toward somebody (e.g., an aristocrat) who is not classed with him. Such feelings of sympathy or kinship, of course, influence the way Javanese act toward one another.

The alus-kasar system specifies things which Javanese ought to do and things they ought not to do. In most situations Javanese regard alus acts as ideal, good, morally desirable, beautiful (the Javanese word, *saé,* means both "good" and "beautiful").[11] Kasar acts are seen as undesirable and ugly. Therefore, the Javanese strives in most situations to be alus and not kasar. When alus behavior is regarded as ideal, the Javanese who acts kasar is punished by his fellows, and he is likely to experience the shame that is the Javanese equivalent (but intensified) of the American's sinking feeling in the pit of his stomach. If the Javanese acts fittingly alus and so do those around him, the result is a delicate dance of smoothness and grace which creates "calmness in the liver" of everyone.

The distinction between "desirable" and "desired" is relevant

---

[9] Durkheim and Mauss, *Primitive Classification,* p. 81.
[10] Emile Durkheim, *The Elementary Forms of Religious Life,* pp. 170–75.
[11] Anderson, *Mythology,* p. 24.

here. Desirable and desired acts or qualities may be the same, but are not necessarily so. A Javanese may desire to do something kasar, such as bellow out a dirty word, but his culture proclaims such an act morally and aesthetically undesirable in most situations. On the other hand, a cultural definition of the desirable need not always stymie a man's desire. It may also legitimize it. We shall see that ludruk participants legitimize certain homosexual fantasies which, from the standpoint of some moral codes (for instance, Islamic) are immoral, by calling them "alus."

What I have said about alus and kasar also goes for the madju-kuna categories. Like alus and kasar, madju and kuna serve to classify discrete elements of reality and add meaning to them. Traditional customs that are going out and modern customs that are coming in can be labeled, related, and so rendered meaningful in terms of the madju-kuna scheme. Not only that, but by being classified with such luminous images as "nation," "Sukarno," and "Revolution," madju action takes on a special glow of cosmic significance and moral worth, thus stimulating many Javanese to act madju. Also, when Javanese class themselves as "madju," they feel special sympathies with others also classed as "madju." As with the alus-kasar system, the madju-kuna system divides up the social network and organizes the sentiments which people feel toward one another. Finally, because madju labels signal "morally desirable," in terms of a certain world view, Javanese who do things (such as refusing to speak polite Javanese) that are bad by alus-kasar standards justify such actions by calling them "madju."

By shifting, then, from an alus-kasar to a madju-kuna way of viewing the world, the Javanese changes the total frame within which his existence assumes meaning, he shifts his social loyalties and sympathies, and he acquires a new base from which to make moral judgments or legitimize his actions. Clearly, insofar as ludruk encourages this shift, it encourages a moral, social, mental, and emotional revolution of depth.

CHAPTER

14

Singers and Listeners

LISTENERS, TRANSVESTITES, ALUS SYMBOLS, AND SEX

Transvestite singers stimulate their male beholders to utter remarks like these:

> If she were a true woman, I'd like to marry her!
>
> If she moves her breasts, they show. They look big. This one is dark and sweet, yeah? (His friend replies, "Too bad, kid, it's a man.")
>
> Delicious, this fellow.
>
> Whee! She's voluptuous, kid!
>
> Whee! She's sexy, kid!
>
> The one doing the ngremo dance is truly a woman. I would enjoy being given that person. She is beautiful.
>
> Those buttocks are big as a jug — and wiggling sexily!

Sexy singers are also greeted with shouts like "Marilyn!" (Marilyn Monroe) and "Bomber!" or by screams and whistles which one Javanese dramatically characterized as "screams and whistles of passion." Men's introspection reports tell of erotic thoughts about the songstresses, and several say they have dreamed about them. Many tales are told — which, true or not, fascinate Surabajans — of the spectator (usually an aristocrat) who becomes infatuated with a singer while watching her perform and initiates an affair with her or even abandons wife and child to settle down with her as his "wife."

Why do the songstresses arouse men? Men are excited by transvestites who (with the help of padding and rouge) display big, shaking breasts, voluptuous bodies, dancing, shimmying buttocks (accompanied by drum slaps which accelerate as the dance nears its end), nice voices, and beautiful faces. Also, transvestites reveal, their alus songs of lost love contain veiled words designed to arouse men's desires. Finally, the sheer strangeness of the transvestite (who, like the Greek satyr, combines bodily elements not ordinarily combined)[1] shocks and fascinates: people exclaim "God Damn!" or "Tjèk!" or "Fuck!" when the transvestites step out on the stage. (Since shock is expressed by exclaiming, "Fuck!" shock and sex are related.)

A ludruk actor whom I shall call "Aspari" tells a tale that gives a clue about the transvestite's attractiveness. Aspari went to an agricultural junior highschool in a mountain town, where at age twenty he experienced "my first love." He says he was never alone with his sweetheart, but did manage to confess to her his love for her and she reciprocated. Shortly after that exchange, the girl was forced to leave school, for her parents would not agree to her marrying Aspari. Aspari was depressed and could not study, so he went home. His father attempted to marry him to a "very rich" girl, but Aspari refused.

Aspari, a handsome fellow, then began playing romantic roles in ludruk. "Many girls fell in love with me," he says, but he had no interest in them, for he still thought only of his "first love." Parents tried to marry their daughters to him. Daughters threw

---

[1] Transvestites often accentuate the fact that they combine male and female elements by clearing their throats in a gruff bass, and spectators never tire of discussing the fact that the transvestite singer is really a man, although he looks like a woman. Emphasis of the fact that the singer's facade covers a male body (the hybrid "culture over nature" aspect) almost seems to enhance the spectators' attraction to the character.

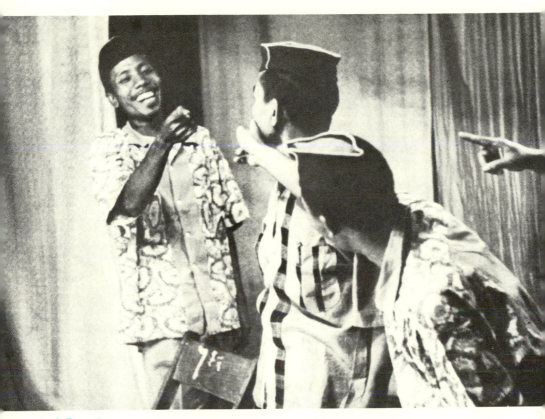

12 Reprobates

13 Victims and victimizers

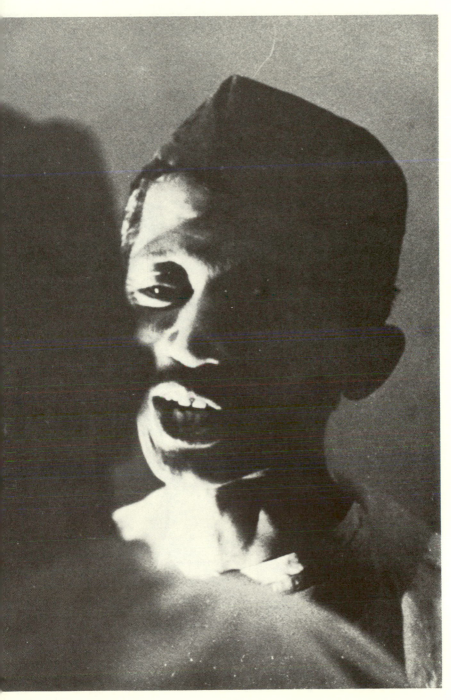

14 Dialogue

15 M-plot hero and heroine

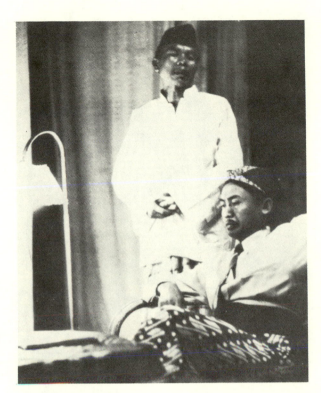

16 T-plot master and servant

17 Tense scene in an M-type melodrama

18 Piet and Toebi, clown-servants in "O Sarinten"

19 Submissive husband and domineering wife

20 Transvestite Ngremo dancer on a kampung stage

21 and 22 Transvestite between-scene singers

themselves at him. But, after refusing to marry a rich girl, he married a poor peasant girl whose father was gone and mother dead. He did not "love" her, he says, but felt ashamed because his old sweetheart had married and was pregnant, while he was still single. Aspari was then twenty-four.

After being married awhile, Aspari awoke one night, told his wife he yearned to send a photograph of himself to his old sweetheart and get the sweetheart's photograph. He left for the sweetheart's house. That very night, he says, the sweetheart fought with her husband and requested a divorce. But Aspari says he hesitated to divorce his wife to marry his sweetheart because he feared parents and neighbors would disapprove. So, the sweetheart married another man and had more children.

One night Aspari played in ludruk at a celebration which his sweetheart attended. After watching him on the stage, she immediately asked her husband for a divorce, and invited Aspari to marry her outside of town, since she knew the neighbors would not approve of the marriage. Again Aspari hesitated. "I did not have the heart to divorce my wife," he says, "for I knew she loved me." So Aspari and the sweetheart again failed to marry.

At this point Aspari became infatuated with a ludruk transvestite singer, and his wife became pregnant.

Now Aspari's sweetheart has married again. Aspari has recurrent dreams in which he meets his sweetheart while both are in junior highschool. During the dreams, he says, he feels "extremely joyful" but after waking feels "extremely depressed." He has hopes of meeting his sweetheart again, but says, "I just leave it to God. Maybe it can happen in the next world."

Lately Aspari has been having dreams just like the ones in which he meets his sweetheart back in junior high. But instead of his sweetheart, it is the transvestite singer whom he meets. Again he is extraordinarily happy during the dream, but very sad afterwards, for he realizes that "she" is just a man.

Aspari has written a play called "Meet Again" which he says is based on his own life, except that it ends like his dream: he meets his sweetheart. He says, and it is true (I have seen the play), that the singer with whom he is infatuated, and with whom he has had some manner of homosexual relation, plays the part of the sweetheart.

Now, this tale categorizes similarly: the transvestite singer with whom Aspari is infatuated; Aspari's youthful days of junior high pre-family-responsibility; and Aspari's teen-age sweetheart.

In chapter 10, Supii recounted how his teenage love affair had ended unhappily. Now Supii is burdened with a wife for whom he does not feel affection, but to whom, he says, he feels bound because of his responsibility for the welfare of his child. As Supii watched a certain transvestite singer perform, he wrote:

> When I watch, I can't help but think of my life with my wife and feel that I would be happier with the transvestite. How soft her voice is. I dream frequently of a wedding and living with a wife who is very beautiful and just right. . . . I desire greatly to take her [the songstress] as a lover for her face is more beautiful than that of a real woman. My sexual appetite is aroused.

A week later, at a kampung performance of ludruk, fantasy became reality. An incident occurred. Transvestite singers did not appear onstage when the time came for them to perform a group dance. The director went backstage to see what was holding things up, and the parted curtain revealed Supii, with his arm around a transvestite singer. (Immediately, plates piled with rice were sent backstage, apparently in the hope that food could be substituted for sex so the show could go on.) Now, since Supii idealizes his teen-age romantic experience as "what could have been" much as the actor, Aspari, idealizes his and feels toward his wife much as Aspari does toward his, perhaps there is some equation in Supii's case, as in Aspari's, of "transvestite lover" and "remembered teen-age lover." At any rate, the teen-age fantasy and the transvestite affair are similar in that both furnish escape and regression from real-life family burdens. Both promise romance without family responsibility; the transvestite offers that because he is womanly, but without power to give birth.

Probably the transvestite's relationship to the kampung male's family life enhances the transvestite's attractiveness. To a man living with a tough "meddlesome mouth" household boss, the gentle transvestite must look good. Also the transvestite, because she can spawn no child, does not bid to become a household boss; much of the power of the kampung wife depends on the importance of her role in managing her household's children. Finally, since all commercial ludruk is located outside the kampung, the transvestite is a creature of the extra-kampung world, thus contrasting with the kampung dweller's wife, who is boss of an intra-kampung household. To kampung women the transvestite is a siren from outside who threatens to allure husbands from their intra-kampung responsibilities.[2]

A special type of transvestite singer, different from the more frequently appearing type we have discussed thus far, combines the roles of whore and mother. I shall call this type of songstress the "sucking harlot." Here are descriptions of two "sucking harlots":

> Riamin shimmies up to the microphone, talking in a shrill falsetto: "I understand you. I treat you like my own clients . . . I was married many times, but my old husbands just die, die, die!" The listeners scream and whistle. Riamin moves his mouth in an exaggerating sucking gesture, lips alternately protuding outward then pulled inward. (Sometimes while making such motions, the harlot singers say, "I can eat up ten men!") He continues, "I'm very confused. Living alone is all right, but sometimes lonely. Which type of man do I prefer? I prefer old men. Young men just talk, talk, talk." Riamin moves his mouth in and out again. "Old men don't talk so much — but they give money." He flips a hip at the audience, which laughs and whistles. Somebody yells, "How much is your price?" The laughter which follows (an informant says) is only heard around prostitutes. Riamin moves his hips again, in a motion an audience-response recorder described as "wriggling movements that are sexually attractive" and sucks in and out with his mouth some more. "How refined you are!" a listener screams. "Everybody knows I'm a man!" shrills Riamin.
>
> Meler is funny looking — high waist, scrawny short arms, big flabby buttocks, no neck, big head. He acts very nervous, alternately smiling and grimacing, saying nothing, pointing first to himself, then to the audience. Finally he clears his throat in a deep bass. Listeners laugh loudly. Another series of screams smiles and grimaces, then another throat-clearing, followed by laughter. Now Meler sings a refined introduction: "Be comfortable everybody . . ." and concludes by shrilling, "Allow me to introduce myself. I am Meler from Tambakredja (a red-light district)." This evokes a shout: "Hey Meler — you whore!" Meler retorts, "Can you pay the price?" A man screams back, "You ask for the sword (*ngedjak anggar*)!" (It is said that this alludes to a "duel of two penises"; I am not sure what the "duel" implies.) Meler slings an imaginary wad of spittle

---

[2] It may seem contradictory to say both that the males are marginal to the household and that they feel household affairs are a burden, but these facts emerge clearly from the data. Probably the male's susceptibility to the wiles of seductresses is related to his intermediate position — enough obligation to the household to feel burdened by it, yet not enough practical involvement to feel a part of it.

from mouth to the floor as the percussions crash. There are shouts of "hoohoohoo!" and a curse "Really fuck!" Another person says, "Truly affected and put-on."

After this kind of bawdy prelude, the harlots sing children's songs! They sing songs like "Mixed Flowers," "Night Watch," "Dum-dee-dum Sugar Cane," "Ferocious Giant," and "The Little Motor Car." The words to "Mixed Flowers" go:

> Afternoons, afternoons, in the yard with friends.
> Much merriment and singing, just what I like.
> Come on friends, all together, be careful.
> Don't be careless.
> Come on, go round the village.
> CHORUS: It's you you you who do do do.
> It's you you you who do! [Repeat]
> SECOND VERSE: Just from the store, got a bronze Simplex
>   [bicycle] with a lamp.
> Step aside, sir, step aside!
> Look at me dance!
> Dance in the gladness-place!
> CHORUS: *Tapé* [a fermented food] from long rice, *tapé*
>   from seeds [Repeat]
> O–o Yes! É Mambo! [Repeat]
> THIRD VERSE: Everybody jumping aside.
> Surprised to see my bicycle!
> Beep-beep. Bret-bret.
> Beep-beep! Bret-bret!

"Dum-dee-dum Sugar Cane" begins with a verse in which girls tell boys to go look for wood:

> Alawaja [rhythm word] look, look together!
> Alawaja, look, look together!
> O–i–o look together!
> Though search boys, do not climb! [Repeat]

Then the boys answer:

> Alawaja, climb-climb anyway!
> Alawaja, climb-climb anyway!

Thus, it goes, the girls pleading "don't," the boys answering "I will," repeating twice what the girls have said "don't do" and what the boys "will do." After awhile the boys sing that they will climb to the top of a tree. The girls sing several warnings, each answered by the boys, until finally the girls sing:

Though fall, boys, don't die.
Alawaja, die, die anyway
Alawaja, die-die anyway!
Though dead, boys, I cry for you!

This is like the children's song "Found a Peanut" both in its building to a climax by repetition and in its laconic ending — death.

In all songs by the sucking harlots, there is much repetition of sounds simply for the oral joy of it. "The Little Motor Car" ends with the line "The pig senggrak-senggrok [grunts]. Ngok grog, ngok grog, Ngok-ngok, grog-grok, ngok-ngok, grokgrok." And the last line of "Ferocious Giant" goes

His eyes plerak-plerok [switch left to right]. Rok, rok, ro–o–o–k [voice changes to a growl, slides down to a low note on the last letter].
His skin is kerok [rough], rok, rok, ro–o–o–o–o–o–k [again growling down to a low note].
Jo! It's skin is rough!

As far as I can determine, these songs are children's songs in the same way that "Mary Had a Little Lamb" or "Little Boy Blue" are. Yet the "sucking harlot" is singing them to an audience composed mainly of adults. It appears that, by having children's songs sung to them, the audience is being treated like children, allowed to regress to an earlier role. A harlot singer of Tresno Enggal, Soelkan, when asked what a ludruk audience desired from his performance, replied: "Movements, moral advice, and to be fed like a child."

The transvestite is regarded by Javanese as the most illicit element in ludruk. Santri vehemently condemn ludruk transvestites because, they say, it is a sin for male and female elements to mix in a public performance. No santri can legitimately act in ludruk, and santri are not even supposed to watch such things. (Interestingly, there are several ludruk transvestite singers, one an Arab, who were brought up as santri, rebelled against their santri fathers, became ludruk transvestites partly out of spite, and as a result were beaten by their fathers but encouraged by their mothers, who gave them money and dresses.) Even the abangan or "backslider" Muslims consider the transvestites and the fantasies or actions they evoke morally suspect: an abangan kampung man characterized the ludruk transvestite as a "rough spot" in Javanese society. Kampung women condemn the transvestites because the transvestites threaten to seduce their husbands (and kampung men excuse their infatuations by claiming that the transvestites hire sorcerers who help them bewitch men). All of this suggests that the transvestites, and liaisons with them, are regarded by kampung dwellers as illicit.

The transvestite's illicitness undoubtedly stems partly from the fact that he evokes fantasies of *sexual* escape from adult responsibilities. He is mixed up with forbidden fantasies of returning to adolesence, returning to childhood, eroticism without procreation, and oral sex: mouths, breasts, sucking.

The transvestite is ludruk's most illicit figure. He is also ludruk's most alus figure. The transvestite singer covers himself with far more alus symbolism than does any other ludruk character. Further, the "sucking whore" who displays the most explicit illicit imagery of any transvestite singer (he talks out loud about his promiscuous and homosexual nature and exhibits blatant oral and pseudo-genital sexual imagery) also displays the purest alus imagery of any transvestite. He is the only transvestite who presents intact a pure imitation of alus art. Ordinary transvestites insert shreds of alus songs and dances into their songs and dances, but the harlot, after singing children's songs, renders entire classical songs, such as Kinanṭi.

We find, then, a correlation between alusness and illicitness: the more illicit the impulse associated with a ludruk figure, the greater the amount or purity of the alus symbolism associated with that figure. How might we explain this correlation? One hypothesis is suggested by Devereux. The stylized, beautiful, alus front put forward by the transvestite singer allows him to be classified (by others and by himself) as alus art. By their actions singers put themselves forward as artists; and singers and listeners speak of the transvestite performance as "art" or even "subtle, difficult, *apik* [fine], and alus art." As alus (or *apik*) art, the singer's actions are, in terms of Javanese cosmology, legitimate.[3] Under the cloak of this legitimacy, illicit impulses (which are pre-genital

---

[3] See George Devereux, "Art and Mythology: A General Theory." But the Javanese case is complicated: "Pure" Javanese tradition does not condemn homosexuality and regards a very wide range of behavior, from he-man to rather (in our terms) "effeminate," as properly masculine. Therefore, Javanese who condemn the transvestite are probably doing so from the standpoint of Javanese morality influenced by Islam, but the transvestite legitimizes himself in terms of "pure" (non-Islamized) Javanese ideals of alusness.

in base, Devereux says)[4] can escape the censure of singers' and listeners' superegos and so be enjoyed with little guilt. Singers and listeners can share illicit images while claiming that they are enjoying "alus art."

One can speculate further why "alusness" and "illicit sexual attraction" should go together. The few thoughts that occur to me cluster around the fact that the singer's alus qualities increase her distance from nature and from her beholders. The transvestite singer's aristocratic trappings accentuate her social distance from her proletarian beholders (perhaps this is one reason why these almost never address her directly, the way they address the clown; they refer to transvestite singers [except the harlots] in the third person: "The one who is singing" or "That one"). The singer is, of course, the epitome of distance from nature, for she has gone as far as she can go (culturally) in changing her biological sex by using feminine rouge and padding. Also her alus stylized manner increases her distance from nature — she is like no natural woman. Listeners recognize the unnatural cultural facade of the singer when they say wonderingly that "She looks like a doll" or "Her face is like a picture." Listeners are instantly repulsed when a piece of nature (such as a stiff male movement or signs of age) pokes through the transvestite's alus culture. When that happens, they scream that the singer is old (*tuwèk*), ugly (*èlèk*), like excrement (*taèk*), and is about to die. In various ways, then, the alus trappings of the transvestite singer increase her distance from her beholders and from nature, and when both these distances are suddenly decreased (by decreasing the alusness of the transvestite's culture), beholders' attraction to the singer quickly turns to nausea. Conversely, perhaps, by increasing these distances, through alusifying herself, the transvestite becomes more attractive. What psychology might lie behind all this, aside from the Devereux-type mechanism? I can think of two possibilities. First, perhaps males can let their erotic fantasies run wilder regarding the transvestite

[4] *Ibid.*, p. 375. One piece of evidence for the pre-genital imagery of the ludruk transvestite is difficult to interpret but adds to the picture already presented. I requested an artistically inclined nineteen-year-old, male mental patient, who had worked as an acrobat in a traveling show, to draw pictures of ludruk transvestities as he remembered them. His drawings (see Appendix A of my doctoral thesis) depict the transvestites with grotesquely huge breasts, much larger than those of the real women he drew, and one picture showed a transvestite's mouth facing a detached breast (he stated that it was a breast) floating in mid-air.

precisely because, along with sexy imagery, she displays "separate from beholder and nature" symbolism that reassures males that she neither offers full sexual consummation to them nor demands full sexual output from them; they can just sit back and appreciate her as a "beautiful" objet d'art (the term "beautiful" [*aju*] appears several hundred times in recordings of men's responses to transvestite singers). Note the Freudian insight that genitals — the body-parts which offer consummation — are rarely regarded as beautiful. The other possibility: precisely because the transvestite is stylized, unlike any particular real women, she is super-womanly. This could be so either because the transvestite's stylized womanly mien forms a kind of blank screen onto which males can project fantasy images of qualities more womanly than those of any real woman ("Some men want a fantasy, not a real woman," said a Javanese man, speaking of men who get infatuated with ludruk transvestites) or because the transvestite's stylized womanly mien, being unlike any single real woman, condenses into one image "many women," or at least qualities common to many women.

One development further supports the idea that "alusness" and "illicit sex" are related: we find that as certain transvestites are being made less alus, they are also being stripped of some of their illicit sex.

As some alus elements of the transvestite's act (the veiled songs of love) are being replaced with madju elements (political lyrics) an attempt is being made in the name of "progress" to clean up the transvestite's sexual image. The most madju troupes discourage homosexuality among its transvestites, and it is considered madju for ludruk female impersonators to confine their feminine role to the ludruk stage. As I have noted, Shamsudin says he originated this idea:

> Impersonators wore hair down their shoulders and switched their hips around all day, so I told them there would have to be revolution — haircuts and no more girlish behavior. "Model your actions after Hsun Hwei Shang" [the Chinese Communist female impersonator], I said.

Today several progressive young ludruk directors regard transvestite manliness offstage as madju; so do some of the transvestites themselves:

> A transvestite from Tresno Enggal, Asmari: "Formerly I let my hair grow to my waist. After playing I would coil it [he makes motions with his hands] and put a kerchief around it — nice — no

need for switches. But now . . . [he smiles, perhaps sadly] progress [madju]. We had to get haircuts."

Another transvestite from Tresno Enggal, Hery: "Like other players I once had hair halfway to my waist. I curled, arranged it like a girl — but then came embarrassment [*malu*] and progress [madju]. I cut it off."

The haircut seems to have been a particularly traumatic part of the Revolution. Perhaps long hair had an especially potent meaning for transvestites since it is the only gross male body-part that can be made more womanly by natural process — letting it grow. Other womanly qualities must be produced by powder and padding, but hair is peculiarly between body and culture, having attributes of both. Also, unlike dresses and rouge, long hair was a womanly ornament which the transvestite could not take on and off as he moved on and off the stage: long hair may have signified a more sustained commitment to the womanly role than does interest in extra-somatic feminine trappings.

Ludruk transvestites have traditionally shown more than professional interest in playing feminine roles. Almost all are markedly effeminate offstage. They wear women's clothes at home, sometimes in public. They paste pictures of themselves — made-up as women — on their mirrors. They work at jobs such as tailoring women's clothes. Some become "wives" of men, living lives not unlike that of the Plains Indian berdache. Many endure parents' discomfort and strangers' taunts to keep the role "woman." Most whom I interviewed have taken feminine roles since childhood. Typically, a transvestite began to play girl's games as a child. He helped his mother in the kitchen. He was classed by the community as female or feminine: Ahmari's neighbors changed his name to "Asmari" because he was soft and weak, Riamin's teacher seated him with the girls, and Sudiardi helped in the kitchen at weddings instead of sitting in the customary male place, under the awning outside the house. The strong, childhood-rooted craving of the transvestite to be women in all aspects of their lives conflicts, then, with the ideal of reformers like Shamsudin that transvestite's should only take female roles when doing so serves the national cause. Offstage transvestites should be men, onstage they can play women while they sing songs that help build the nation.

The attempt to politically regiment the transvestites produces bizarre scenes, such as the following which occurred as Tresno Enggal was departing from Brawidjawa Army headquarters to play for troops stationed near Djombang:

The actors were sitting at tables in the downstairs pool hall of army headquarters, waiting for a truck to get ready for their departure. The female impersonators were laughing and chatting gaily, wearing little straw hats they had bought during an engagement in Bali. Suddenly a tough-looking sergeant marched in and bellowed that all actors should line up for inspection. The transvestites leapt up, minced and flopped over to get in line, snapped to attention along with the other actors; then each lisped, "Prepared," when his name was called by the sergeant. When all names had been called, the sergeant did an about-face, saluted his commanding officer, and reported. The officer briefed the troupe on their mission, then dismissed them. The transvestites walked on out to the truck to embark for Djombang, where they would carry out their "duty."

TRANSVESTITE AS PREACHER OF MADJU IDEALS

The transvestite singer is the only ludruk performer who regularly and directly exhorts an audience to be madju and loyal to the nation. The transvestite's messages are phrased as exhortations: "Come on . . ." "Let us!" "Organize!" "Advance!" But in all the performances I attended there was never a verbal on-the-spot reaction to a transvestite's political message. There were neither responses such as "We're ready!" nor comments about the transvestite's message. This lack of reaction is in marked contrast to the audience's stance toward the clown's critical political lyrics. There were thousands of responses to these lyrics; as we saw in the last chapter, listeners literally hold social-political discussions with the clown singer.

One reason why the ludruk audience does not respond to the transvestite's nationalist verses may be that the audience whom the transvestite addresses is often outside the ludruk theater. The transvestite frequently pleads, in the ludruk audience's hearing, for a set of elements external to hat audience to get into harmony. For instance, the singer implores "Indonesia, all my folk" to stop quarreling. He begs "Nationalists, Communists, Religionists" to be one. He beseeches "all ethnic groups" to be united. Now the ludruk audience is not "Indonesia." It does not include Nationalists, Communists, Religionists or all ethnic groups. It is composed of Communist (probably no Nationalist or Religionist) Javanese (probably no Sumatrans, Ambonese, Balinese, etc.). Most of those the singer addresses are not present. He does not directly address those present. He never implores, "Surabaja proletarians" (or "abangan Javanese Surabaja kampung dwellers") to "join the national effort!" The transvestite addresses a system, the Nation, of which the ludruk audience forms a small, rather marginal, part. The singer asks this system to get into harmony. The transvestite song is like a prayer, voiced by a priest, overheard by a silent congregation, directed to a symbolic system largely external to the congregation, requesting this system to get ordered. The song is more reminiscent of certain Javanese rites than of sledgehammer "arouse-the-masses-to-action" propagandizing.

Some of the transvestite's verses do directly exhort an unspecified audience, which could be the ludruk audience, to action. The transvestite sings, "Get up! Open your eyes!" "Let us move upward. Let us reach our national goal!" "Come on, let us make a better effort!" Such songs seem to call for action and response. But do not forget how the transvestite sings them: to the tune of a slow, droning, repetitive chant, accompanied by soft instruments, while smiling a fixed smile, and moving in decelerated, flowing fashion against a dreamy mural of a quiet palace courtyard. The alus symbols surrounding the singer's verbal message are more calculated to produce calmness of heart than fiery response. Such symbols might have better suited the alus verses that tell of "constant thinking about and remembering" lost love than the madju verses that call for people to "be active," "work," and "fulfill the Revolution!" A young Javanese said that when he heard the music accompanying these verses, he remembered a lullabye his mother used to sing to him when he was sick, and the term "unify" in the nationalist verses made him think of being one with his mother! The particular *bonang panerus* ornamentation played during the transvestite song, very slowly, is also played, in similar style, during scenes showing a girl crying on her mother's knee.

The only kind of spontaneous response to transvestite nationalist verses that I heard was by pedicab drivers, on quiet midnight streets, pedaling home to bed, or by beggars and sellers preparing to bed down on the sidewalk. These worthies sang songs which were apparently taken from the transvestite — same words, same tune, and same falsetto voice. The following two were heard most often:

> Indonesia, all my folk,
> Islam, Christian, Buddhist, and Hindu,
> Come be together. Do not quarrel and argue.
> Remember this is an era of progress! [Heard 8 times]

> Don't scorn folk of your own nation
> Who are still ignorant.
> Give knowledge if you can. [Heard 6 times]

It is significant that the transvestite nationalist verses are not sung in work contexts, during the day, but in tranquil contexts when work is done, no challenges need be faced, and the singer is ready to go to sleep. The nationalist songs are sung as lullabyes.

Although the nationalist songs sung by the transvestite do not seem likely to arouse excitement and action, they may be better suited to fill what Sukarno calls the Indonesian need for "a myth, a superbelief." [5] The transvestites' lyrics define human and social goals, paint a picture of the utopia that will exist when these goals are achieved, and frame that picture with a system of charismatic symbols, such as Sukarno, Pantjasila, Manipol-USDEK, Mother Kartini, and "the lap" — the Constitution of '45. The symbols seem to lend an aura of sanctity and morality to the goals and utopia. Perhaps the transvestite song revives that dim feeling that a sacred and good kingdom is coming; present suffering is just a step toward salvation. Seen in this light, the transvestite's lyrics look less worthless. Their job is not to arouse, but to fortify and console, by explaining the meaning of present suffering.[6]

The foregoing analysis leaves unanswered a number of questions, such as: How does the fact that the preacher of ideologies is a *transvestite* affect the congregation's attitude toward the ideologies he preaches? Does the metaphor of transition implicit in the transvestite's image make him a walking advertisement for an ideology of transition? Does the demonic love which some men feel for the transvestite prod them to "fall in love" with the transvestite's ideology? How does the transvestite's illicitness affect his listener's perceptions of national ideology? If the transvestite's

[5] J. M. Van der Kroef "The Realist Convergence in Indonesian Political Life," p. 289. Also note Sukarno's aim of giving Indonesians an "identity." Sukarno has spoken often about bringing about "spiritual changes," giving Indonesians "new values," and so on. Guy J. Pauker, "Indonesian Images of Their National Self," pp. 305–24, upon examining writings by Indonesians that were entered in a contest sponsored by a Djakarta publisher to select the best Indonesian writings on "Indonesia's mission in the world," was struck by the fact that the writings were always phrased "in moral rather than political terms" (p. 322). They based their hopes for good government on moral reform and moral qualities of Indonesian leaders rather than on improvement of decision-making or administrative process.

[6] Much of this section was stimulated by Robert N. Bellahs' seminal paper, "Some Suggestions for the Systematic Study of Religion," p. 1.

ideological utterances mainly explain and console, does this necessarily imply that they lack power to influence action? (Persons initially converted to Christian ideologies in order to find consolation were later, under proper circumstance, inspired and guided by them to choose and act.) And finally, have we accounted for the generally amazing fact that the dominant ludruk preacher of nationalist ideology is the transvestite singer?

The transvestite is essentially aesthetic (alus) in deportment and attitude. An alus, aesthetic attitude says, "It is good to appreciate the surface of present existence." This contradicts the madju notion: "Current conditions should be viewed only with respect to their potential as means toward achieving future goals." Does not, therefore, the transvestite's general stance contradict the verbal message he proclaims? How does this contradiction affect the audience's attitude toward that verbal message? Does the aesthetic aura rub off on the verbally expressed utopian image, causing that image to be contemplated for its beauty rather than seized as a charter for action? "Explaining" means going beyond appreciation of surface appearances to formulate a conceptual framework in terms of which visible events can be classified; hence, does the transvestite's esthete posture discourage listeners from doing what I suggested, above, that they might do: draw from the transvestite's lyrics a conceptual system in terms of which to explain their existence and suffering? Similarly, moral judgment implies stepping beyond surface appearances to formulate a set of principles in terms of which visible events can be judged "good" or "bad." Might the transvestite's esthete presence — love of appearances — discourage the moral judgments that his lyrics conceivably could evoke? Max Weber argued that art competes with religion in that it offers "ersatz salvation." Like religion, art offers escape from the practical world, but unlike religion, art does not require its communicants to earn their escape by obeying a set of moral precepts which form the basis for "a brotherhood of men." Therefore, to religion, art is always "a deceptive bedazzlement . . . a realm of irresponsible indulgence and secret lovelessness." [7] Thus, the transvestite — the essence of ludruk as "art"? [8]

---

[7] Max Weber, "On Religious Rejections of the World," p. 1129.

[8] This, of course, is not the end of speculation about the relation between the transvestite singer's persona and the ideals he sings about. Could it be that *any* ideal is best presented by a person with alus attributes, since alus is "ideal" and non-alus is not? So even madju ideals are best presented by the transvestite, who, at least for a moment, is alus. Yet such presentation would be a joke because

CLOWN SINGER AS THERAPIST

The transvestite focuses on utopia, but the clown singer talks about daily problems. The clown presents himself as everyman, in an everyday setting, talking everyday language, in everyday street-corner style. The conventions of such conversations apply. The clown does not preach idealistically nor blurt out deep id-fantasies. All that is allowed is opinionated description of observables such as fads, prices, stores, and young hoodlums. As the clown talks, the audience replies, "True, brother," or "That's the way it is, pal." Audience and clown converse.

By so doing, audience and clown publically share privately felt tensions about such mundane matters as prices. Then the clown conjures up scapegoats on which to blame the tensions. Audiences react by "laughing until they have to urinate."

This is pure cathartic therapy. The clown proposes no solutions to his patients' problems. He just helps them let go. He is no depth-therapist. He makes no try at delving into the unconscious to draw out deeply repressed conflicts. The problems he talks about — prices, corruption, innovation — are practical problems (ego-problems) of which everybody is fairly conscious, even if they do not depict them so vividly and publically as the clown does. By talking openly about these problems, the clown does flaunt a censor — but a social, not a psychic one. No Javanese

---

everybody knows the transvestite is not "really" alus — he has just assumed an alus facade on the stage. But then, "alusness" is in part itself the essence of facade — the spiritual, unreal, the attitude that momentary appearance is what counts. So sham is necessarily linked to the transvestite, and therefore to the madju ideals which he vocalizes — such a quality being further communicated by the stereotyped, schematic, excessively simple and vague nature of the madju slogans themselves. Since the madju ideals are presented theatrically, there is a necessary ambivalence built into the situation — everyone knows that what is presented theatrically will turn out disappointingly different in reality. There is a great deal of irony involved in the transvestite's madju preaching. Further, by presenting the madju ideals via a "motherly" figure, who often symbolically suckles her audiences, the feeling may be evoked that, "I receive these ideals passively, as one receives mother's milk." The trick now is to shift from this passive stance of receiving ideals to the active stance of applying them. Perhaps this shift could be facilitated by the motherly transvestite's quasi-genitality (she gives a facade of offering satisfaction to the male's genital drives); she is the soft, seductive female, who asks for active male advances. Thus, it is interesting that Surabaja proletarians (and elite) tell tales about the most active and aggressive leaders of Indonesia's nationalization and modernization (men like Sukarno and Subandrio) being seduced by ludruk transvestites.

represses worries about prices the way he might repress fears about his masculinity, but a social censor — the government — does suppress complaints about high prices and government failings. The transvestite, via art, expresses illicit, psychically repressed impulses — the clown, by wit, just gripes.

Part 4

Conclusion

Ludruk as A Rite of Modernization

Now it is time to summarize, interpret, and define more formally the modernizing trends which ludruk encourages. The trends that I shall treat — specialization, bureaucratization, and so on — emerge in many societies and are defined by general theories of modernization (the theory that guides this chapter's analysis is that set forth by Marion J. Levy, Jr., in *Modernization and the Structure of Societies*),[1] but I shall accentuate the distinctive way

[1] Levy, *Modernization,* vol. 1, defines several social trends which go along with increasing technological modernization — increasing specialization of social units, decreasing self-sufficiency of social units, increasingly universalistic ethic, generalization of markets and media of exchange, centralization, bureaucratization, increasing idealization of the multilinear nuclear family, and increasing emphasis on "rationality," "avoidance," "functional specificity," and "universalism" of social re-

ludruk contributes to these trends as they manifest themselves under the unique conditions of Javanese society. Even so, since the definition of modernization which guides this chapter is one put forward by a theory intended to apply to all societies, the reader should not be surprised to find that the discussion is at a more general level than that of earlier chapters.

I shall not repeat in detail earlier points about ludruk's role in the modernization process. Rather, I will use these points as springboards from which to jump into more general analyses.

To highlight ludruk's role as a rite of modernization, I shall, from time to time, contrast ludruk with slametan, the traditional rite with which we have already had some acquaintance and which Clifford Geertz regards as "the center of the whole Javanese religious system." [2] In many ways, slametan plays a role exactly complementary to that of ludruk.[3]

SPECIALIZATION

The Javanese kampung dweller has increasingly come to move in terms of extra-kampung social units that specialize in economic functions (e.g., markets, factories, stores), in education (e.g., SMA schools), politics (e.g., SOBSI or People's Youth), and recreation (e.g., the ludruk theater). Increasingly, economic, educational, political, and recreational activities have been removed from the kampung and taken over by extra-kampung specialized units. The kampung's role in its inhabitants' lives is shrinking, a trend symptomized by the decline of rites and symbols (bersih désa, danjang) that signal the importance of kampung (or village) as a social unit.

---

lations. While all the modernizing trends that I shall treat in this chapter are defined in accordance with Levy's theory, I shall not always use his somewhat cumbersome terminology, and sometimes the trends that I name involve only part of what Levy's definitions imply; for instance, I use the term "conjugalization" to refer to a trend that is part of Levy's "increasing idealization of the multilinear nuclear family" and "monetization" to refer to a trend that is only part of what Levy means by "increasing generalization of markets and media of exchange." I organize this chapter in terms of Levy's framework because, first, I have found it helpful in drawing together much of what I have to say about ludruk and Java, and second, phrasing case studies in terms of a general scheme can help refine the scheme.

[2] C. Geertz, *Religion of Java*, p. 11.

[3] This complementarity is the main subject of my paper, "Ritual, Entertainment, and Modernization: a Javanese Case," forthcoming in *Comparative Studies in Society and History.*

By and large ludruk supports the tendency for kampung dwellers to get increasingly involved in extra-kampung specialized units and less involved in the kampung. Since all five of Surabaja's commercial ludruk theaters, all built since World War II, are located outside the kampung, ludruk literally draws kampung dwellers out of the kampung, seducing them into taking part in a specialized entertainment unit — the ludruk theater. More importantly, perhaps, since the days before Durasim, when ludruk Besut was performed in the kampung and depicted only kampung characters, ludruk has concentrated on idealizing extra-kampung society and denigrating that of the kampung. In its dagelan, ludruk ridicules kampung-affiliated figures and values; in its melodramatic tjerita (such as "The Robber's Nest of Djakarta") the kampung is a dark place of suffering from which those who are lucky rise; and in its clown songs, ludruk brands the kampung an arena of poverty and corruption. The degree to which ludruk avoids idealizing kampung life is striking. Transvestite songs, which specialize in picturing ideal societies (utopia under Guided Democracy), never mention the kampung. Final scenes of melodramas, which customarily depict happiness and ideal situations, almost never are set in the kampung; out of eighty-two final scenes that I say, only one was situated in a kampung. The kampung is not the spot where ludruk builds its utopia.

Given PKI's emphasis on improving kampung life (with the help of RKKS), it is interesting that ludruk, which has some links to PKI, does so little to idealize life in the kampung. One would think that the Youngblood Hawke-like ludruk fantasy of lowly individuals rising to join the elite contradicts the Communist ideal of the proletariat as a group rising in revolt against the elite.

Many ludruk goers are too old to embark on real-life "quests" from kampung to extra-kampung realms, but the experience of vicariously enjoying the quest of ludruk heroes helps them glamorize the "quests" on which their children or their neighbors' and relatives' children have embarked or will embark. In this way ludruk diminishes elders' tendencies to inhibit youths' ambition to rise from the kampung.

Ludruk is a complement to bersih désa and slametan rites. Bersih désa and slametan are what Van Gennep might identify as "rites of incorporation"[4] in that they sacralize the kampung or groupings of neighbors within the kampung, and ritually sym-

[4] Van Gennep, *Rites,* p. 11.

bolize the kampung dweller's spiritual participation in the kampung or its neighbor groups. Ludruk is, in Van Gennep's terms, a "rite of separation." *Ludruk carries its participants through a series of symbolic actions which separate them from the kampung.*

Ludruk participants sense the complementary roles of slametan-bersih desa and commercial ludruk; for they regard these two types of "rites" as mutually repelling. Actors do not regard it as fitting to hold slametan at commercial ludruk theaters in places like the People's Amusement Park, and the two times, out of eighty-two performances, that the actors portrayed slametan on-stage, they ridiculed it. Bersih désa was never mentioned by ludruk.

The lower-class household is inside the kampung. Therefore, any extra-kampung orientation that ludruk encourages is also extra-household. But some ludruk elements particularly focus on evoking anti-household sentiments. The transvestite zeroes in on the household. Whore-like, princess-like, adolescent-lover–like (note the case of Aspari), and offering sexual pleasure minus family responsibilities such as those imposed by the kampung household, the transvestite is, not surprisingly, famous for seducing men's thoughts, and occasionally bodies, from loyalty to household, wife, and children.

Type-M plots glorify the proletarian youth who rises in status without parents' help. Since such youths attain a style of life different from that of their parents, their parents can be of limited aid in teaching them "how to act." Thus, M-plots encourage youths or youths' parents to devalue the role of household and parent as teacher of social skills. Ludruk songs have the same effect by calling for the young to learn reading, writing, and Manipol-USDEK — knowledge best acquired away from home, at school or at Pemuda Rakjat meetings.

In sundry ways, then, ludruk encourages its participants, or stimulates its participants to encourage their children, to disengage themselves from kampung and household and engage themselves in specialized units of Surabaja society. Thus ludruk promotes a society of increasingly specialized units.

CENTRALIZATION

We have seen one trend toward centralization that kampung dwellers are experiencing: the kampung's lessening autonomy and its incorporation into city and national government. Related to this trend, city-nation-kampung rites (e.g., the Independence Day

General Slametan) and symbols (kampung gates adorned with pictures of West New Guinea Battles) are replacing purely kampung rites and symbols (bersih désa, slametan, danjang).

Ludruk is part of this trend. It serves in a way like a supra-kampung slametan. As the Javanese abangan kampung dweller stirs outside his kampung, he increasingly comes into contact with ethnic, religious, and political factions other than his own: Ambonese, santri, army, and so on. Traditionally, he has placed great emphasis on rites that symbolize harmony among people with whom he associates: the slametan is such a rite. But, as Geertz remarks, the slametan is not equipped to harmonize the diverse groups and social types which the kampung dweller encounters, especially outside his kampung, in urban society.[5] Slametan was designed to harmonize homogeneous village society. What rite can do for the heterogeneous extra-kampung society what the slametan once did for the village? Ludruk tries to be such a rite. The transvestite singer generalizes the idea of rukun to the national level; he calls for and depicts harmony among the various ethnic, occupational, religious, and political factions of Indonesia, many of which are represented locally in Surabaja and form part of the extra-kampung, urban social experience of the kampung dweller. Thus, the transvestite, (in somewhat perverse fashion) makes an attempt at replacing kampung rites wich national rites, kampung community with symbolic national community, and kampung loyalties with national loyalties. Other parts of ludruk, as we have shown, encourage similar trends.

Not only by replacing localized rites but also in more humble ways, ludruk contributes to the centralization of Javanese life. Each ludruk troupe circulates among five theaters placed in five different districts of Surabaja, exposing all these districts to the same jokes, language, costumes, stories. Perhaps by disseminating a uniform popular culture ludruk helps to build informal communalities and consensus among proletarians that give a basis for unifying them in more practical ways (e.g., centralizing the market, legal, transportation, and educational systems in which they are involved). In this regard, it is significant that ludruk disseminates common images of buying, selling, dealing with police, going to school, riding the trolley, getting a job, marrying, divorcing.

Perhaps ludruk contributes most significantly to centralization by fostering empathetic skills. Consider a contrast between ludruk

---

[5] C. Geertz, "Ritual and Social Change: A Javanese Example," pp. 36–37.

and slametan. Ludruk focuses mainly on roles which ludruk participants do not play in real life ("Dutchman," "Chinese," "Islamic trader," "Djakartan"), but slametan focuses on roles which its participants do play in real life; during the slametan each person plays the role "neighbor." Therefore, ludruk is better fitted than slamentan to exercise its participants' skills at empathizing with strange persons and situations. In this way ludruk trains its participants to operate in a large-scale, non-face-to-face, centralized society — to buy and sell with strangers and foreigners (notably Chinese), to empathize with political leaders whom one does not know personally and with issues involving foreigners and foreign situations (such as Cuba and Malaysia), to manuever a pedicab in downtown traffic. All of these activities require wide capacity to empathize with strangers and strange situations. By contrast, the slametan, which is adapted to needs of kampung life, does not have to promote such skills, for within the kampung (or at least within the *gang,* the subunit of the kampung within which most collective activities are organized) everybody knows everybody else fairly well, and the situations are familiar. Ludruk is better adapted than slametan to giving practice in mental skills necessary for living in an increasingly centralized, as opposed to localized, society.

UNIVERSALIZATION

We have already shown how the shift from T- to M-plots and from alus to madju symbolism in jokes and songs encourages "universalism" — increasing emphasis on doing and on judging people according to what they can do rather than according to who they are (their class origins). It could be argued further that ludruk's denigration of the slametan directly encourages "doing"; by weakening faith in the slametan, ludruk weakens faith in the animistic complex — of which slametan is the prime symbol — based on the belief that evil spirits enter a disturbed heart, a belief that discourages action (for instance, yearning, which leads to doing, is discouraged on the grounds that it disturbs the heart). Also note that the helpless abandoned child and passive, submissive heroine vanish as ludruk replaces T-plots with M-plots; symbols of inability to do anything give way to characters who can do things.[6] This type of symbolic shift parallels trends in other

---

[6] I have stressed that the M-plot increasingly depicts goal-striving that results in reward and, simultaneously, innovation. Gregory Bateson's "Bali: the Value Sys-

fields, such as the increasing tendency among youth to paint grasping fists rather than the languidly curved fingers of classical art.

Note that the experience which ludruk provides contrasts with that furnished by slametan. Slametan give their participants the experience of feeling in harmony with persons. Ludruk supplies the experience of successfully, actively manipulating persons (sexually) to achieve higher status for oneself. Slametan exercises emotions fit for the kampung, where rukun ideally reigns. Ludruk teaches attitudes useful in the extra-kampung arena, where relatively universalistic values increasingly reside and struggles for status and profit occur.

Ludruk's espousal of universalism does not directly affect the ethics of the elite who control Javanese society, since ludruk (with the exception of Marhaen) is seen only by proletarians (although some elite occasionally listen to ludruk on the radio). But proletarians who have vicariously enjoyed the rewards of action in an M-plot society with a universalistic ethic may be spurred to goad their children to take advantage of those fairly universalistic systems (such as schools) now emerging in Indonesia.

RATIONALIZATION

"Rational" man justifies actions by showing that they are adequate means for achieving a given end, rather than by claiming that they are traditional.[7] When ludruk condemns such madju actions as modern youth's loose sex, the condemnation is justified on traditional, not rational, grounds: "X madju action goes against tradition, therefore is bad." When ludruk praises madju actions,

---

tem of a Steady State," emphasizes the contrast between this kind of action and Balinese action. Bateson writes that the Balinese see life not as sets of conative sequences ending in satisfaction, but as rote sequences inherently satisfying in themselves; Balinese feel some vague dread about the world and try to escape it by endless rote ritual and courtesy, fearing to innovate in any significant way (p. 46). The parallels between this sort of orientation and the alus action of Javanese are clear. M-plots move away from this sort of action toward the type Max Weber finds distinctive of Puritans (*The Protestant Ethic and the Spirit of Capitalism*. pp. 98–128): the Puritans were distinctive in the degree to which they systematically organized their behavior in a disciplined manner toward a goal, allowing no tension-release irrelevant to the goal — no idle talk, hedonistic indulgence, ostentation in decorating one's body, or sensuous expression (as in ritual). The contrast between this type of action and Balinese, alus Javanese, or T-plot action is clear.

[7] Levy, *Modernization*, 1:139.

such as speaking Indonesian, it does not always justify its praise on rational grounds ("X is the most adequate means for achieving a given end"); often ludruk simply says, "X action is good because it is modern — that is, not traditional." It appears, however, that ludruk justifies madju actions rationally more frequently than it does kuna actions. For example, note the *in order to* form of the transvestite song ("In order to get cheap food we should. . . ."). The form of the justification is instrumental or "rational." The action in question is justified by calling it a way to achieve the goal "food."

The rise of rational values encourages a decline in alus values. To judge an action alus is to judge it for itself — its beauty, religious aura, or the social harmony immediately surrounding it. The rational temper judges an act not for itself but according to its use as a means toward some goal. If the goal at hand is a practical one, aesthetic, social, or religious aspects of the act may appear useless frills. Thus, when society demands that the person who wants to buy a screwdriver think only of the most efficient way to buy that screwdriver, alus etiquette aimed at keeping harmony with the clerk, expressing metaphysical notions, and creating beauty may be judged useless and may be omitted. So ludruk's progressive omission of alus symbols may reflect tendencies toward rational thinking (such tendencies are encouraged by PKI doctrine, youth culture, and the relatively commercially rational "business is business" atmosphere of Surabaja) and at the same time help lull the public mind into forgetting symbols which represent values opposed to rational ones.

Ludruk's questioning of animistic magic (such as wish-granting) is conducive to rational thinking. Ludruk (particularly Marhaen) asks of such magic, "Does it work?" rather than accepting it as a ritual which always has been performed and therefore always should be. Ludruk concludes that the magic does not work, hence ridicules it.

One can see in commercial ludruk a movement toward what Max Weber called "freeing the world of magic." Commercial ludruk kindles by its play content and staging arrangements (see chapter 3 on "animism") a decline in the belief that a magical force pervades all objects. When objects lose their magic, it becomes possible to view them rationally — as means to some end. (Ludruk also supplies an ideology which makes certain ends — national ends — sacred; as sacredness comes to "reside" in these abstract ends, particular objects of the physical world tend to lose their sacredness; so they can be viewed rationally as means toward the sacred ends.)

In general, encouraged by its theatrical setting, apartness from the kampung, and secularism, ludruk promotes anti-traditionalism. At the same time, ludruk is by no means the most anti-traditionalist element in the lives of kampung dwellers. As Samidin, a cook's son, said, "Youths consider ludruk rather old-fashioned compared to movies," and the ludruk audience is populated with parents rather than youths. Ludruk's role is that of buffer between the most traditionalist and anti-traditionalist agencies which the adult kampung dweller encounters. While ridiculing village and kampung, ludruk also criticizes movies, fads, and youths. Thus, for adults who feel a bit constrained by traditional institutions yet fearful of youth's radical anti-traditionalism, ludruk is good therapy.

SPECIFICATION

The more obligations a given social relationship imposes on those who take part in it, the less functionally specific (and the more functionally diffuse) the relationship is.[8] Thus, as one moves from "relations among rural villagers" to "relations among urban kampung dwellers" to "relations among members of a ludruk audience," one moves toward increasingly functionally specific relations. Co-members of a ludruk audience have few dealings with each other outside the theater, and during the show about their only mutual obligation is to let each other enjoy the show. Co-dwellers in a kampung have many more mutual obligations: to jointly guard against thieves, help each other in time of sickness or debt, jointly elect officials, cooperate in clean-ups or in repairing roads. Co-residents of a rural village have all the mutual obligations of co-kampungers, plus others. For instance, each villager is obligated, through an elaborate system of agreements, to help his neighbors harvest their crops or do other work. There is no similar labor exchange in the kampung. Male co-residents in a kampung do not go as a body on Monday to help one of their number who works in a glass factory, on Tuesday jointly to lend a hand to one of the neighbors who works in a lumber yard, and on Wednesday en masse to help a neighbor sell in the market. In spheres other than that of labor exchange, similar contrasts could be made,

[8] *Ibid,* 1:144. My definition differs somewhat from Levy's.

demonstrating that rural villagers share many obligations which kampungers do not.

I would like now to relate these differences between rural village, urban kampung, and the ludruk audience to a theory set forth by Max Gluckman. Gluckman speaks of a "ritual of social relations" by which he means

> a stylized ceremonial in which persons related in various ways to the central actors, as well as these themselves, perform prescribed actions according to their secular roles; it is believed by the participants that their prescribed actions express and amend social relationships so as to secure general blessing, purification, protection, and prosperity for the persons involved in some mystical manner which is out of sensory control.[9]

The slametan fits this definition. It is a stylized ceremonial whose actors perform prescribed actions according to their secular roles: during the slametan they play "neighbors" just as in secular life. And those who celebrate the slametan believe that it will harmonize their social relations and so guard them from evil spirits, bless their house, and in other ways protect and bless them in some mystical manner.

Now Gluckman hypothesizes that such a ritual will most likely be performed, have greatest importance, and be thought to have greatest mystical efficacy by a group whose members have functionally diffuse (what Gluckman calls "multiplex") relations with one another, whereas such a ritual will decline in importance or cease to be regarded as having mystical efficacy by a group whose members' relations with one another are functionally specific. How does this hypothesis fit our case? The slametan is important among Javanese villagers, and they do see it as capable of maintaining social harmony and so in suprasensory ways preventing disturbance of the heart, penetration of evil spirits, and illness. It appears that among urban kampung dwellers, related to one another in less functionally diffuse ways than the villagers, the slametan is less important, and its mystical powers to bless and protect are not so highly regarded. Finally, among members of the commercial ludruk audience, whose relations to one another are extremely functionally specific, the slametan is not practiced at all, and it is ridiculed. The "rite" which this commercial group celebrates is ludruk, which is the opposite of a ritual of social relations in that its central actors play roles strikingly unrelated to their everyday roles and it

[9] Max Gluckman, "Les Rites de Passage," p. 24.

is not regarded as having any suprasensory power to restore cosmos or nature to harmony or to bless the group. Thus, the "ritual of social relations" (slametan) declines as relations among the practitioners become more specific until finally a kind of anti-ritual of social relations (ludruk) emerges.

Gluckman's explanation for this would apparently run as follows. Default from any functionally diffuse relation involves default from many obligations. The rural villager who betrays his neighbor betrays his co-worker, co-land-holder, co-recreator, and so on. Default strikes not just at one isolated role, but at many roles. Moral judgments of a default apply to many of a man's roles, not just one. Because default from an obligation strikes so deeply at the social order, people see such default as a cause not only of social but of natural and supernatural disorders, such as illness, crop-failure, drought (and in the Javanese case, penetration of evil spirits). Therefore, a ritual which works in supernatural, suprasensory ways is required not only to redress (or prevent) a tear in the social fabric but also to restore (or maintain) natural and supernatural harmony.[10] The rural village community needs the slametan. Extending the argument, co-kampungers need the slametan less; co-ludruk spectators need it least — for as a group's social relations get less and less diffuse, disturbing them bothers the cosmos less and less. Accordingly, disturbances in relations among the ludruk spectators are so unlikely to disturb the cosmos that the spectators need not worry about symbolically ordering their relationships so as to order the cosmos. Hence, in place of a rite of social relations, one has ludruk, which does not bother to symbolize the particular relationships that exist among its onlookers. Ludruk mainly depicts relations among personages not in the audience.

Admittedly, this argument is schematic. But perhaps it is plausible enough and complete enough to suggest that ludruk is a child not only of the "revolutionary uterus," as Shamsudin would have it, but of its audience's social complexion.

One final speculation along these lines. The national community is a group of non–face-to-face members related to one another in functionally diffuse ways. Members of a national community are related to each other as co-workers for a cause, co-worshippers of symbols, co-speakers of a language, co-residents of a space. Accordingly, the transvestite's quasi-prayer to the nation comes closest of

---

[10] *Ibid.*, p. 29.

any ludruk action to being a ritual of social relations, aimed at redressing, by mystical plea, disharmony in the national community.

Aside from being, perhaps, a product of functionally specific relations, ludruk acts in one striking way to foster such relations. In the dagelan, ludruk portrays buyer-seller, creditor-borrower, employer-employee relations — relations involving very narrow and specific obligations, such as paying for what you buy and supplying what you get paid for. Might the narrow, unidimensional nature of these relations be reflected by ludruk's portraying them on the halfstage (whereas family relations are always fullstage)? Perhaps ludruk goers are learning to *see* the social world in a modern way.

AVOIDANCE

The more a social relationship minimizes emotional display and personal contact or involvement, the more "avoidant" (and the less "intimate") it is.[11]

By negating the importance of the kampung household, ludruk undermines some of the most intimate Javanese relationships — those of mother-child, brother-sister, grandmother-grandchild. Perhaps to fill a gap left by declining blood relationships, ludruk affirms intimate non-blood relationships such as friendship and romantic love. By encouraging people to break with parents, speak Indonesian, be egalitarian, join national groups, go to school, follow youth-ways, ludruk fosters the flowering of friendship as an institution. Ludruk also encourages friendship by romanticizing it. Particularly in tales of the Revolution, the bond between comrades-at-arms is glorified much as in German songs and tales. M-plots glamorize romantic love, as we have seen. Ludruk's satire of alus values ("Ludruk knows no shame," said a servant, speaking of ludruk's parodies of alus ways) encourages Javanese to drop the idea that relations between persons must be restrained (alus). And, in fact, M-plots are sprinkled with distinctive displays of interpersonal emotionality; for instance, an M-plot lover suddenly bursts forth: "My love is like fingernails! If cut off, it will grow

---

[11] Levy, *Modernization*, 1:62. I do not phrase this heading as a trend but simply as a quality. This is because with increasing modernization many types of social relations become *less* avoidant, not more so. Therefore, in this section I diverge from Levy and speak of a trend toward a certain *kind* of avoidance (avoidant-specific relations) as part of modernization, with a parallel trend toward a certain kind of intimacy (intimate-diffuse relations).

back!" Along with exhibiting forms of interpersonal emotionality absent from T-plots, M-plots lose some T-plot symbols of narcissistic emotional expression. The pathetic woman who weeps with self-pity disappears, and the clown who smiles and symbolically masturbates while dancing with himself is seen no more.

It may be that by fostering a decline in alus symbols and a rise in madju symbols, ludruk is encouraging relations that are avoidant and functionally specific and discouraging relations that are avoidant and functionally diffuse. Alus symbols are often used by Javanese to insure harmony of diffuse relationships by phrasing such relationships as avoidant. The master-servant relationship is diffuse in that the servant depends on his master for many things — food, housing, protection, and social education — and the master is obligated to furnish these things. The traditional relation between employer-employee is similar to that of master-servant, as is the traditional relation of father-child. In all these cases the inferior uses alus language, gestures, and mien to place the superior on a higher plane than himself, to "build a wall around him," and thus to avoid direct contact with the superior. In this way the relationship, which if disturbed would disrupt many threads of the participants' lives, is harmonized. Since in each case the relationship itself is venerated, the manners surrounding it are ritually and aesthetically elaborated until they become ends in themselves.

Madju manners are often used either to phrase functionally specific relations as avoidant or diffuse relations as intimate. Lovers or friends use Indonesian language and madju oratory to express intimate feelings toward one another. Clients and officials customarily use Indonesian language, brisk manners, and madju implements such as uniforms, notebooks, and desks to keep distance between each other. (Thus, people laugh when a clown, Amat, treats his relation to the official as intimate, saying, "I hate to leave you because you look so sad.") Ludruk recognizes the specific as well as avoidant dimension of official relations. In scenes such as the one in "Wave of TRIKORA," which shows an official who posts a sign reading "Talk only when necessary," ludruk takes note of the ideal that the official-client relation should involve only the specific problem at hand — that is, it should be functionally specific.

By displaying madju symbols, then, and failing to display alus symbols, ludruk encourages people to think in terms of avoidance-specific (or intimate-diffuse) relations rather than avoidance-diffuse relations. Insofar as ludruk discourages avoidance-diffuse relations, it cuts at the roots of alus etiquette and the alus art complex which is an extension of that etiquette. Therefore, ludruk can be seen as contributing to the demise of alus art such as wajang,[12] while promoting the rise of vulgar madju art, such as ludruk.

MONETIZATION

Ludruk encourages Javanese to extend the range of phenomena that they will exchange for money. By being commercial, ludruk is helping Java monetize in one way — it is encouraging Javanese to buy and sell recreation. Also, ludruk is increasingly encouraging people to buy and sell love: in M-plots ludruk phrases romance in monetary terms much more than in T-plots. For example, in "The Last Impression," both the hero and the Arab blatantly court the gentle heroine's favor by offering her money. Full-fledged prostitutes appear in M-plots more than in T-plots. In the ludruk prologue pals phrase their relationship as that of borrower-lender. The prologue swindle is monetary (note how Anton's and Amin's relationship to their stepparents is cast in monetary terms, neither Anton and Amin nor the parents being concerned about anything quite so much as their money), and the final prologue harmony is effected by giving the victim's money back.

It should be noted that in certain ways Javanese proletarians have monetized social relations more than Americans have. For example, at a Javanese wedding guests give the host money, and sometimes the host has a woman on hand to write down how much the guest gives, so that the host can reciprocate with an equal or greater amount when the guest has a wedding. On the other hand, Javanese appear uncomfortable about dealing with money in public, but not explicitly commercial, contexts. In such situations money is hidden in envelopes while it changes hands.

[12] In addition to suffering some loss of popularity the wajang seems to be losing its alus values. Anderson, *Mythology*, p. 27, says that increasingly there is a tendency for wajang stories to be interpreted as a simple conflict of good and evil rather than as a very complex amoral interplay of different life styles and that the younger generation tends to see Ardjuna — epitome of the alus, beautiful, and heroic — as effeminate. The youths glorify Bima, closest thing in wajang to the movie he-man. (But I have heard an *older* Javanese say that the trouble with Sukarno is his identity with Bima rather than Ardjuna.)

BUREAUCRATIZATION

In a bureaucracy of the sort idealized by Max Weber,[13] official should relate to client in his official capacity only, personal connection's should not intrude. Clearly ludruk is wary of such relations, as is indicated by jokes; thus, the official's pronouncement, "I am here in my official capacity," is greeted by Piet, the clown, "I am here in my unofficial capacity." Although clown's jokes express misgivings about bureaucracy, however, perhaps they ease ludruk participants' tensions regarding bureaucracy and acclimate them to the increasingly bureaucratic atmosphere of Indonesia.

Ludruk's concern with bureaucracy has probably been stimulated by its bureaucratization. Tresno Enggal is now a wing of the government; it is employed by the army. The newest ludruk theater (People's Amusement Park) is run by the city government. And Marhaen and Tresno Enggal are trying to turn their transvestites into civil servants.

CONJUGALIZATION

The barbarism "conjugalization" refers to a trend toward emphasizing the husband-wife relationship and de-emphasizing the parent-child relationship.[14] As we have seen, the shift from T- to M-plot mirrors, romanticizes, and perhaps stimulates such a trend in Javanese society.

Ludruk not only idealizes romantic husband-wife relations; it also strikes at the matrifocal household symbol — the domineering woman. This woman's power is strongly based on the parent-child relationship. By control over her own children and strong ties to her parents or to sisters, cousins, nieces, and nephews related to her through her parents, this woman strengthens her household position. The father lacks bonds like the mother's, thus weakening his household position. Therefore, by weakening the moral value of the parent-child bond, ludruk bids to weaken the power base of the mother and give the father a chance for a stronger household position. Also, by undermining alus symbols, ludruk encourages a shortening of the traditional alus distance between father and child, which is to say, it encourages a shortening of the father's distance from household affairs which focus on the child. Finally,

---

[13] Levy, *Modernization,* 1:72.
[14] *Ibid.,* 1:75.

by supporting romantic "partnership" between husband and wife, and ridiculing the wife who dominates her husband, ludruk encourages husband and wife to be "partners" in household duties.

All of these tendencies are in the direction of encouraging the father (husband) to get more immediately involved in household affairs. What might be some of the consequences if the father should move in this direction? For one thing, the father might take a more direct hand in punishing the child; and being raised by a punishing father rather than a distant father (and punishing mother) could conceivably affect the way Javanese proletarians relate to employers. The Javanese employer-employee relation has traditionally been consciously patterned after the father-child relationship. The traditional pattern, sometimes called by moderns "fatherism," calls for an employer who is treated by the worker with alus respect and who should only in the most drastic circumstances fire or reprimand the worker. A more intimate, directly sanctioning relation of father to child would furnish a new model for employer-employee relations.

The ideal household depicted in the final M-plot scene is rather bourgeois: new rich husband and wife sit happily together in their parlor enjoying their conjugal privacy. It is interesting that, in spite of its Communist links, ludruk expresses in its shift toward the M-plots a shift toward bourgeois ideals. Perhaps ludruk, being commercial theater, tends to attract persons who, though of the working class, are a bit bourgeois in their aspirations. If so, it is noteworthy that Surabaja's commercial theaters have quintupled since the Second World War. (One wonders if, in some oblique way, this bourgeoisation of ludruk reflects general social tendencies that have recently culminated in the dramatic massacre of the Communists and rise of bourgeois forces in Indonesia?) [15]

We can say, "Many of the themes, forms, and experiences which ludruk increasingly provides are such as to encourage, in sundry

[15] I should note that my conclusions about the bourgeois trend in ludruk content and other anti-Communist trends in East Java were recorded in a doctoral thesis, submitted, bound, and placed in the Harvard University Archives before the Communist massacre of Fall, 1965 (See "Javanese Folkdrama and Social Change," chap. 4 and pp. 220–23, 234, 236). I certainly do not claim to have forecast the dramatic upsurge of anti-Communist, bourgeois forces and the resulting massacre of several-hundred-thousand Communists which occurred in 1965; but my analysis of ludruk 1962–63 revealed a trend toward bourgeois attitudes among Javanese proletarians at a time when their official Communist ties still seemed strong and even seemed to be growing stronger.

ways, the modernization of Java," if, following Marion J. Levy, Jr., we define modernization as a process having as its social dimensions: increasing centralization, rationalization, bureaucratization, monetization, specialization of units, and increasing emphasis on conjugal, avoidant, and functionally specific relationships. The final chapter says more about *how* participation in ludruk performances stimulates participants to think, feel, act, and judge in ways conducive to these trends.

CHAPTER

16

Symbolic Action and Society

Only when we have a theoretical analysis of symbolic action comparable in sophistication to that we now have for social and psychological action, will we be able to cope effectively with those
aspects of social and psychological life in which religion (or art, or
science, or ideology) plays a determinant role.[1]

CLIFFORD GEERTZ

Ludruk is symbolic action; that is, ludruk shows exhibit a type of
action distinct from that sometimes called "technical." Ludruk action is more directly oriented toward creating beautiful or stimulating form and expressing emotions, moral ideals, or conceptions

[1] "Religion as a Cultural System," p. 42.

234

of reality than toward achieving empirical economic, political, or social ends. If ludruk depicts peasants sowing their seeds or a family resolving its conflicts, that is not the same as real peasants striving to sow their seeds (striving to achieve an empirical economic end) or a real family striving to resolve its conflicts (striving to achieve an empirical social end). The ludruk actors are not really struggling to make crops grow onstage or to resolve a quarrel among themselves; their main concern is to entertain (to create stimulating form), to portray a conception of reality (a conception of the nature of peasants or families or human existence), to express emotions, and perhaps to make a moral point. Although this symbolic action may ultimately have economic, political, or social consequences, it is not so immediately and fully oriented toward economic, political, or social ends as is seed sowing, family discussion, or bargaining, voting, and warring.

Many social science endeavors can be seen as attempts to analyze relations between symbolic and technical action. Max Weber's study of Calvinism and capitalism[2] is a famous example of one type of approach to this problem. Weber was concerned to show that action which laymen usually classify as "technical" is actually strongly symbolic. The puritan capitalist's economic action, Weber argued, was not strictly oriented toward such empirical ends as making money. Such action had a strongly symbolic component. It was a sacred calling, aimed at achieving religious salvation and expressing the idea of God's glory. It was a worldly equivalent to the monk's ascetic devotional practices.

A second approach to analyzing the relation between technical and symbolic action is exemplified by my study. Whereas Weber showed that the same action combined both symbolic and technical components, I deal with relations between symbolic and technical actions separate in time and space from each other, but carried out by the same individuals. I have tried to show how the symbolic actions which Javanese proletarians carry on inside the ludruk theater are related to the more or less technical actions (I shall often refer to these simply as "daily" actions) which they perform outside the ludruk theater. To establish the nature of such a relationship, we must perform the following operations: define the nature of the symbolic action occurring during the ludruk show; analyze participants' responses during the show; on this basis of both action and response analysis. construct hypotheses

[2] *The Protestant Ethic.*

about what participants learn during the show — what they take away when they leave; analyze patterns of participants' daily social life; compare daily social patterns with those patterns which, according to our hypotheses, participants learn at ludruk (such comparison would proceed both statistically and structurally, both by noting correlations between trends such as the rise of anti-kampung experiences at ludruk and the decline of inter-kampung ritual and by noting such formal congruences as that between arranged marriage satire at ludruk and arranged marriage custom at home); on the basis of these comparisons construct hypotheses about ludruk's contributions to its participants' lives (for example, ludruk might teach parents to comprehend children's resentment of arranged marriage); flesh out these gross comparisons and hypotheses with casestudies of individual ludruk participants (see, for example, the analysis of Supii); ask participants what ludruk does for them (although the notion that the native can tell the anthropologist *all* the meaning a practice has for his society is a naïve one, controverted by various investigations and theories).[3]

By following these steps, I have constructed an argument regarding the nature of ludruk's relationship to Javanese social life. I have already presented most of this argument, and shortly I shall state a few more parts of it. But first, I would like to make a few general remarks about the nature of the relationship that I am proposing.

In some ways the safest type of relationship to argue for would be one of "reflection." It is clear that ludruk's symbolic action reflects trends in Javanese social life (more in the fashion of a prism or lens than a mirror, for the symbolic actions are analyzed and condensed representations of their participants' social lives rather than carbon copies of them). An extension of this argument could be that ludruk not only reflects daily Javanese social life, but that it also reveals aspects of it which cannot be seen by observing it. Because daily actions must take place under conditions not totally of the actors' choosing, the actors cannot totally express their ideals through their daily actions; daily conditions will not allow them to. But on the ludruk stage, they can construct, in fantasy, any conditions which they wish, so they can

---

[3] Robert K. Merton, *Social Theory and Social Structure,* pp. 19–84. I also notice that many literary critics regard the man most native to a work — its author — as the one most inept at grasping its implications. See, for instance, G. Wilson Knight, *The Wheel of Fire,* p. 6.

construct conditions which allow them to express their ideals in rather pure form. Therefore, we could argue, by studying ludruk, we can see those invisible ideas which Javanese proletarians are unsuccessfully struggling to express in daily life. Thus, ludruk might be viewed as a sort of X-ray machine. It lays bare aspects of Javanese existence that cannot be seen with the naked eye. It leads to a more acute diagnosis of daily Javanese life.

One example is appropriate here. Suppose that we wish to analyze goal-seeking social behavior (social action) of the type in which anthropologists have recently shown interest.[4] If it is agreed that Javanese individual's conceptions of social action are vital determinants of their social action, then it seems that ludruk stories could reveal much about that social action. Ludruk stories portray social action more colorfully and concretely than do most media; Javanese aphorisms regarding law and morals may abstractly define social goals or ideals, but ludruk stories concretely depict actors struggling to actualize such ideals. Consequently, such stories are uniquely fitted to shed light on the nature of Javanese conceptions of social action, and illuminating Javanese conceptions of social action should illuminate Javanese social action.[5]

But this book has not taken as its primary aim "the study of ludruk as a means of understanding Javanese daily social action." Rather than studying ludruk as a way of gaining insight into daily

---

[4] See Leach, *Political Systems;* Raymond Firth, *Essays on Social Organization and Values,* pp. 35, 45 ff.; Victor Turner, "Witchcraft and Sorcery: Taxonomy Versus Dynamics," p. 317; Eugene Ogan, "Nasioi Marriage: An Essay in Model-Building," pp. 172–93.

[5] One interesting piece of intellectual history suggests that viewing symbolic performances as portrayals of social action and viewing social behavior as "action" go hand in hand. The sociologist, Talcott Parsons, and the literary critic, Kenneth Burke, (the first dealing more with daily behavior, and the other more with symbolic performances) both use the label "action" or "social action" to refer to behavior analyzed into "goal" or "purpose," "means" or "agency," "actor" or "agent," and "situation" or "scene" components. See Parsons, *The Structure of Social Action,* pp. 44–45, and Burke, *A Grammar of Motives,* pp. xvii–xxv. Burke and Parsons are aware that their schemes coincide. It is interesting that several decades earlier there was another case of a famous literary critic and sociologist (Georg Lukács and Max Weber) formulating rather similar views of society and symbolic performances, Weber's being the basis of Parsons' "action" scheme. One wonders what influence Weber and Lukács had on one another, since Lukács' 1914– article on dramatic action and society was published in a journal partially edited by Weber (See Georg Lukács, "Zur Sociologie des Modernen Dramas," pp. 303–45, and compare Max Weber, *The Theory of Social and Economic Organization,* pp. 87–123; Weber's book was published in 1922 as *Wirtschaft und Gesellschaft*).

actions, I have viewed ludruk as itself an action. I have approached ludruk as an active agency within Javanese society, a force that influences the course of Javanese social change. I have argued that ludruk performances encourage the modernization of Java.

At a conservative level, it seems that this argument has been supported. We have shown that ludruk helps its participants classify, clarify, and crystallize in their minds the nature of the modernization process in which they are engaged. Such a state of mind surely helps the participants carry on those daily, technical actions which are increasingly of a modern sort; ludruk helps them understand what they are doing, and understanding what they are doing probably helps them do it. But even if not, by contributing to such understanding, ludruk is pushing forward the process of modernization, since becoming modernized is not only a matter of increasing ability to perform modern-style technical actions, but also involves coming to think in terms of "modern" premises like "rationality" and "universalism." Thus, if we claim only that people think more in a modern vein while they are at ludruk, my major argument — that ludruk contributes to the modernization process — is substantiated, for spending time thinking modern is *part* of the modernization process.

Another way of making the point: we have shown that ludruk furnishes therapy for people engaged in modernization. Ludruk portrays these people's daily conflicts in such a way that it "cures" or relieves tensions which they develop as a result of such conflicts. Having been cured, they can return to their daily chores with renewed spirit, or decreased anxiety and resentment. They also may be less likely to quit their chores, which is another way of saying that they may be less likely to rebel against the increasingly modernized daily patterns in which they are involved. Hence, by providing therapy for tensions stemming from modernization, ludruk makes it easier for those involved in modernization to stay with it: ludruk increases the likelihood that modernizing trends will continue.

We see, then, several ways in which ludruk has been demonstrated to contribute to modernization. But an argument I have pursued earlier, and wish to pursue further now, is different, and perhaps more perilous. It is that the experience of participating in ludruk actively *molds* the values, ideas, and emotions of participants in such a way that they are likely to act, think, and feel "modern" in daily life. Theoretically, one could make the point by an experiment: take two groups, comparable in all respects, expose one of them to ludruk, but not the other, and show that the exposed group develops more modern attitudes than the unexposed group. As may be suspected, I am in no position to follow such a procedure, and in fact, as far as I am aware, studies which have attempted to do so have dealt with extremely superficial and simple performances and effects.[6] My study has been more clinical than experimental. I have tried to analyze the totality of the experience which ludruk provides its participants; I hope that this analysis has rendered at least intuitively plausible the notion that ludruk molds its participants' attitudes in a modern direction. By way of conclusion, I will present a synthesis of ludruk seen as communicative process: a capsule portrait and interpretation of some striking aspects of ludruk's symbolic action, participants' involvement in it, and the peculiar manner in which this experience molds participants' values, ideas, and emotions.

LUDRUK AS SYMBOLIC CLASSIFIER

The first strokes in my portrait depict the ludruk transvestite's way of presenting his symbolic classifications:

It is tempting to follow major anthropological thinking about symbolic classification,[7] and write as if ludruk men were philosophers, who classify reality in terms of symbols for purely cognitive reasons, but our study of the transvestite shows that the natives sometimes classify an object in a particular category for quite a different reason — sex. One of the primary motives underlying the transvestite singer's struggle to get himself classified "alus" seems to be that of legitimizing his role of communicating illicit sexual messages. After covering himself with alus symbolism, the transvestite and his listeners can freely savour his particular offerings.

The transvestite's song illustrates an interesting relationship between verbal and non-verbal symbolic categories.[8] On the basis of the transvestite's lyrics, the content of which is action-packed, pleading for movement and organizing efforts, we classify the

[6] See Carl I. Hovland, Arthur A. Lumsdaine, and Fred D. Sheffield, *Experiments on Mass Communication*, pp. 201–27.

[7] See the "primitive classification" writings listed in Needham's introduction to Durkheim and Mauss or the writings on "ethnoscience" discussed at various places in A. Kimball Romney and Roy Goodwin D'Andrade (eds.), *Transcultural Studies in Cognition*, as well as in Lévi-Strauss, *The Savage Mind.*

[8] This is a type of relationship the ethnoscientists have largely ignored. See Romney and D'Andrade, *Transcultural Studies.*

transvestite song as madju. But non-verbal symbolism accompanying the lyrics belies their message. The non-verbal signals — soft music, alus setting — frame the lyrics in such a way as to transform their meaning. The non-verbal signals say, in effect, "Be calm" even as the lyrics say, "Act!" This appears to be one reason why there are no on-the-spot reactions to the lyrics. The only response occurs in quiet places after the show. In these places, nationalist lyrics verbally calling for action are sung as lullabyes.

The transvestite does not confine himself to presenting a single symbolic classification nor does he follow the "syncretic" pattern allegedly characteristic of Southeast Asians — chaotically mixing a number of symbolic classifications.[9] Not only does the transvestite set forth two distinct symbolic classifications of separate origins, traditions, and import, but he expresses both at the same instant! This he does, not by mixing the two classifications but by separating them into distinct channels (alus-kasar into non-verbal channels and madju-kuna into verbal channels). One wonders if close analysis of other so-called "syncretic" systems would not reveal similar subleties of communicative order and distinction.

Changes in symbolic classifications are usually phrased by social anthropologists as shifts in "native thought" or as reflections of changes in social structure. But the transvestites call to mind other interpretations. The transvestite's alus-kasar and madju-kuna categories are embodied in material objects such as sarongs, chignons, jackets (alus) and short skirts, pony tails, blouses (madju). Therefore, the question: what would happen to the native's "categories of thought" if changes occurred in such material forms (which have been shown to change according to laws of their own)? To put the question a bit flippantly: what happens to the category "alus" when transvestites start wearing short skirts?

In addition to the points about the transvestite, we note a general feature of the symbolic oppositions that ludruk presents: each represents a number of values. Take, for instance, the contrast between slacks and sarongs, dramatized by the clown song and the melodramatic villainess, Inem. Tight slacks stand for various madju values: sexual freedom, romantic love, self-choice of spouse, pan-Indonesian cosmopolitanism, urbanism. Sarongs represent

---

[9] See Kenneth Perry Landon, *Southeast Asia, Crossroad of Religions*. This point and others regarding the transvestite as "symbolic classifier" are expanded in my article, "Javanese Clown and Transvestite Songs: Relations between 'Primitive Classification' and 'Communicative Events' ", pp. 64–76.

various kuna values: traditional norms of sexual and marital conduct, provinciality, rurality. We can analytically distinguish a number of value-contrasts called to mind by the single symbolic contrast: sarong versus tight slacks.

By expressing these values via symbols such as "sarong" and "slacks," ludruk phrases the values so that they are apt to powerfully affect beholders. As Turner notes, symbols combine abstract moral values with sensory substance.[10] The values are saturated with the gross emotions evoked by the symbol's sensory aspects and at the same time the gross emotions are "enobled" by contact with the moral values; tight slacks render the notion of pan-Indonesianism somehow more sensuous and, perhaps, the slacks are enobled by contact with the ideal "One Nation." By being expressed via ludruk's sensuous (lascivious) symbols, madju values doubtless affect Javanese viscera more than if they (the values) were simply mouthed.

EMPATHY

Ludruk spectators empathize with ludruk action and characters. This is shown by their responses during performances, their dreams about ludruk stories, their own accounts of their empathy, etc.

Ludruk performers are concerned that spectators empathize with them. One evidence of this: a performance's content varies less to support political factions with which the performing troupe is affiliated than to match the sentiments and social experience of the spectators at hand, whoever they may be (see chapter 4). Apparently, empathetic and dramatic considerations count more to ludruk actors than do formal political ties.

Since ludruk participants themselves create ludruk, one would expect that they would find it easier to empathize with ludruk than if it were a canned medium made and marketed by aliens. Yet it is striking that many ludruk characters are socially different from ludruk participants; the characters are often elite, the participants proletarian. The ludruk clown serves — as does the clown in Javanese and Balinese wajang — to mediate between elite characters and proletarian spectators. The clowns — of proletarian origin but moving in aristocratic circles — often interpret elite characters' actions to the audience, but they seem to do less of this in later ludruk stories than in earlier ones.

[10] Victor Turner, "Three Symbols of Passage in Ndembu Circumcision Ritual," pp. 135–36.

Participants' empathy with ludruk has some striking qualities. The audience is very vocal in their response to onstage action. Sometimes they appear deeply absorbed with eyes glazed as if in a trance. But their attention flickers on and off, and they can leave the world of the stage with little transitional ritual. The fragmented quality of the audience's concentration is paralleled by the disjointed quality of onstage action. It is riddled with jokes. It is composed of "prefabricated" pieces loosely stuck together. All of this may have to do with ludruk's accent on bodily motion and imitation. Perhaps it is easier to slip in and out of bodily (tactile) empathy and imitation than in and out of deep identification with development of a character and struggle toward a goal.

The clown epitomizes the fragmentation, comedy, and bodily emphasis of ludruk.

Ludruk's type of empathy mirrors pan-Southeast Asian and pan-Javanese patterns of behavior. Apparently the prefabricated form is typical of Southeast Asian drama, and the ludruk participant's ease of slipping in and out of concentration resembles such things as the Balinese capacity to slip in and out of trance, the Javanese, Balinese,[11] and Thai ability to slip easily in and out of extraordinarily deep sleep, and perhaps the Javanese and Thai tendency to slip easily in and out of social roles (note the Javanese woman's pride in being totally santri while she lives in a santri neighborhood, totally abangan while living in an abangan neighborhood). The bodily focus parallels the emphasis on bodily learning (as opposed to learning by verbal instruction) in Bali and Java and the tremendous Balinese and Javanese emphasis on dance; note Geertz's theory that Javanese identity is more bound up in dance than in any other art [12] (and I was struck by the fact that at the Youth Hall of Surabaja, thirteen of twenty-one paintings supposed to depict "scenes of Surabaja" depicted Javanese dances — the other seven paintings showing Surabaja harbor, main street, and similar scenes). It is also significant that the mental disease, *latah,* compulsive bodily imitation, is found so widely in the Malay-Indonesian area. Finally, the clown, who epitomizes all these patterns, occupies a grotesquely important place in Javanese culture.

Ludruk's empathetic patterns appear to be changing. Young directors and commercial theaters are condensing and integrating

[11] This and other remarks about Bali in this paragraph are derived from Bateson, *Balinese Character,* while the statements about Thailand derive from a conversation with A. Thomas Kirsch regarding his field research in that country.

[12] C. Geertz, *Religion of Java,* p. 282.

onstage action. This should affect the way audiences attend to such action.

Several contrasts must be made between ludruk's way of influencing its participants and the techniques of many religious or political performances. Ludruk, unlike speeches in a party cell or sermons in a sect, is not tightly bound to an organization with sanctioning powers: that is, commercial ludruk performers and their audiences do not form a corporate group such that ludruk can apply sanctions if its audiences do not act as ludruk tells them to act. Ludruk must rely on purely dramatic techniques which draw its participants into empathy with it, thus seducing them into "making themselves over in the image of ludruk imagery."

Unlike religions such as those of the Puritan West or Tokugawa Japan, as analyzed by Weberian sociologists,[13] ludruk does not influence action by saying, "If you act this way you will achieve other wordly salvation" or "If you act in this way, you will achieve mystical union with an ultimate being." Ludruk influences by empathy, form, and dramatic technique rather than by other-wordly promises. There is, however, one parallel with the religious technique of influence. Just as religion incites action by symbolically linking such action with mysterious supernatural realms and rewards, so ludruk lures its audiences into empathy by saturating its onstage actions with glitter and romance of a non-mundane sort. If ludruk were a copy of everyday life, it would perhaps lose influence.

Ludruk stories do not possess ethical authority. Javanese stress that ludruk is "not religion" but "just entertainment". Javanese rarely cite ludruk stories to justify a political or moral stance, although they do employ wajang stories ("which," they say, "are religion") in this way. Ludruk is not sacred. Ludruk is aesthetic, amoral, even wicked. Ludruk stories do not achieve their major impact by serving as ethical, theological, or legal charters for action as do myths, according to social anthropology.[14] Rather,

---

[13] Weber, *Protestant Ethic,* and Robert N. Bellah, *Tokugawa Religion.*

[14] Consider two of the most influential modern anthropological studies of myth: Claude Lévi-Strauss's analysis of the Oedipus myth appearing as part of "The Structural Study of Myth," and E. R. Leach's chapter in *Political Systems of Highland Burma* — "Myth as a Justification for Faction and Social Change." Leach emphasizes that Kachin myth serves to validate the social status of clans or per-

ludruk stories affect participants by seducing them into experiencing certain types of social action, empathizing with certain goals, means, and dramatic forms, and so developing within themselves dispositions to favor these goals and means, and to act in increasingly linear, continuous fashion, in accordance with the forms.

Our notion that ludruk influences by empathy leads us to accord its social impact more importance than would an analyst who follows the traditional social anthropological assumption that symbolic performances achieve social impact primarily (or purely) by furnishing theological, ethical, or legal validation for social institutions. If a social analyst believes that, he will pay more attention to religion than to art, as, in fact most social anthropologists do. If we widen our picture of the social role of symbols to include the subliminal ways by which symbols influence behavior (by inducing empathy and imitation), however, we easily see the social role of art. One might even argue that art works a powerful influence on society precisely because its modes of influence *are* undercover. By being unsuspected, artistic influences might be more powerful than the religious ones that everybody is aware of (and therefore on guard against). Religion makes no bones about the

---

sons. Lévi-Strauss has the opposite approach; he argues that the Oedipus myth, by showing that Greek social ideas and cosmology are structurally parallel, "validates cosmology." The myth makes cosmology seem "true," (p. 216). Thus, Lévi-Strauss and Leach both stress the validation function of myth.

Further insight into this characteristic social anthropological stress on myth as a sanctifying or validating element can be found in Bronislaw Malinowski's famous essay, "Myth in Primitive Psychology." This essay has guided social anthropological thought for decades and is undoubtedly one source of the "validation" emphasis in Leach's analysis of Kachin myth, even though Leach's chapter is intended as a rebellion against Malinowskian functionalism. In his essay, Malinowski divides Trobriand tales into three types. Two types he regards as socially unimportant: "fairy tales" told just "for amusement" and "legends" told to "satisfy social ambitions," (p. 107). Now some of the fairy tales and legends which Malinowski cites happen to portray individuals struggling toward goals — a hero rescuing a woman, a youngest son struggling daily toward eventual victory over a giant fish, and in Malinowski's own words, "extraordinary economic achievements" (p. 105). These are portrayals of social action with which the natives empathize. But Malinowski hardly bothers with these tales. He says these portrayals are much less important than a third type of story (e.g., of tribal origins) that validates tribal institutions, that furnishes a "warrant of antiquity" for rites and moral rules. This type of story is by far the most important, says Malinowski (p. 107); he labels it the *myth* and devotes most of his analysis to it. Thus, in the very *ursprung* and mythical charter of current social anthropological thought about myth, we find that the action-portrayal and empathy aspect of stories is underplayed and the legal or religious validation aspect is emphasized.

social message it preaches, but by publically claiming that art carries no social message ("art for art's sake") the artist may increase acceptance of the social message (influence) that art, in fact, does carry. This is not to say that the artist deliberately works it so that his art will have powerful social impact. As is well known, symbols have latent functions. Precisely what people do not intend them to do is what they may do. One wonders if the social anthropologist has underplayed the social role of art because he has mistaken what the natives say it does (or does not do) for what it does, in fact, do?

By thinking of ludruk's social role as that of teaching attitudes by drawing people into empathy with its action, I have naturally been drawn toward emphasizing the total *form* of the ludruk performance. For example, I have stressed that the melodrama, by musical climax, narrative movement, passage imagery, and other formal devices lures ludruk participants into joining a motion toward particular experiences (such as entry, vicariously, into a bourgeois M-plot household, celebrated by screaming at a scapegoat); that by getting involved in such motions the participants learn to act and orient toward the world in certain ways (such as lineally, continuously, innovatively). This emphasis on the total form of a dramatic performance as a determinant of social attitudes and behavior is absent from the work of social anthropologists, like Leach, who treat symbolic performances as validators. When one is concerned to show that symbolic performances are statements, oral equivalents of legal documents, which validate institutional or personal claims, one naturally places emphasis on the content of the performances — what they state; thus, Leach does not deal with the form of Kachin myths, except to note briefly how each is divided into sections. He confines himself to showing how the myths are statements about genealogical relations among certain kinsmen, spirits, and ancestors, each statement being cited by a particular clan to validate its claim to superior status.[15] In general, social science has paid more attention to the content of symbolic performances than to their form (as is signified by the presence of an established social science field, "content analysis" and the absence of a social science field called, "symbolic form analysis"), but perhaps this will change with the influence of men like Marshall McLuhan, who emphasize that a medium's social impact inheres less in what it says than in its form.

[15] Leach, *Political Systems,* pp. 264–78.

At this point I must speak further of the nature of our evidence that ludruk induces its participants, through empathy with its action and form, to take on dispositions toward particular actions or throughts. My position is this: numerous correlations between what is expressed at ludruk performances and ludruk participants' daily behavior have been demonstrated. Unless we deny that such basic psychological processes as stimulus-generalization and response-generalization occur among the Javanese (and these processes have been shown to occur among rats, pigeons, monkeys, as well as humans), it is inconceivable that what goes on at ludruk fails to affect the behavior of ludruk participants away from ludruk. Our situation is something like that of an observer who has noted correlations between the frequency with which milers on a track team exercise at times other than track meets and the endurance they exhibit during track meets. If the observer does not deny that such physiological processes as "decrease in pulse rate in response to repeated exercise" occur among the milers he studies, it is difficult for him not to conclude that the milers' exercise away from track meets influences their running at the meets. With respect to our situation, ludruk is the exercisor of psychological capacities (as McLuhan would say, "the medium is the massage") and daily life is the track meet.

Note that this example does not take account of the fact that we also have some direct evidence of ludruk affecting daily behavior. Boys at school imitate sayings heard at ludruk. People at work sing ludruk songs. These are signs that persons who have been exposed to ludruk carry with them "in their heads" traces of that experience; presumably, such memory-traces affect their daily actions even when they are not giving verbal expression to those traces. Finally, some people explicitly claim to have learned things from ludruk (such as to be kind to one's spouse), and ludruk actors sometimes explicitly define ludruk as a "torch" or "example" to teach people how to behave, thus locating ludruk within an esteemed Javanese tradition: that the highest calling is that of teacher, and drama is a major source of emotional and moral education.

Possibly, ludruk's power as a teacher of attitudes is increasing; it can be argued that the newer M-plots are more likely to incite their participants to imitate their action after the show than are the older T-plots apt to incite imitation of *their* action. This argument runs as follows: Aristocratic characters appear more frequently and initiate action more often in T-plot than in M-plot narrative, whereas proletarian characters appear more frequently and initiate action more often in M-plot than in T-plot narrative. Therefore, if ludruk audiences, being proletarian, identify more fully with proletarian than with aristocratic characters, then ludruk audiences identify more fully with M-plot than with T-plot narrative. That is why, I have suggested earlier, the clown-servant appears more frequently in T-plots than in M-plots: clown-servants, who are one with proletarian audiences but hobnob with T-plot aristocratic characters, mediate via jokes between the audiences and these characters from whom the audiences feel psychically set apart. Now, these T-plot clown-servants evoke empathy which differs from the empathy evoked by the serious characters (heroes, heroines, and the like) who propel the narrative of M-plots. A perusal of about forty audience-response reports shows that the serious characters often evoke responses linking them to narrative action sequences, whereas the clowns never evoke such responses. Spectators anticipate how the serious characters will be involved in future narrative sequences ("Wah! This person will be kidnapped!"), recall past narrative involvement ("This one earlier became a spouse of that one."), and perceive that the characters have just completed a narrative sequence ("They are finally married."). In no case, in the forty reports, did spectators respond in any of these ways to clown-servants. Spectators respond strictly to clown-servants' action of the instant. They greet the clown ("Meler! Meler!"), remark on his appearance ("Lho! This is the one with the deformed lip!"), judge his artistry ("He doesn't fit his dance to the gamelan."), describe his immediate situation ("Wah! He is given something!"), imitate his sayings, or classify him in terms of a scheme of character-types rather than in terms of the ongoing narrative ("He is like Djanaka." [a wajang character]). Thus, my earlier argument that clowns are in many ways set apart from narrative sequences is extended by comparing the way audiences respond to clowns versus serious characters; clowns evoke empathy with momentary actions; serious characters evoke empathy with narrative sequence. Since clown-servants appear more frequently in T-plots than in M-plots, we conclude that participants in T-plots spend more time in momentary-action empathy than do M-plot participants, whose narrative-sequence empathy is less often interrupted by clown-servants. Further, I argue that not only are M-plot participants more caught up in M-plot narrative sequences than are T-plot participants in T-plot narrative sequences, but also M-plot participants are likely to feel more compelled than T-plot participants to complete, offstage, the narrative sequences in which they have gotten involved. This is so not only because of the greater narrative involvement of M-plot participants but also because of M-plot content; whereas the T-plot ends by ordering everything harmoniously (causing some spectators to say, in their introspection reports, that they feel "relieved, "relaxed," "happy"), the M-plots end uncompleted. All M-plots but one end before the hero and heroine have produced children, although they have married or are about to marry, and since Javanese tend — much more strongly than Americans — to perceive the act of marriage as incomplete until children have been produced, participants in the M-plots perhaps leave the theater with a feeling that the M-plot action is not yet finished. Since these participants have (for reasons mentioned above) empathized with the M-plot action, perhaps they feel some vague desire to complete that uncompleted action after they leave the theater. This is not to say that M-plots stir Javanese proletarians to go home and produce children. Rather, we were shown earlier, certain broad values underlie the specific actions (courting, marrying, setting up a household) of M-plots. These values are "modern." M-plots define a type of action that is innovative, relatively rational, self-initiated, and so on. Therefore, I would argue that M-plots build into their participants a mental drive or set to engage in and complete *any* action — be it domestic, occupational, or whatever — that is "modern": innovative, rational, self-initiated. But will the M-plot participants, in actuality, be able to accomplish such actions? Earlier (chapter 10) I showed that the M-plot participants are distinctively *not* in a position to accomplish such actions, but that their children, increasingly, are. Accordingly, our argument must be that insofar as the M-plots help build into ludruk participants a drive toward completing "modern" actions and insofar as this drive is frustrated, the likelihood that the participants will try to get their children to fulfill the drive will increase. This is the type of psychology, we might argue, that stimulates proletarian parents to say "the Youth will build the bridge from Banjuwangi to Gilimanuk" and to encourage their children to go to the University or to "struggle for rewards from time of birth rather than simply absorb that which flows from the mother's breast" (Basman claimed to be training his son this way).

Since we have embarked on a speculative (but conceivably testable) argument, perhaps the reader will allow a few more wild remarks about the advantages of M-plots over T-plots with respect to inciting social action. A few pieces of evidence suggest that ludruk participants see the T-plots as more like slametan and other rites than are the M-plots. T-plots are older than M-plots and more like the old Besut plays, which were, as we have seen, closely linked to slametan. Like slametan, T-plots move toward establishing social and psychic harmony; M-plots are less oriented toward these ends. Like wajang, which in many kampung and village contexts functions like slametan, T-plots place considerable emphasis on alus "ritual of manners"; M-plots exhibit much less of this emphasis. Clowns, who are much more characteristic of T-plots than of M-plots, are more closely connected in Javanese minds (and also historically) with slametan ritual and animistic beliefs than are serious characters of M-plots; the only onstage portrayals of slametan were by clowns, and the only onstage actions which evoked writers of introspective reports to mention slametan were clowns' actions. In sum, Javanese seem to see more similarity between slametan and T-plots than between slametan and M-plots. Now, slametan and similar rites are conceived as affecting the environment via supernatural channels: one performs the rite, and automatically, regardless of what technical actions one performs after the rite is finished, the cosmos becomes ordered, bodies become healed, houses are made safe. Consequently, to the degree that T-plots are seen as slametans or rites, T-plot participants will feel that *they* are not responsible in their daily actions for making T-plots come true: simply by performing the "T-rite," they set in motion supernatural forces that will automatically make the story come true or in some magical way affect the environment. By contrast, to the degree that M-plots are perceived as lacking the ritual qualities of slametans, M-plot participants are forced to conclude that the only way M-plots can affect the world is for the participants, themselves, to go forth and apply the plots' teachings. Thus, our earlier argument that social anthropology overestimates the power of religion to influence attitudes and actions, and underestimates the power of secular art, finds another line of support; whereas Durkheim argues that religious ritual serves powerfully to mold social attitudes even though the natives claim that its primary function is to supernaturally affect the environment, I suggest that when the natives feel this way about a symbolic performance its power to mold attitudes is weakened and that secular art, since it is not regarded in this way thus has one attitude-molding power that ritual lacks.

This is a good place to stress that I am not claiming, here or anywhere else in this book, that ludruk is the only, or the most powerful, stimulant of ludruk participants' modern attitudes (nor do I deny that in some ways ludruk inhibits rather than stimulates such attitudes). Probably the safest thing to say is that ludruk "reinforces" modern attitudes that are stimulated by many sources other than ludruk. But the cliché "reinforce" does not eliminate the question of causation; to say that ludruk "reinforces" social attitudes that are stimulated by sources other than ludruk is to say that ludruk's effects on its participants' social attitudes parallel effects which derive from sources other than ludruk. We are still left with the task of tracing out ludruk's "effects." I have tried to show that these might be more far-reaching than one would at first expect.

The word "effect" may carry too much flavor of sledgehammer impact, evoking an image of ludruk plays pounding values into soft Javanese skulls. But "effect" can be more subtly defined. If ludruk were not present, one channel for expressing modern attitudes would be absent, hence the attitudes would be less exercised and (to extend the analogy) would be more likely to atrophy than they are since ludruk is present. Ludruk serves as a mental gymnasium — a place where proletarians can exercise and so preserve attitudes that are at this time not fully utilizable by Javanese society.

This notion leads back to the idea that ludruk's most important effect is on the way its participants raise their children. Although research of a variety and extent impracticable for the Indonesian conditions under which I found myself in 1963 would be necessary to strongly support this hypothesis, still it is possible to state a plausible case.[16] Following is a final attempt to do so.

First, ludruk participants are, it seems, in a better position to change their child-training practices than, say, their on-the-job behavior or other non-domestic behavior. It may be true that the ludruk participants have more emotion invested in child-training practices than in most non-domestic behavior, but it is also true that they are socially in a better position to change the former than to change the latter; because they are proletarians, their behavior at work is often controlled by somebody other than themselves, but at home, they, as parents, rule. This is especially so

[16] These paragraphs on the relation between ludruk and childrearing benefit from a discussion with Stephen L. Klineberg and Robert A. Scott of Princeton University.

since the nuclear, rather than extended, family household is the ideal in Surabaja kampung; although as in Basman's case a grandmother may live with the parents and try to tell them how to rear their children, such a relative is regarded as an appendage to the house of which the parents are bosses and not as an elder manager of the house as is the case in some tribal households. Therefore, if parents want to change their ways of rearing their children, nobody within their household has authority to stop them. And, since, as I have shown, the importance of intra-kampung solidarity is decreasing. neighbors' control over each others' households is decreasing.

Assuming, then, that parents who take part in ludruk have some freedom to change their child-rearing practices, are they so inclined? To a striking degree they are. As we have seen, Surabaja society is youth centered. Youth is a focus for social and political life, and we often find youths performing while parents watch (note that the M-plots, although watched by parents, are mainly concerned with depicting youths' adventures and have almost no scenes depicting, say, parents at work). As part of their concern with youth, Surabaja parents talk about youth as the hope of the future; youths will do what parents have not done. (As we have seen, ludruk goers' children and young acquaintances are in a distinctly better social position to carry out the success fantasies depicted on the ludruk stage than are the ludruk goers themselves.) To prepare youth for their achievements, parents are tremendously concerned that they be educated; this concern with children's education is manifested from the lowest levels of society to the highest and correlates with the tremendous strides Indonesia has made in education by comparison with her low development of industry; this generation of Indonesian parents is more oriented toward teaching than doing. Nor do parents restrict their educational concerns to formal schooling; Indonesian mothers form panels to discuss child-rearing practices designed to prepare youth for the future, and lowly kampung dwellers show a surprising awareness of the need to change patterns of punishment and feeding in order to be madju and raise children fit for the future. Basman talks about schedule feeding rather than demand feeding; women talk about spanking children as "the modern way," and so forth. I am not sure to what degree these changes are being put into practice, but at least they are being talked about. At this point, then, we have argued that parents who take part in ludruk have some freedom to change their child-training practices (more freedom to do that than to change certain aspects of their non-domestic behavior) and that these parents show some inclination to make such changes and feel to some degree that such is necessary to create a generation which will make the success fantasies of the ludruk stage (and other media) come true.

Ludruk participants' attitudes, ideology, and situation dispose them, then, to modify their child-rearing customs and to rear their children to do what they cannot do. How might ludruk help stimulate such a process? The ludruk show exhibits an interesting dialectic. The prologue draws kampung dwellers out of the kampung household, which manifests traditional values. The M-plot follows the prologue, concluding the show by putting kampung dwelling parents back inside a home — but an extra-kampung one manifesting modern values. Insofar as parents who enact and observe ludruk identify with the young heroines and heroes of M-plots, they are in the following condition when they leave the ludruk show: they have just finished vicariously achieving social success; they have just vicariously gotten married — so now they are prepared to produce children, since for Javanese marriage implies procreation; and since they are ready to produce children, they are also, by implication, ready to nurture them. Possessed of this mental set, the parents go to bed to dream (say some). Next morning they arise still a little entranced with the social fantasy they experienced the night before: that is, they *had* achieved social success. Daily life abruptly reminds them that they themselves cannot make that fantasy come true. They feel a touch of sadness about that. At this point, might the second disposition induced by ludruk (toward nurturing children) come into play, helping to stimulate a new thought: I will raise my child to do what I cannot?

In other ways too ludruk may help summon this thought. First, ludruk induces its participant-parents to remember themselves as youths. Introspective reports of parents watching ludruk are full of remarks like, "This reminds me of myself at age sixteen." By evoking parents' nostalgic memories of their youth, ludruk helps such parents identify with the imagined adventures and successes of their children as youths. Second, ludruk induces its participant-parents to remember themselves as children. During ludruk, parents empathize with childlike clowns, address each other as "child," and listen to children's songs. Perhaps this experience, coupled with others thrust upon the parents by Indonesian culture (as proletarians they are sometimes called "children" by speakers like Shamsudin, and they themselves sometimes call themselves "children" of organizations like Tresno Enggal), helps these parents imagine themselves in their children's shoes.

If ludruk spurs parents to fantasize about their children's success, does it inspire them to take steps toward training these children to succeed? Paradoxically, one of the modern values which ludruk teaches parents to teach their children is that parents' teaching is limited in value. The image of the next generation which ludruk presents is of youths who are schooled and politicized away from home, and who adopt a life style suitable to a status higher than that of their parents. Thus, says ludruk to its parent-participants, "Your children as youths will behave so differently from you that you should teach them now to 'achieve on your own, don't depend on us.'" If parents take this idea to heart and start teaching children independence by strongly rewarding them for accomplishments they achieve on their own, this would be a radical shift from traditional custom. Proletarian Javanese parents have traditionally been wary of clearly rewarding children for unique achievement (in so-called singing contests on Independence Day parents never declare a winner, for example); parents instruct not by giving a child a chance to try a task for himself, then rewarding him for his success (or punishing him for his failure), but by a constant stream of talk and bodily manipulation which guides the child's every action and allows him little chance to either fail or succeed on his own. Perhaps, ludruk-going parents, having themselves identified with ludruk heroes and heroines, then identified their children with themselves, are a bit disposed to treat their children as M-plots treat their protagonists; if so, they will reward their children's personal achievements to a greater degree than traditional Javanese parents do. (Note here that ludruk with all its tactile, bodily content is a good medium for influencing those patterns of bodily response — cuddling, massaging, shoving, bending, sucking — which are so crucial in Javanese patterns of rewarding and punishing children.)

Ludruk furnishes catharsis for parents worried about the way their teen-age children are developing. As we have seen, much of the clown's song concentrates on the loose sex, frivolous study, faddish dress of modern adolescents. To these songs, parents respond, "Yes, that's the way children are," thus sharing and relieving their anxieties about the younger generation. Ludruk perhaps serves the dual function of kindling parents' wishes to rear children in new ways and soothing parents' anxieties about what is happening to the new crop of children.

An amplifying effect could occur as ludruk's teachings pass from ludruk to parent to child. Let us imagine that every time a parent comes home from ludruk he is steamed up enough so that for a short time he responds differently to his child than he would had he not been to ludruk; perhaps, like Basman, inspired temporarily by an image of success, he makes his son fight a little for his rewards in hopes that this will make him ambitious. Now since the ludruk-going parents are adults whose personalities and values are pretty well set it does not seem likely that even repeated exposure to ludruk will bring about permanent and deep restructuring of their personalities and values. But if such a parent goes to ludruk often and if each time he goes he is temporarily stirred to respond in a non-traditional way to his child, might these repeated patterns of parental response not have strong effects on the *child?* — for the child's personality is still malleable. Also, if it is true that parental acts often mean more to children perceiving them than to parents doing them, slight and temporary changes in parental behavior could have deep meaning to the child. Again, slight changes in parents induced by ludruk might amplify as they are passed down to children.

Now a final point about ludruk and empathy. Historians and philosophers have remarked that art is particularly useful in forecasting social trends; art expresses emerging values and attitudes that later get worked out institutionally (by the artist's audience's children?)[17] Social scientists have retrospectively shown that art foreshadowed significant institutional changes; for example, Krakauer[18] argues that Nazi ideals were expressed by German movies decades before they became manifest in German politics, and Lowenthal[19] shows how a scene from "The Tempest" foreshadowed coming changes in Western class structure. My 1965 analysis of ludruk, mentioned earlier, which revealed a trend toward bourgeois attitudes among ludruk participants before the emergence of anti-Communist outbreaks in Indonesia, might be taken as further example of the way analyzing symbolic performances can aid comprehension of emerging social trends.

But to accomplish such an analysis it is necessary to take note of the nature of participants' empathy during the symbolic performances. For the concern is with those ideas and attitudes which

---

[17] John Dewey, *Art as Experience*, p. 345.
[18] Kracauer, *Hitler*.
[19] Leo Lowenthal, *Literature, Popular Culture, and Society*, pp. 144–49.

are novel — those which do not yet manifest themselves in society's daily life. And if ideas expressed during a symbolic performance are not yet practiced daily by the performance's participants, how can we tell if these ideas are influencing them? At least one clue is given by the nature of the communicative behavior occurring during the performance. What sort of empathy do the participants display? Although ludruk goers do not choose their mates in real life, that they clap and cheer when ludruk characters utter the ideal "self choice of mate" suggests that the onstage ideal is not without influence on their attitudes.

Still the analyst must beware of assuming that participants' reactions during performances relate in any simple way to their attitudes away from performances. Sometimes the relationship appears direct: Geertz gives the example of the Plains Indian exercising a certain bravura during his vision quest and so reinforcing his tendency to live flamboyantly day-to-day.[20] Sometimes the connection is less direct: Mass media psychologists point to the "sleeper effect" (a person reacts negatively when first exposed to a symbolic medium but later changes his attitude to match that expressed by the medium).[21] One thing the student of symbolic performances in changing society might note is disillusionment; if the ideals expressed by the performance are novel — not yet manifest in society — then the artist or spectator may feel disillusioned when he turns from performance to society. To my knowledge, no social scientists have yet explored this phenomenon, but undoubtedly disillusionment follows empathy at the ludruk theater. After the show, or during it, one glimpses the sham of the transvestites' beauty or of the madju ideals they profess and perceives that the elite who parade onstage are not elite; nor, indeed, are genuine elite — those who could make the M-stories true — present to watch the spectacle, or (usually) even aware of its existence.

A few paragraphs back, we stumbled again into the posture that ludruk is an X-ray machine; social trends were regarded as the phenomena with priority, as that which is to be understood, and ludruk was treated as a "gimmick" for understanding them. But a wider perspective is possible. It is that which I have tried to sustain during much of this book: ludruk and society are assigned equal weight, and analysis of their interaction is an essential way

[20] C. Geertz, "Religion as a Cultural System," p. 9.

[21] William W. Lambert, "Stimulus-Response Contiguity and Reinforcement Theory in Social Psychology," p. 84.

of grasping the dynamics of changes in either. Lack of fit between social reality and symbolic definition of that reality is seen as a powerful stimulus of change in either the reality or the definition, since participants in both the reality and the definition strive to bring about fit between the two. To grasp the total dynamics of the Javanese scene, we must grasp the dynamics of daily social life *and* of symbolic performances, such as ludruk, analyzing each conscientiously in its own terms and then analyzing interactions between them. The social scientist tends to pay too little heed to the dynamics of the performances, to report from the performances only those tidbits of content which lend support to his portrait of the values and organization of the society in which the performances are found; he cites a few proverbs or song lyrics to illustrate values and roles which are, he decides after analyzing the native's daily social behavior, the dominant ones in the society.[22] This kind of analysis, which fails to grasp the essence of symbolic performances, can yield no full appreciation of social dynamics.

But what is our final position? Must we give equal priority to "society" and "symbolic performances?" Ultimately, one might argue, priority must be given to that which means most to the participants. In places like Java, where social bonds are shifting, vague, and taken rather lightly, it sometimes seems that artistic events mean more than daily groupings and loyalties. The social scientist's assumption that "social system" (networks of roles, statuses, and social relationships) is the most viable framework within which to view a group's existence often seems, in Java, a bit absurd. In Java, as in other places,[23] social scientists might lay less stress on representing groups' lives as "social systems" or even as "cultural systems" (logically related beliefs, values, and symbols), and more on perceiving the dynamics of important communicative events;[24] a portrait of Java might well be a portrait of symbolic *action* patterns which the natives regard as moving, funny, beautiful.

[22] Most any of the ethnographies by British social structuralists fit this description, as do most attempts by social scientists to present a picture of a "total" community or society.

[23] Charles Keil, *Urban Blues,* argues that symbolic actions such as blues singing are more a focal point of Negro social life than are social institutions such as church and family, which serve as centers for white bourgeois society (see pp. 15–18).

[24] The phrase "communicative events" is from Dell Hymes, "Introduction: Toward Ethnographies of Communication," p. 13.

Afterword, 1987

During the twenty years since this book was published and the twenty-five years since the research on which it is based was carried out, notable changes have occurred both in the object of study and in scholarly perspectives on such study. In fact, object and perspectives have moved in opposite directions. Indonesian popular culture, my focus of study, has shifted from a Marxist to a more bourgeois, developmental orientation, while American social science, including social anthropology, has shifted in precisely the reverse direction, at least in some circles. An ironic lesson, for those who record dialogues between "us and the other"! This re-

I gratefully acknowledge helpful comments from Karl Heider, Dorothy Holland, Stuart Marks, and Ruel Tyson.

lationship and others are suggested by reflections on the original context of my study and on changes since. Such an account, limited and biased though it may be, can provide a small case study of the effects of theoretical, methodological, circumstantial, and personal constraints on ethnographic analysis—a topic more current at the moment than when *Rites of Modernization* was published in 1968.[1]

The twelve months during which I did the Indonesian fieldwork for *Rites*, spanning 1962 and 1963, led into the "Year of Living Dangerously," as President Sukarno called it: the eve of the most momentous eruption in Indonesia's history as a new nation. At this time, Indonesian Communism was at its peak; the Indonesian Communist Party (PKI) was the largest Communist party in Asia outside China, and it had deeply pervaded popular culture, including the working-class drama that I studied, the *ludruk.* In the port city of Surabaya, the center of ludruk and of my fieldwork, twenty-six of twenty-seven districts were under Communist control. Communist takeover was expected by some. But an allegedly Communist-led coup launched in 1965 provoked a military takeover. An estimated half-million people were killed, many but not all of them Communists or Communist sympathizers. Many more were imprisoned or otherwise punished, and President Sukarno was replaced by General Suharto. By the time I returned to Indonesia, on New Year's Eve 1969, Suharto's "new order" was in place: a more technocratic, capitalistic, materialistic, and military-dominated order than the mass culture nationalist-socialist "Guided Democracy" of Sukarno.

The effects on the ludruk, as far as I could tell from a brief return visit to Surabaya in 1970, were in part what one might expect of a shift from a socialistic to a military government. Some of the actors had been killed or imprisoned, including the Marxist idealogue Shamsudin, who headed the most famous troupe, Marhaen. Marhaen and all the other troupes existing during 1962 and 1963 had been disbanded, while new troupes had been formed under military control. When in 1970 I presented a copy of *Rites of Modernization* to the currently playing ludruk troupe at the Surabaya People's Amusement Park, it was to an entirely new group of actors, and the presentation was overseen by a soldier. The basic

---

[1] See George E. Marcus and Michael M. J. Fischer, *Anthropology as Cultural Critique: An Experimental Moment in the Human Sciences* (Chicago: University of Chicago Press, 1987). A simplified statement of the perspective is in James L. Peacock, *The Anthropological Lens: Harsh Light, Soft Focus* (Cambridge: Cambridge University Press, 1986), chap. 2.

pattern and form of the plays remained, however, except for a reduction of explicit political criticism.

The conceptual equipment that I took to Indonesia in 1962 was similar to that of many other anthropologists and social scientists of the time. "All you need to know is Boas and the French" was the advice given my class of graduate students by one of our revered teachers, Clyde Kluckhohn (in lectures on the history of theory, his last seminar at Harvard University, during late Spring 1960). By "Boas" Kluckhohn meant the American tradition of cultural anthropology passing from Boas through Kroeber, Benedict, and others, which taught a holistic appreciation of cultural configurations. And by "the French" he referred to the Anglo-Gallic tradition of social anthropology, passing from Durkheim through Radcliffe-Brown to Evans-Pritchard, Lévi-Strauss, and others, which taught a similarly holistic sense of the way elements functioned within social systems or were logically positioned within symbolic structures. Such structural-functionalism/configurationalism was, then, the dominant view in sociocultural anthropology. Stirrings could be detected which signaled intensified attention to symbolic patterns as independent entities: the structuralism of Claude Lévi-Strauss, for example, and the culturalism of Clifford Geertz. At this point, however, Geertz was still working within a structural-functionalist mold strongly inspired by Talcott Parsons, who, with the young Robert Bellah, provided the primary theoretical resource I too found as a graduate student. Though friendly and supportive in general, my anthropological mentors were a bit doubtful about my plan to violate the more holistic, structural-functionalist approach by focusing so intensely on a single symbolic form, the ludruk, and, in fact, rejected my initial research proposal. Geertz, to whom I sent a copy of my proposal, gave encouraging and extremely helpful advice while warning about the delicate political/social position of the ludruk.[2] Seeking ideas from outside anthropology, I read literary criticism, especially Kenneth Burke, who gave courage to focus on what would probably be obvious to humanists: the dynamics and thrust of the aesthetic form itself. But I went to the field with a structural-functionalist orientation.

---

[2] The following letters were of great significance to me as I prepared for fieldwork. On November 6, 1961, John Pelzel, my temporary advisor, wrote from Harvard:

> Your proposal . . . was of very great interest to me. It has the core of an extremely original and significant problem. . . . The third element—as I see it—of your proposed study, analysis of the art form itself, is, so far as I

Perhaps owing to this orientation, as well as to limited funding and other practical difficulties, I had not planned on extensive audio and visual recording of the performances, and was not well-equipped. In 1962, portable and inexpensive video cameras were not yet available, and the secondhand 8 millimeter camera that I took turned out to be defective, as was my cheap tape recorder. Consequently, I brought home few cinematic or audio recordings or transcriptions, though I did take numerous photographs, a few of which appear in this book. Most importantly, I laboriously typed out detailed, blow-by-blow descriptions of the eighty-odd performances that I saw; this material, most of it still unpublished, was the core of my dissertation and book.

When I first began analyzing my data, I attempted an exhaustive analysis of sociocultural themes and only gradually came to

---

know, hardly done by anthropology at all. Am I forgetting something? If not, I think you are on your own in devising both categories and methods of analysis. How you might go about it, and make the results ultimately relevant to the broader culture, I frankly don't know now. [Now follows an evocative portrait of forms in relation to landscape in India, illustrating the elusive relationship between form and context and the significance of form, ending with a comment on the backward state of anthropological inquiry into art forms.]

On May 22, 1962, Clifford Geertz, writing from the University of Chicago, began a three-page letter on the subject of the fieldwork, which he encouraged with suitable warnings:

I think a study of the *ludrug* such as you outline would be most useful and I think probably feasible. The main doubt as to feasibility stems, of course, from political considerations. Not only is Surabaya the reddest area of Indonesia by far, but the ludrug companies are themselves in the leftist camp and how they will receive an American who (he says) wants to study them is problematical to a degree. There isn't much you can do about this, I suppose, but try; but you need to realize that politics is for keeps these days in Indonesia and the domestic situation generally is very tense indeed. Surabaya and the ludrug companies are not the place for political naiveté, and you may have some corking rapport problems (the fact that the companies also tend to be homosexual havens doesn't make the situation any easier either). But, on the other hand, the Javanese, even Communist Javanese, when last I worked with (or was it against?) them remained remarkably civil and I don't say that the job is impossible, merely that I myself would prefer studying French-Moslem relations in Oran.

Once in the field, I received encouragement from Cora DuBois and David Maybury-Lewis, while Robert Bellah and Thomas Kirsch provided especially helpful comments after I got back. But as my advisor, DuBois, was herself in the field during my writeup, my dissertation was much under my own control—which I found exhilarating.

frame my analysis in terms of the ludruk form—the plots, songs, jokes, and the like—which imposed itself on me, overriding my holistic propensities. Perhaps partly because I had arrived at this conception of the ludruk against predispositions—my own and those of my discipline—I emphasized the integrity and power of the ludruk as an aesthetic and symbolic form, apart from any social or cultural value and function it might have. Nevertheless, the influence of structural-functionalism as well as undergraduate training in experimental psychology (and, no doubt, some vague philosophy of pragmatism) led me to heavy-handedly force an argument that ludruk was not just entertainment, that it had an effect on attitudes toward modernization: it was a "rite of modernization." While I realized that to demonstrate such an effect was empirically difficult if not impossible, the attempt, I think, was useful in that it encouraged analysis of the communicative process—the aesthetics as well as content of performance and the dynamics of audience response—what Hymes, in a formulation influential for me, termed the "communicative event."[3]

Reviews of the book were divided suggestively between those focusing on the analysis of the drama and those concentrating on the sociocultural analyses. James Brandon, a scholar and practitioner of cross-cultural drama, exemplified the first type, predicting that the book would become a "minor classic" in analysis of theater.[4] A similar emphasis was manifest in the anonymous review for the *Times Literary Supplement,* which explicitly contrasted the dramatistic and anthropological focus, stating, flatteringly but disturbingly: "Perhaps in his next book Mr. Peacock will be able to write just on the theatre, a field in which he displays a truly remarkable talent, and escape from the clutches of anthropological professionalism."[5] The professional anthropologists, in the second type of review, tightened their clutches by emphasizing the issue of how drama relates to society and culture. Edward Bruner, in the *American Anthropologist,* was concerned about an overemphasis on the performances and their effects on modernization, which "prevents him from maximizing some of his insights into the dynamics of Javanese family and social life."[6] James Fox, in *An-*

[3] Dell Hymes, "Introduction: Toward Ethnographies of Communication," *American Anthropologist* 66 (1964): 13.

[4] James Brandon, "Review of *Rites of Modernization,*" *Modern Drama* 12, no. 4 (February 1970): 439–40.

[5] "Pop Theatre of Indonesia," *London Times Literary Supplement,* Feb. 1969.

[6] Edward Bruner, "Review of *Rites of Modernization,*" *American Anthropologist* 71 (1969): 537.

thropos, echoed the same concern, concluding by referring to the study's contribution to the anthropological study of urban society.[7] The point is not to contest the reviews, which were generally careful, insightful, and generous, but to note with interest the continuing anthropological emphasis on sociocultural function, in contrast to the dramatistic focus on the symbolic form as such.

Since the time of my study, "symbolic" anthropology has become an acknowledged subfield; in fact, this volume was the first in a new but short-lived series entitled "Symbolic Anthropology"; it helped launch that subfield. Symbolic anthropology is being refined into yet more literary, aesthetic, and philosophical approaches, and anthropologists now lavish attention on the subtle issues of interpretation of texts and other symbolic expressions without guilt. Structural-functionalist and neoevolutionist theories such as "modernization" have given way to or share the stage with other approaches to understanding social forces and change such as the Marxist view, or others combining historical and hermeneutical perspectives.

Were I to rewrite *Rites,* it would doubtless reflect some of these new sensibilities, though many of them were nascent in the work, while some are not, in my view, necessarily an advance. I would deemphasize the analysis of "effect." But, as noted, this emphasis, or overemphasis, did have the advantage of pushing toward analysis of the communicative event. The prevailing anthropological approach to analysis of symbolic forms, under the influence of hermeneutical concerns, including the Geertzian "culture as text" model,[8] is to emphasize the epistemological premises embodied in the form rather than the communicative process of which the form is part. This kind of epistemological emphasis is seen in recent (and excellent) interpretations of the sacral Javanese drama, *wayang kulit.*[9] Keeler explicitly contrasts my search for "effects" of the ludruk with his approach to the wayang kulit. Keeler states, "My contention is that both social life and aesthetics develop out of deeply held assumptions about the world, and that neither one need be seen as cause or effect of the other."[10] Certainly this

[7] James J. Fox, "Review of *Rites of Modernization," Anthropos* 65 (1970): 336–37.

[8] Clifford Geertz, "Deep Play: Notes on the Balinese Cockfight," in *The Interpretation of Cultures* (New York: Basic Books, 1973), 459–90.

[9] A. L. Becker, "Text-Building, Epistemology, and Aesthetics in Javanese Shadow Theater," in *The Imagination of Reality: Essays in Southeast Asian Coherence Systems,* ed. A. L. Becker and A. A. Yengoyan (Norwood, N. J.: Ablex Publishing Corporation, 1979), 211–43.

[10] Ward Keeler, *Javanese Shadow Plays, Javanese Selves* (Princeton, N.J.: Princeton University Press, 1987), 18.

model evades difficulties of causal or functional approaches; on the other hand, it can lead to an overly intellectualistic view of dramatic performances, at the extreme treating them more as philosophical treatises than as drama—a tendency that Burke and Frye warned against. Burke ridicules the "savants" who would "catalogue for us the 'thoughts of' a stylist like Milton, by stating them simply as precepts divorced from their stylistic context,"[11] while Frye refers to the "existential fallacy," which is to assume that philosophical assumptions generate the form when, in fact, the reverse may be true in drama.[12] Keeler himself, at the end of his study, seems to echo this concern when he writes, "Only when we treat the performance as an event, as an experience of great evocative power rather than as some elaborate heuristic device, do we escape the intellectualistic prejudices and expectations we bring to the study of texts . . ."[13] In fact, Keeler's fine study is richer than his somewhat intellectualistic initial statement of purpose would suggest, for he treats wayang kulit as a performative experience which in its totality distills the social and cosmic world of the Javanese. But the general point is that if anthropologists have made strides in their hermeneutics—in reading twitches as winks, cockfights as texts, plays as epistemologies—they can still enrich the model by fuller analysis of the performance experience itself, of which, from a certain viewpoint, the "deeply held assumptions about the world" are only a facet. *Rites* broke with the totalizing, holistic tradition that still prevails in anthropology by dissecting "culture" and "ritual" into components of communication as part of a dynamic process of social change.

The ludruk plays are oddly placed, from the standpoint of both Indonesian culture and sociocultural anthropology. The plays are not the sacred rites that have long been the dominant concern of both the culture and the discipline; rather, ludruk is an antirite, on the edges, profane, not to say obscene and suspect: the haven of clowns, transvestites, and raucous social criticism. Ludruk is hardly what national tourist bureaus glorify, and I have heard that my descriptions of ludruk were once cited by a journalist of the "New Order" as an exposé of bizarre behavior during the old. Yet I have also heard that a certain Surabayan politician, in a speech

[11] Kenneth Burke, *The Philosophy of Literary Form* (New York: Vintage Books, 1957), 168–69; Northrup Frye, *The Anatomy of Criticism* (Princeton, N.J.: Princeton University Press, 1957), 63–64.

[12] James Peacock, *Consciousness and Change: Symbolic Anthropology in Evolutionary Perspective* (Oxford: Blackwell's; New York: John Wiley, 1975), chap. 6. develops this point in general terms.

[13] Keeler, *Javanese Shadow Plays,* 267.

on Surabaya's Hero's Day, quoted the book with relish, saying that it captured something of the "Surabaya character"—presumably the raw crudity of which Surabyans, in contrast to wider Javanese ideals of refinement, are perversely proud. Within anthropology and other disciplines, students and colleagues have reportedly gleaned from the book some hints useful in studies of theater, ritual, even sports and politics.[14] It will perhaps take its place in the effort by the late Victor Turner and others to extend our anthropological understanding beyond orthodox ritual and intellectualist hermeneutics, to include a range of symbolic forms and modes of studying them. Others have apparently found the study useful in teaching, perhaps because the ludruk epitomizes in microcosm such a range of issues, from aesthetics to hermeneutics to the social dynamics of the Third World: issues which remain pressing. Such was the spirit in which the book was written—not just to describe a little-known working-class play, but to confront understandings that ludruk embodied and issues raised by the effort to understand *it*. I am pleased that a paperback edition will permit wider use of this kind.

[14] Ruth McVey, "The Wayang Controversy in Indonesian Communism," in Mark Hobart and Robert H. Taylor, eds., *Context, Meaning, and Power in Southeast Asia* (Ithaca, N.Y.: Cornell University Southeast Asia Program, 1986), 32–37. McVey disagrees with my emphasis on the positive, modernizing effect of ludruk while underlining its critical purpose, a perspective with which, to some extent, I agree. For a perceptive criticism of *Rites* from this standpoint, see the review by Ved Prakash Vatuk, *Journal of American Folklore* 83 (July–September 1970): 364–65.

Appendix
A
Musical Lines

Although the following musical lines have been discussed in the text, some further explanation seems necessary here. Line A shows the sléndro tonal system in accord with which the ludruk gamelan is tuned. B, C, and D show the nuclear themes of the three compositions most frequently played by the ludruk gamelan: Djuladjuli, Srepegan, and Sampak. E shows the basic vocal line which all clown singers follow during the first part of their opening song (see chapter 12), although different singers add different improvisations to this basic line. This first part of the song includes the clown's stereotyped introduction and welcome to the audience, during which he begs the audience's forgiveness in case he makes mistakes, and gives any serious messages (such as advice about living a good life, cooperating in the household, or contributing to the government); the second part of the song (F and G) is the part that draws responses — laughter and murmurs of agreement (see chapter 12) — and it includes the clown's critical comments. F is the vocal line most frequently sung after the first part of the song, but G is occasionally sung then also. H depicts the vocal line which all transvestite between-scene singers follow during their "regular" songs (i.e., when they are not singing children's songs or kinanṭi songs); as can be seen, the amount of ornamentation in this song is high by comparison with the clown song, but the amount shown here is typical for the "regular" transvestite song.

KEY:

    Λ raised a quarter tone
    V lowered a quarter tone
    ▬ emphatic beat
    ◡ non-emphatic beat

A. TONES OF SLENDRO SYSTEM

B. NUCLEAR THEME OF DJULA-DJULI: PATET SLENDRO MANJURA

C. NUCLEAR THEME OF SREPEGAN: PATET SLENDRO MANJURA

D. NUCLEAR THEME OF SAMPAK: PATET SLENDRO MANJURA

E. VOCAL LINE OF CLOWN: PART I

F. VOCAL LINE OF CLOWN: PART II

G. VOCAL LINE OF CLOWN: VARIATION ON PART II

H. TRANSVESTITE SINGER'S HIGHLY ORNAMENTAL VOCAL LINE

Appendix B
Outline of A Commercial Ludruk Performance

The following is an outline of events occurring during a performance by the troupe Tresno Enggal which featured the story "Revenge in the Night" and took place at the People's Amusement
Park theater on April 5, 1963, between the hours seven-thirty
P.M. and midnight. This outline is abstracted from my field notes,
and it also corresponds to a tape recording of the total performance and an outline of the performance written by an Indonesian.
The outline is schematic; its purpose is only to set forth the *sequence* of events that occur during a total performance. More
detailed information on specific parts of the performance can be
found in chapters 4 and 8.

Prelude: Gamelan music.

Curtain opens: Sanjoto, ngremo dancer in male clothes, appears. He
dances, then begins to sing while standing still. He sings a welcome

to the audience in high Javanese language and begs their forgiveness in case there is a mistake. Then he sings a number of verses: The first says that Javanese have experienced hard times so that they will someday find good fate. The second says Javanese should live carefully to arrange for good future lives. The third says that the singer prays for the nation to become honorable. The fourth says all (Indonesians) should make an effort to do better. The fifth says the singer cannot forget the image of a past lover. Sanjoto concludes by singing, "That's all I have to say. Whether it is good or not is for you to decide." He dances some more, sembahs. Curtain drops.

New scene: Amin appears, sings the clown song: First three verses say that the educational system of Indonesia should be improved, for with improved knowledge the development plan for Indonesia can be quickly carried out. Fourth verse says that women's fashions have gone to the extreme. Fifth verse says that girls who cut their hair fail in school. Sixth verse says youths should study more diligently. Seventh verse says young men and women should not be sexually promiscuous. Eighth verse says an unmarried girl who is impregnated suffers a sad fate. Ninth verse says such a girl will be ejected from home and wander the streets. Tenth verse says the girl will finally end up in Potter's field. Amin concludes by singing, "This is the old people's advice. That is all I have to say."

Amin soliloquizes about his poverty and misery. Piet, a second clown, appears and engages in a dialogue with Amin. He induces Amin to go with him to steal. Amin and Piet practice stealing, Amin playing the part of a kampung guard and Piet playing the role of the thief. Amin loses this "duel," because he immediately says, "You win" when Piet challenges him to fight. Piet and Amin practice stealing again, then set off to steal.

New scene: Piet and Amin enter Wiro's house in a kampung. They steal a large trunk from the house. Curtain drops.

New scene: Piet and Amin, now on the street, open the trunk. A ghost leaps out. (Laughter.) Curtain drops.

Song interlude: Muchtar Rijamin is the singer. He sings three verses. First: laborers, peasants, and other groups should unite to defend the national claim. Second: "Sujudana is the king of Ngastina, Sengkuni is the Prime Minister; Bung Karno is our President, the flag is red and white." Third: "As water may spill from a coconut shell dipper, so may one lose a spouse." Rijamin dances a little in stylized walking motion, continuing to sing. Fourth verse: "As friends we are brothers. Who knows when one of us will depart?" Fifth verse: Indonesia, composed of many religions, should be united "for this is an era that is madju." Curtain drops.

New scene: The feature story "Revenge in the Night" begins. The scene is in a rural village house. An old man, Pak Rusman, is quarreling with his nagging wife, Mbok Rusman. After several minutes, Inem, Rusman's daughter-in-law, enters. Young Rusman, her husband, has decided to go to the city to seek work, since he cannot make a living in the country. Inem and Rusman leave for the city. Pak Rusman (comically) commands his wife to go to her room. Curtain drops.

Song interlude: The singer is Soerjadi. He sings the children's song, "The Little Motorcar." Dances. Curtain closes. (In this case the singer of a children's song is not of the "sucking harlot" type.)

New scene: The city home of Bapak Kusbijantoro, aristocrat. Amin, a servant, is dusting furniture. Bapak Kusbijantoro enters. After a typical "master-servant" joking session, Amin exits and Bapak Kusbijantoro's wife enters. Husband and wife talk about their young son, Kusbijantoro. He is just playing around all the time. The father says he is going to arrange for the son to marry his cousin, Sulastri. Father and mother exit. Sulastri enters. Kusbijantoro enters and tells Sulastri he is to marry her. He twists her arm and tells her she will have to obey his command. He exits. Curtain drops.

Song interlude: The singer is Hery Soeparno. First verse: Djoko Tingkir rides a crocodile to the palace; "don't think of your lover, it won't work out." Second verse: "He's not of the family, but he cannot be forgotten. Women should beware [of seducers] if they want to be good mothers." Third verse: "Tjakraningrat is prime minister of Sampang. . . . You pass by but do not stop to visit; a heart is broken." (There are more verses about love and fewer about politics in this performance than is usual for Tresno Enggal performances.) Singer dances a little. Curtain drops.

New scene: Kusbijantoro and a modern girl, Mientje, meet on the street. Mientje promises to arrange for Kusbijantoro to meet Rusman's wife, Inem, who is Mientje's friend. Kusbijantoro gives Mientje one of Sulastri's sarongs to give to Inem. Curtain drops.

New scene: Rusman's house in the city. Piet, the servant, is talking about how extreme Inem is in her modern, city ways. Rusman enters, and Piet complains to him about Inem. Inem enters in her wild, modern clothes. Piet exits. Rusman tells Inem she should be more conservative. Piet enters. Rusman exits. Piet and Inem argue about her having lost her old village ways. Inem exits. The modern girl,

Mientje arrives at the door and enters, dancing around. Piet exits. Inem enters. Inem and Mientje talk. Piet enters, mocks Mientje. Piet exits. Inem soliloquizes about how Kusbijantoro loves her. Curtain drops.

New scene: Kusbijantoro and Inem meet on the street near a movie theater, and decide to run away together. Curtain drops.

New scene: House of Rusman. Piet and Rusman are worrying about Inem's spending so much money. Inem enters, exits. The police come, asking for Rusman. Piet denies that Rusman is home. Kusbijantoro enters, asking for Inem. Piet goes to get her. Inem and Kusbijantoro run away together, after Inem tells the police where Rusman is. The police arrest Rusman for embezzling (to pay Inem's bills), leaving Piet with Rusman's and Inem's child. Curtain drops.

Song interlude: The singer is Sjamsuri. First verse: "Indonesia, composed of Islamic, Buddhist, Christian, and Hindu religions . . . should be united and not in conflict." Second verse: "He [Javanese pronouns do not specify gender] is no kinsman, but if he dies, you will miss him" (implying that the person being spoken of is the singer's or listener's lover). Third verse: "Oh dear girl, who is your lover now? It does not matter if he is ugly, just that he is honest." Curtain drops.

New scene: A city street, where Pak and Mbok Rusman, who have come to town seeking their child, Rusman, meet Piet. Piet tells them what has happened to Rusman because of Inem and Kusbijantoro. Pak Rusman, angry, leaves for the house of Kusbijantoro's parents. Curtain drops.

New scene: The house of Kusbijantoro's parents. Rusman appears at the door with Piet. Rusman asks Piet whether he should speak krama or ngoko to Kusbijantoro's father. Piet advises him to speak naturally. Rusman recounts to Bapak and Ibu Kusbijantoro all that Inem and young Kusbijantoro have done. Curtain drops.

New scene: A new house where Rusman, now out of prison, lives in luxury with Sulastri, whom he has married since her spouse and his spouse ran away. Rusman and Sulastri are amiably talking when two blind beggars appear at the door begging. They turn out to be Kusbijantoro and Inem. Upon realizing where they are, the beggars crawl away. Rusman and Sulastri shout in unison, "Revenge in the night!" Curtain drops. The end.

Appendix
C
The Field Research

The field research was carried out from September, 1962, to September, 1963, in Surabaja, an East Javanese city. During this year I saw performances of ludruk and collected information on the social life of ludruk players and spectators.

COLLECTING DATA ON LUDRUK PERFORMANCES

I saw eighty-two ludruk performances. Most of these were in the five commercial theaters in Surabaja. The seven best-known troupes in Surabaja took turns playing at each of these theaters. I saw a number of performances by each of these troupes at the most popular and newest commercial theater, in the People's

Amusement Park (THR) of Surabaja. I also went to one or two performances at each of the other theaters in Surabaja: Banguredjo, in a shantytown famous for its brothels; PBRI, near the Unilever factory; Wono Kromo, in a market district by that name; and a theater in the "Night Market" on Pandergiling street. It was very easy to watch a ludruk performance at a commercial theater; usually I just bought a ticket and sat in the audience, although in some cases I sat backstage with the actors. In addition to commercial performances, I saw a few all-night performances at celebrations in kampung, three ludruk performances at meetings of Communist-affiliated mass organizations, two performances at rural villages, and several benefit performances arranged by political-cultural organizations, such as the Surabaja branch of the "Garden of Students" (*Taman Siswa*). Unless I state otherwise, all ludruk performances analyzed in this book were seen at commercial theaters.

Onstage Action

Full tapes of the onstage dialogues that occurred during two typical five-hour-long commercial performances were made. Numerous eight-millimeter films of dance sequences and other sequences where body movements were important were taken. Verbatim texts of most of the ludruk songs were obtained.

Aside from these "literal" recordings, I made detailed notes on each of the five-hour performances that I saw. Most of these inevitably selective notes aimed at describing coherently each sequence in which audience expectations were built up and gratified; for such sequences seemed to be the building blocks from which ludruk performances were constructed. An instance of such a sequence: a clown makes a speech in Indonesian language, building up volume until suddenly he substitutes for the appropriate Indonesian word *ibu* (mother) a Surabaja Javanese word for mother (*mbok*), at which point the audience roars with laughter. In my notes on this sequence I tried to set down the climactic pun word, the gist of the speech preceding, the general pattern of facial expressions and postures leading to the climax, specific expressions and postures accompanying the pun word, and striking orchestral accompaniments such as the "whomp" of the drum when the pun word was uttered. Thus, for a given ludruk performance, my notes consisted of more or less verbatim transcriptions of songs plus an outline of the story and skit preceding the story and rather detailed notes on particular climax sequences (mainly jokes) that punctuated the skit or story and notes on anything else that struck me as important that I had time to write down.

There are, of course, a number of schemes for characterizing in detail face-to-face interactions.[1] I did not use any of these, partly because such schemes tend to require more elaborate personnel and facilities than could be had easily by a lone anthropologist in Indonesia, where rather uncommon economic conditions made it troublesome to exchange money, get supplies, and pay assistants. Also, these schemes did not seem to fit the kinds of interaction that took place on the ludruk stage. They are designed for systematic observation of "real" groups. Groups on the ludruk stage are representational groups. The ludruk groups are not primarily oriented toward solving practical problems or harmonizing themselves. They are trying to present a show, to represent certain aspects of the world in such a way that they entertain spectators by arousing their expectations and resolving them. I thought that my own method — reporting the gist of arousal-fulfillment or "climax" sequences during ludruk performances — would better allow me to report the acts around which ludruk performers themselves organized their performances than would standardized schemes developed for reporting other types of interaction.

Since I was the only investigator, there may be questions about the reliability of my observations. There were, however, some checks. On occasion I asked several Javanese high school students to make outlines of performances on which I also took notes. I also obtained some story outlines which ludruk actors themselves had written to guide their performances. By and large my notes and the actors' or students' outlines jibed. It is also interesting that my plot summaries were about the same length as the actors' outlines, which suggests that they and I abstracted from the performances to about the same extent. My wife also took notes on some performances; her notes more or less fit mine. I tested my grasp of some of the ludruk jokes by repeating them to polite Javanese friends, and usually they laughed at the punch line. As I began categorizing onstage action, I tried to explain my categories to ludruk actors and spectators, who seemed to find my categories comprehensible, even though it often happened that they had not yet applied to ludruk performances the labels that I applied. For

[1] Roger W. Heyns and Ronald Lippit, "Systematic Observational Techniques."

example, I described to prologue actors a few features which appeared to me to distinguish all prologue characters whom I have labeled "victim" from those whom I have labeled "victimizer." The actors had apparently not created a label to distinguish all victims from all victimizers. But when I presented this distinction to them, they spontaneously spoke of cases that fit the distinction and they named additional features that distinguished victims from victimizers. For instance, one actor, who played the role victimizer, said that victims are always kuna.

At this point I must mention a special problem with respect to correlating my labels of ludruk action and the labels of ludruk participants. In some chapters I label certain onstage ludruk actions (such as a clown's pun which contrasts a low Javanese word with a high Javanese word) a "contrast of alus and kasar cagegories." Other actions I label "a contrast between madju and kuna categories." Now it was rare for an actor to apply the labels "alus," "kasar," "madju," or "kuna" to an onstage act at the time such an act was performed. A clown who had just made a pun did not ordinarily stop and say, "I just made a pun which contrasted a kasar word with an alus word." To explicitly apply such abstract labels would ruin most jokes. Rather, the clown contrasts a number of concrete symbols which everybody hearing him knows are correlated with certain abstract labels. For example, every Javanese knows that certain words are ngoko or "low" and others krama or "high" just as a German learns that certain words go with "die" and others with "das". Javanese categorize words explicitly as ngoko or krama. Further, Javanese seem to agree that "kasar" is an appropriate label to apply to ngoko words and "alus" to krama words. Therefore, if I heard a clown make a pun which contrasted a ngoko word with a krama word, I felt justified in saying that the pun was a contrast along the alus-kasar dimension, even though the clown did not utter the words "alus" or "kasar" at the time he made his pun.

The main rationale, then, according to which I classify certain onstage actions as "a contrast along the alus-kasar dimension" or "a contrast along the madju-kuna dimension" is as follows. There were certain pairs of words, acts, locales, and other symbols which Javanese, in interviews or on other occasions explicitly labeled as alus-kasar or madju-kuna contrasts. If during a ludruk performance such symbols were contrasted — even if the words alus, kasar, madju, or kuna were not voiced at the time the contrast was made — I usually felt justified in classifying such a contrast as "along the alus-kasar dimension" or "along the madju-kuna dimension." I say "usually" because I was not overly mechanical in following this rationale. In some cases, even though the symbols were some which informants had labeled "alus" and "kasar", if the spirit or emphasis of the contrast was clearly along some other dimension, I did not classify the contrast as alus-kasar or madju-kuna.

In some cases, after deciding in the fashion just described that a given ludruk action turned around an alus-kasar or madju-kuna contrast, I questioned ludruk participants about that action. Usually, their remarks verified my conclusion. One of the most gratifying verifications, for instance, went along the following lines. I saw a joke onstage in which a clown mocked his master's manners by asking guests to "slurp up" their coffee, instead of politely asking them to "please drink" the way his master would have. In my field notes, I described the joke and indicated some of the ways in which the contrast seemed to be between alus manners the master would have used and kasar manners the clown did use. Later I talked to a Surabajan about the joke. I described the scene to him. He laughed. Then he said the joke was funny because —

> it was as if we stepped up high then looked down. The word for slurp [*disruput*] is a kasar word, used only to describe something like the way Arabs drink coffee. It would not fit to invite somebody to drink with a word like that because ordinarily you would say in krama Javanese "Please drink" [*Mangga dipun undjuk*]. Putting "disruput" with "mangga" would be peculiar and therefore funny just like a joke my friends and I used to make. We would combine an alus word like "pandjenengan" [krama for "you" or "your"] with a crude word like *raèn* [face] and say *raèn pandjenengan* ["your face"]. Ludruk jokes are often of this sort.

Audience Responses

Even as my eyes were onstage, I always kept an ear open for the jeers and laughter frequently issuing from the audience sitting behind me; one disadvantage of being a foreigner was that theater managers insisted on seating me in the front row of the theater, the row for guests and dignitaries. This position made it hard for me to observe the spectators. Occasionally, however, I lurked behind the fence at the back of the theater, observing the audience inside.

I also employed audience-response recording teams. Each team consisted of students from a Surabaja high school for the liberal arts (SMAA). There were four teams of three students each which took turns accompanying me to performances. One student would sit in class-one seats, another in class-two, and a third in class-three. Each was instructed to record verbatim all responses to onstage action which he heard in whatever language such responses were uttered (usually ngoko Javanese) and to note the onstage action which evoked the response. All submitted their reports to me after the performances. I read through the reports, underlined the words I did not know, then had a session with a Javanese informant who explained these words to me.

It soon became clear that most vocalized responses were derisive or simply described what was happening onstage (e.g., "His pants are falling off"). Nobody seemed to scream out his inner feelings. Therefore, I asked about twenty ludruk goers whom I knew well to accompany me to several ludruk performances and write down all they felt or thought "inside" (*batin*) while the performance was going on. The most usable reports came from ludruk watchers who were better educated and more articulate than the usual audience, but who had the same occupational status as they. For instance, I was lucky to find a very articulate pedicab driver, who produced some rich reports. These batin reports are referred to throughout this monograph as "introspection reports."

Where recordings of both overt responses and inner thoughts left gaps, I directly questioned ludruk goers on occasions when they were not at ludruk. For example, I would quote a line to a well-known ludruk song and ask, "What do you think when you hear this line?"

A few ludruk goers were asked to draw sketches of ludruk characters. The hope was that this might reveal something about the way they perceived such characters.

Finally, I looked for elements of ludruk in life outside the theater. For instance, pedicab drivers could be heard singing ludruk songs as they pedalled home at night. I noted these songs when I could understand them.

Language

Language, of course, was a major problem in gathering data on onstage action or audience responses. According to the situation portrayed, ludruk characters spoke either Surabaja Javanese language, crude form (ngoko), Javanese language, polite form (krama), or Indonesian, the language taught in schools and spoken all over Indonesia. They also spoke a few words of Chinese, Arabic, Japanese, English, and Dutch. In certain plays featuring Madurese heroes, they spoke Madurese, a language from the isle of Madura across the bay from Surabaja; I deal only in passing with these Madurese plays since my main interest is in aspects of ludruk akin to Javanese society.

Some ludruk plays were almost entirely in Indonesian. In all ludruk plays soldiers, policemen, government officials, criminals, youths, prostitutes, Europeans, non-Javanese Indonesians, Arabs, Japanese, and Chinese spoke Indonesian. I had studied Indonesian intensively for six months in the United States and after three months in Surabaja was able to accurately follow those ludruk plays or those portions of ludruk plays that were in Indonesian. I could do this partly because most ludruk actors did not have a very elaborate Indonesian vocabulary, since their schooling was limited and Indonesian was mainly learned at school. Some actors, however, were quite articulate in Indonesian.

Most wordplay in ludruk was in Surabaja ngoko Javanese, as were almost all audience responses. Therefore, I concentrated my language study on ngoko. This study I carried out with the help of an interpreter-teacher, A. Soetjito. Soetjito, a gifted natural linguist who was, unlike most Javanese men, rarely silent, gave a running translation of all portions of ludruk performances that were in Javanese. He also gave rapid-fire explanations of all wordplay. The aim of Soetjito was for me to learn as much ngoko Javanese as possible by watching ludruk with him and practicing ngoko with him outside the theater. Unfortunately, since I was a foreigner, it was not appropriate for me to use ngoko in ordinary conversation. Hence I was placed in the awkward situation of needing most to comprehend that language which I could use least. In spite of this enforced passive learning of ngoko, my comprehension of it did grow until, after several months, I could grasp the gist of much said on the ludruk stage. But every performance would unearth dozens of jokes and other utterances that I could not catch, so I relied on Soetjito throughout my study. I do not think I could have comprehended much of the ludruk wordplay, without Soetjito, even if I had stayed in Surabaja three times as long as I did.

Polite Javanese uses a totally different vocabulary from ngoko. Krama is rarely used in ludruk, except in courtly scenes and stereotyped exchanges such as greetings. I learned to comprehend the stereotyped exchanges fairly well after hearing them again and again.

I learned about theater settings simply by going to theaters and looking around. Most of what I learned about ludruk troupes was by similarly informal methods. I sat around backstage with the actors and observed how they ran their troupes during performances. I went on several trips with the troupes. I questioned the actors a little about their troupe organization, but not very much, since this was not one of the main things I wished to study.

Toward the end of my stay in Java I began collecting life histories of the ludruk players. I arranged through the directors of two troupes, Tresno Enggal and Suara Baru, for actors to come to my house to be interviewed. Typically, an actor would arrive, talk for about two hours about his life story, eat a meal with my wife and me, tell his tale for two or three hours longer, then depart. I collected about twenty of these life histories. All the histories were narrated in Indonesian and my questions were in Indonesian (except for Javanese terms denoting certain customs). All the actors, who were mostly young men, twenty-five to thirty years of age, were competent in Indonesian language. The actors seemed to enjoy telling their stories and were very faithful in keeping their appointments. There was only one case of an actor failing to appear, and he sent word beforehand that he could not come; later I learned that he had decided to get married that night.

I by no means collected all the information that I could have regarding religious and artistic influences on ludruk, since I regarded such information as secondary to my central problem. Although a number of amateur culture historians in Surabaja enjoyed speculating on the religious and artistic beginnings of ludruk, I did not seek them out as much as I could have. One document, largely written by such persons, however, did furnish me with much information on the cultural traditions lying behind ludruk. This was a typewritten copy over a hundred pages long of speeches and discussions that composed the Seminar Ludruk held at the Balai Pemuda (Youth Hall) of Surabaja, from December 25 to 28, 1960. The main participants were Javanese intellectuals (most with Communist leanings), ludruk actors, and officials from the Ministry of Information, who were interested in folk plays as a vehicle of mass "education." The seminar included three speeches by Javanese culture historians on the history of ludruk.

I did not ask many direct questions about political influences on ludruk. Mainly I just noted what ludruk actors told me during conversation, watched the troupes in political contexts (such as Communist-affiliated meetings), and looked for political messages voiced during performances. Almost all that I learned about political influences on ludruk was from the viewpoint of ludruk players, rather than from the viewpoint of influencing agencies such as the Ministry of Information. This had the advantage of giving me the player's view regarding the sources and extent of political influences on his play rather than the official's view of how much influence his agency was exerting on the play. The trouble was that the actors seemed a bit vague on the machinery lying behind the political influences brought to bear on them; officials could have given me a fuller picture of this machinery.

COLLECTING DATA ON THE SOCIAL LIFE OF LUDRUK PARTICIPANTS

From the start of my project my intention was to study all aspects of the social life of ludruk participants that seemed directly relevant to ludruk. It quickly became clear that the social universe of the participants was a very broad one, far transcending the kampung in which the participants lived. Like most city dwellers, the kampung dwellers spend a large amount of time away from their residential neighborhood. They work, shop, and seek prostitutes, beer, or ludruk away from their kampung. This poses special problems for the ethnographer. The ethnographer who studies a rural village which encompasses most of its inhabitants' activities — work, play, worship — can sit in the village for a year or so, then leave, feeling with some justification that he knows the general nature of the social life of the villagers. But to sit in the kampung is to miss the center of action for kampung dwellers — the factories, markets, and streets. Yet to study these extra-kampung domains is extremely difficult. A village includes within a bounded and limited spatial area a set of roles that form a coherent system of face-to-face interaction, but the extra-kampung roles of the inhabitants of a kampung form no such face-to-face interaction system. Such roles (e.g., mechanic, carpenter, laborer, pimp, thief, fun-seeker, patriot, student, marketing housewife) are sprinkled all over town, part of many different face-to-face interaction systems in many different places. This aggregate of roles forms a rather sprawling universe.

Observing these scattered (and hence hard to observe) extra-kampung activities was my first problem in the study of kampung dwellers' social life.

Each ludruk troupe playing in commercial theaters included players from many kampung, since such troupes recruited from amateur troupes based in many different kampung, and each ludruk theater, being outside kampung, drew customers from many kampung. Therefore, since ludruk participants came from many different kampung it seemed unwise to generalize from a study of a single kampung population to the population of ludruk participants. Even the population of actors and spectators involved in a single play came from many kampung. Hence, my second problem was to learn something about several kampung and about ludruk participants from several kampung.

The third problem was that to probe into as many aspects of ludruk participants' social life as possible, I should beware of repeating the same question or observing the same event too often (it would be dangerous to narrow the range of questions too soon to ask the same question to many people, for this might cause me to overlook some aspect of society that would be a key to understanding ludruk), yet to know to what degree a given answer to a question or a given event was typical of the population of ludruk participants, I needed to ask each question or observe each event a reasonable number of times.

I do not think my procedures furnished optimal solutions to these three problems. What I did can be briefly summarized as follows:

I adopted a compromise solution to the first two problems. I lived in a single kampung for a period, then spent another period getting acquainted with other kampung groups and surveying a wide range of extra-kampung activities of kampung persons. My wife and I lived for four months with a family of six in Kampung Gundih, which is slightly more run-down and disorderly than most in Surabaja since many of its inhabitants were squatters and its headman a drunkard. The family, a most admirable group, more or less adopted us, and we got involved in their visits, weddings, ceremonies, trips, and domestic and economic crises, which were frequent, given the incredible economic situation in Indonesia. For the other eight months of our stay in Surabaja, we lived in a small house behind the house of a Javanese psychiatrist. During this time I widened my acquaintance with ludruk participants considerably. I attended celebrations held in various kampung on major holidays such as Labor Day, Mother Kartini Day, or Independence Day, became fairly intimate with three groups from different kampung (some pedicab drivers, a group of ludruk actors, and some young men friends), interviewed about a dozen kampung people who were mental patients at Karamindjangan hospital, had in-depth interviews with some twenty kampung people who did not act in ludruk (the main advantage of the house behind the psychiatrist's house was that it offered privacy for uninterrupted interviews, which had been impossible in the house where we lived in the kampung), wandered around the markets, coffee houses, streets, and kampung of Sarabaja, attended some political meetings, and went to theatrical performances, other than ludruk, which were popular in Surabaja.

To find out about as wide a range of social activities as possible, I made it a policy not to ask the same question or observe the same event very often, but I did scatter my questions and observations. I asked the same question to persons who did not know each other and who represented different age or sex categories. I tried to observe similar events in different contexts.

Two things cause me to have some confidence that the features of social life that I report are roughly true of the social life of most ludruk participants. First, I do have full evidence that most of the ludruk participants are proletarian and Javanese and so am encouraged by the fact that much of what I observed regarding these people fits descriptions of Javanese urban proletarians written by a team of ethnographers who carried out a study much more extensive than mine in a small city in East Java during 1953–54.[2] This similarity between my observations and theirs is not surprising because living and working conditions of proletarians in the various East Javanese cities are roughly similar — East Javanese proletarians speak a common language, intermarry, move about among the towns and cities of the area, and enjoy or endure the same government policies regarding such things as education and politics. Second, I did sample rather fully the ludruk plays of

[2] This team consisted of Alice Dewey, Donald Fagg, Hildred Geertz, Clifford Geertz, Robert Jay, and Edward Ryan, and was directed by Douglas Oliver and Rufus Hendon. A number of publications by members of the team are listed by Hildred Geertz in her bibliography to "Indonesian Cultures and Communities," pp. 486–91.

Surabaja. Since I saw eighty-two performances, each watched by an audience of several hundred, with some variation of audience composition from performance to performance, I estimate that I saw plays watched by several thousand Javanese proletarians — a very large sample. Thus, I do know the kind of entertainment a large sample of Javanese proletarians come to see. It is risky to infer anything about the social life of such people from knowing what they come to see on the ludruk stage. Yet, if there appear plausible connections between what these proletarians perform and watch on the stage and what, according to my data, they do in daily life, and if my data on their onstage activities is based on a big sample, there is a likelihood that my data on their offstage activities holds for the same big sample.

I would like to suggest one advantage which the anthropologist gains by using mass entertainment as a path toward understanding the lives of city dwellers. A virtue of the classical anthropological tradition is that the lone ethnographer who does a full ethnography of a tribe draws together in his one brain many aural and visual scenes of his tribe's life, thus retaining, as Margaret Mead puts it, a sense of "wholeness" that is "part of one's everyday experience" of living in a society.[3] But the modern anthropologist who tries to study urban life may find that to cover the scattered domains of the urbanite's life he must employ a team of assistants administering questionnaires and specializing in different points of urban life; his own job becomes that of administrator of the team and synthesizer of their reports. Thus, the anthropologist, to cover a complex group, loses the classical virtue of seeing and hearing for himself all the scenes and sounds of the group which he is studying. At least from watching mass entertainment in a city, a single anthropologist is able to see, hear, and synthesize scenes which large groups of urbanites with varied and scattered social affiliations find worthy of sharing and vividly displaying when they come together.

[3] Margaret Mead, *An Anthropologist at Work: Writings of Ruth Benedict*, p. 204.

Appendix D
A Performance of "Pak Sakera"

Because of my central problem — modernization — I restricted my attention largely to those ludruk plays which turned around the conflict between traditional and modern values. Hence I had little to say in the text about the most exciting ludruk stories — the "hero stories," which center on abangan-santri and Javanese-Dutch conflict. I briefly summarized two of these, "Sawunggaling" and "Sarip Tambakjasa," but barely mentioned the story which to my mind is the most moving of any of the ludruk melodramas — "Pak Sakera." The following account preserves some of the flavor of this play as performed by Mari Katon at PBRI theater on March 7, 1963.

> *Curtain opens:* It is during the early nineteen-hundreds. Pak Sakera, a Madurese, formerly employed as a foreman at a sugar factory in

Pasuruan (near Surabaja), his face painted bright red to signify his ferocity, is standing on the right side of the stage. A tall, bearded Dutchman stands on the left. Neither speaks. A voice from offstage says that Pak Sakera tried to make peace with the Dutch, but the Dutch would not heed, so finally Pak Sakera was forced to take revenge. Suddenly Pak Sakera erupts into action, slicing the Dutchman with his sickle. The Dutchman utters the first word of the show: "Aaaaaaaaaagh!"

New scene: Pak Sakera is now in prison, at Kalisosok in Surabaja, because he killed the Dutchman and because he had been convicted of stealing funds. He was framed by a village chief and his assistant, who had cheated Sakera out of the funds. As the curtain opens, a Madurese friend of Sakera's, Satia, is talking to a prison guard. Suddenly the gamelan breaks into a lively tune, Djula-djuli. Satia starts dancing in rhythm to the gamelan music, popping his head from side to side in time with each bop of the drum. The prison guard gets seduced into dancing with Satia, also popping his head from side to side in rhythm with Satia.

Amat, a clown, dressed as a prison guard, walks out and is greeted by great laughter from the audience. Amat's face stares stupidly ahead, looking neither to left or right, unsmiling. Then he flutters his eyelids. A fat Dutchman, with much gold braid and other decoration on his uniform, appears, blustering out instructions to Amat. He waits for Amat to answer. Amat utters a crude Surabaja Javanese word. (Laughter.) The Dutchman is infuriated. He instructs Amat some more. Amat suddenly gives the Dutchman's shoulder a jovial shove. (Great laughter.) The Dutchman is angered. Amat leaps away, smiles tensely. Now the Dutchman commands Amat to bring in the prisoners. He does, acting tough (incongruously so, since he is puny in appearance and ordinarily passive in manner); he makes them kneel to him, rattles his gun at them. The Dutchman bustles up, pats Amat on the shoulder. "Ah yes," says he, "That is good. Must show your power." Amat brings in more prisoners, then contemplates his rifle: "This person won't do good, for I often fill it with black spice. This is an old spice-person-rifle!" (Laughter.) Now the Dutchman commands Amat to bring in Pak Sakera. "Don't want to," whines Amat, with a horribly pained expression on his face. The Dutchman insists. Amat goes to get Pak Sakera. Sakera swaggers in, holding a whip, face painted red, bushy mustache, black villager's clothes. (Audience comment: "Pak Sakera is truly cruel.")

The Dutchman quizzes Sakera about places in Surabaja where he has resided. Sakera insists on translating the place-names into garbled and hideous sounds. The Dutchman asks him about *Djembatan Merah,* the "Red Bridge," from which busses depart in Surabaja, and Sakera stumbles: "Dj . . ." "Djembatan Merah!" shouts the Dutchman, correcting Sakera. "Dj . . !" shouts Sakera, louder. "Djembatan

Merah!" screams the Dutchman. "Dj . .!" screams Sakera, much louder. Finally Sakera shouts the Dutchman down. The Dutchman mutters, "Yes," and writes something in a notebook, turning to Amat and blustering that Sakera is a "difficult chap."

New scene: A man leaps into Sakers's path. It is Satia, Sakera's friend. He and Sakera greet each other violently. The friend tells Sakera of illicit goings-on at home between Sakera's second wife, Marlina, and his nephew, Brodin. Angry, Sakera escapes from prison to straighten things out at home.

New scene: Pak Sakera's first wife, Mbok Sakera, is at home, seated with legs spread wide apart, hands on hip, loud voice, tough manner; she is Madurese. Mbok Sakera is scolding Brodin for gambling. "You can't even win," she says contemptuously. Brodin, a dandy, in a bright shirt, sits passively. Spectators scream at Mbok Sakera: "Oh Samson!" (a cry often directed at tough female characters) "She has a face like Ghandi!" "Her walk!" "She doesn't walk, she marches," says a woman. Another woman, who sells fish in the market at Gresik, says of Mbok Sakera, "Wow! She truly talks like a Madurese."

Sakera's second wife, Marlina, enters. She is Javanese, alus, thin, neatly dressed in high-quality *kain baṭik* by contrast to the Mbok Sakera, who is sloppily and cheaply dressed and keeps scratching her belly. As Marlina enters Brodin grins, showing gold teeth. Marlina says she loves Brodin. Brodin sings a Madurese song to her; she sings a Javanese song to him: "Think, think, think, but the one thought about feels nothing." She says to Brodin, "If you were to die, I should feel sad." Brodin asks, "Why?" "If you should die, I'd grab another." (Various audience reactions accompany this dialogue. Somebody asks Marlina, "Is your spouse Sakera or Brodin?" Somebody says of Marlina, "If she sees a handsome man, her eyes switch his way." Somebody shouts at Brodin, "Don't dare to fool with Sakera's spouse! He'll break your neck — but desire enters your intestines!" About Brodin someone says, "This is Brodin, nephew of Sakera. Later he'll be killed." To Marlina: "This is the rainy season. Don't wear such a huge chignon. Later it will slip because of so much lovemaking. Your neck will sink too [i.e., be cut off by Sakera]." Brodin and Marlina embrace, Brodin asks Marlina to give him jewels, and someone laughs, "Ha-ha, she brought a big bracelet." Brodin and Marlina touch each other, and a person comments, "Love-making — an example [i.e., lovemaking is presented as an example of what one should not do]." Brodin tells Marlina she ought not to wear such a huge chignon. "She's certainly show-off," says a spectator, "She has a pretty face, but one can't sleep with her [this presumably alludes to the fact that Marlina is a man].")

At this point, Pak Sakera, who has been standing outside, observing, throws some rocks through the window. The lovers are disturbed, but resume their activity, the girl caressing the male (it is never the reverse in ludruk). Rocks are thrown again. They stop briefly, then resume again. Repeat. (Audience response: "Nice — those two don't feel anything even though somebody secretly watches their lovemaking.")

Pak Sakera bounds in, Brodin flees. Sakera poises his sickle to kill Marlina. (Response: "Who is it that plays Pak Sakera? Not Salimin. Fine acting." "Who plays Brodin?") Marlina kneels to ask forgiveness. (Response: "Ask forgiveness! Ask forgiveness! You want to live!") Mbok Sakera bursts through the door, brandishing a huge knife, and screams, "What are you doing, Pak Sakera, you son of a bitch?" (Response: "That woman is reckless and wild to a point that a man wouldn't dare get smart with her!") Mbok Sakera rushes at Pak for the kill. He grabs her wrist and diverts her thrust toward the wall. Again and again she thrusts and he diverts, so that their fight turns into a dance, Pak and Mbok leaping together, he grasping her wrist, the two following her knife's thrust. Finally, she slaps her knife back into her sash, glares contemptuously at Pak, scratches her belly, leaves.

New scene: Pak Sakera accosts Brodin, gambling, and slits Brodin's throat with his sickle.

New scene: Amat, who earlier played the prison guard, and Slamet, another clown, appear. They are night watchmen in a village. Each is beating a bamboo tube as they make their night rounds. Amat always hits one-too-many beats in the rhythm's sequence. Slamet keeps trying to teach him; Amat keeps hitting too many beats. Each time he does, the audience roars with laughter.

Suddenly Amat and Slamet come upon Brodin's body. Their bamboo-beating suddenly stops short of completing a sequence. Amat says, "Somebody's dead — that means 'dead.'" Amat perceives that Brodin's gambling winnings are on his body. He dives for the money. Slamet warns him, "How about when I tell the police about this? When persons are responsible for a body, they must not pick up money that's on it." (Response: "Hurry and report to the police! Don't pick up that money! Later you will be accused by the police!") Amat throws the money down and Slamet dives for it. "Waaaah," says Amat, frustrated.

New scene: The village headman's assistant, who had originally cheated Sakera, walks by. Sakera wheels, slashes his throat. (Response: "You're so savage, Pak Sakera!" "Good Lord, the person is punished so savagely!")

New scene: Sakera comes to the house of the headman, who helped the assistant cheat Sakera, and slits his throat. (Response: "This one dies seated.")

New scene: Amat and Slamet run to the assistant's house to report Brodin's death, discover the tjarik's body.

New scene: Amat and Slamet run to the lurah's house to report Brodin's death and discover the lurah's body. They are so shocked that they jump. (Response: "Hahahahahaha, they leap!" "Many have been killed. What hit this one?")

New scene: Since the lurah and his assistant are dead, Amat and Slamet list officers of the administrative hierarchy to see who is still living. The *mantri polisi* (police chief)! They go to his office. There they sit respectfully on the floor as he asks them questions (this is proper posture during Dutch rule). Amat answers the first question in English, "Hello." The mantri asks Amat's name. Amat whines, "I'm Amat," in Javanese, then "What's yours?" in English. The mantri, shocked, jumps back. Amat leaps from his submissive floor position and gives him a shove, grinning.

New scene: The police have sent Amat to the house of a *hadji* (devout Muslim who has made the pilgrimage to Mecca), by the name of Jasit, to ask his help in catching Sakera. Amat enters the house, brazenly walks past the hadji's outstretched hands into the arms of the hadji's wife, grasping her as if she and Amat were sexual intimates (thus mocking Muslim sexual piety). After this, Amat produces a giant income tax form and begins narrating at length all the money that the hadji owes. The hadji, who, as in all ludruk stereotypes of santri, is stingy, walks to and fro, in great anxiety. Finally the mantri polisi walks in. The hadji rushes fearfully up to him, asking him how much he owes the government. "Taxes?" asks the mantri, "You owe none." Amat meanwhile has gone outside. The mantri informs the hadji that his reason for coming is to get the hadji to help catch Sakera.

New scene: Jasit, the hadji, and another hadji, Bakri, who have been asked to help fight Sakera, though both were once his friends, are tempted by the police offer of a reward if they help catch Sakera. They appear at the mantri's office. Bakri and Jasit have long been bitter enemies owing to a property dispute. Brought together by the police, asked to cooperate in catching Sakera, they wish to fight instead of shaking hands. (Response: "My goodness, the hadjis don't speak after a quarrel. Hadjis have fought about property until they don't speak anymore.") The mantri's clerk has to threaten them with a pistol to force them to shake hands. Each tries to crush the other's hand.

New scene: The two hadjis meet alone. They argue because Jasit is willing to kill Pak to get the Dutch government reward, which he will use to buy new stalls in the market. Bakri, still Sakera's friend, tells Jasit that Sakera killed the lurah, tjarik, Brodin, and the Dutchman in just revenge. But finally the two agree to set a trap for Sakera in order to get the reward.

New scene: Jasit goes to the house of a *modin* (village Islamic priest), who happens to live near a cave where Sakera is reputedly hiding. The modin's daughter has just come of age, and he is holding a celebration. Jasit asks the modin if he will hold a dance (*tandak*) during his celebration, and invite Sakera to the dance, for it is known that Sakera has a weakness for tandak. The pious modin is greatly against giving the tandak, for that is sinful. He finally agrees, after Jasit threatens government punishment if he does not. Then he begins to like the idea of having the tandak, starts talking about how fine the tandak was which he did in his youth in Gresik, licks his lips while remembering the taste of the palm wine he used to drink in Tuban. (Tuban and Gresik are cities near Surabaja.) All of this evokes a flurry of comments from the audience alluding to illicit drives hidden under the modin's piety. (A bricklayer, laughing, says, "My goodness, the modin knows about tandak, just like that!" Another: "The modin likes to go to the whores, I think.")

New scene: The celebration and tandak is in full swing. Dancing girls keep trying to tempt the pious modin to put the tandak cape on his shoulders and get out on the floor with them. The modin repeatedly wipes himself clean of the cape's pollution. (Response: "The modin's action is that of a person who knows the tandak is forbidden.") Finally, the modin, smiling sinfully, agrees to dance. But now he must place money in the dancing girl's bosom. Painfully, he reaches in his pocket, hating to let loose of money. Finally, he comes up with a tiny sum which he angrily thrusts at the dancer. Now he begins to dance, smiling. (Response: "Later he will hear the sound of the *bedug* [drum beat at the mosque at prayer time].") The modin hears the call of the bedug. Straightway he craves to pray. (Response: "How strange! This character dances in the mosque. The mosque is used as a place to beat the gamelan." Someone else comments, "Sorry outfit this Mari Katon. They are truly kasar.")

Pak Sakera appears, walking in from the back of the auditorium, down the aisles, flanked by his wives. (Response: "What's this! Pak Sakera, the murderer! Where did he come from?") Pak Sakera's achilles heel is his love of dance; the dance has seduced him from hiding. He takes the floor, dancing with the girls and Jasit, all doing a stylized relaxed, slow walking motion, with arms out horizontally. Suddenly, Jasit kicks out his foot in a *pentjak* (karatedance) gesture. The gamelan shifts into a loud, rolling drum beat. Sakera and Jasit whip off their coats, Jasit rolls his sarong to his waist. They will fight. Pak whips out his knife. Jasit dodges. Pak lunges again and again, Jasit dodges. Suddenly Jasit pins Sakera, and the whole crowd at the dance falls on Sakera, even Bakri. A spectator cries, "Ajo! Come on! Get free now or your soul will be done, Sakera!" But it is the end.

Glossary of Indonesian and Javanese Terms

NOTE — This glossary does not include all Indonesian and Javanese terms mentioned in the text; it includes only those terms which after being initially defined are used again throughout the text. Although some of these terms have several meanings, only those which are relevant to the text are given here.

Abangan Javanese who are inactive in Muslim religion or actively hostile toward it.

Alus Refined, civilized, polished.

Batik Method of dying textiles, or cloth that has been so dyed. A design is drawn on the cloth to be dyed; then, by covering first one part, then the other with wax, and dipping the cloth in vats of dye of varying colors, the design becomes multicolored. Cloth dyed in this way and used for making sarongs is often quite alus and expensive.

Bersih désa Ritual, involving food offerings to the danjang (see below), which serves to cleanse the kampung area of dangerous spirits.

Bonang Small gongs, which are like inverted kettles, arranged on a rack.

Dagelan Comic skit presented before the melodramatic story of ludruk is performed.

Danjang Spirit of the founder of a kampung.

Djula-djuli Theme song of ludruk.

Gamelan Ensemble, mainly of percussive instruments. ("Gamelan" originally meant "hammer.")

Gambang kaju A xylophone.

Gendèr barung Musical instrument composed of fourteen bronze keys hanging above sympathetically tuned bamboo tubes.

Kampung Urban slum or shantytown neighborhood with many features of a rural Javanese village.

Kasar Crude, uncouth.

Ketoprak Folkplay, which usually enacts stories depicting ancient Javanese times.

Kendang Double-ended drum, one end played with the left hand, and the other end played with the right hand.

Krama Set of Javanese words, a level of Javanese language, considered high, refined, and formal.

Kris Dagger with symbolic (for instance, phallic) meanings.

Kuna Conservative, traditionalistic, old-fashioned.

Lurah Headman of a rural village.

Masjumi The progressive Muslim political party.

Madju Progressive, modern.

Manipol-USDEK Ideological symbol based on Sukarno's "Political Manifesto of the Republic of Indonesia" (a speech given on Independence Day, August 17, 1959). In early 1960, the central message of this speech was summarized as five ideas: the 1945 constitution, Socialism à la Indonesia, Guided Democracy, Guided Economy, and Indonesian Personality. The first letters of these five phrases (in Indonesian language) form USDEK. "Manipol" is an abbreviation of "political manifesto."

NASAKOM Sukarno's slogan meaning "Unity of Nationalists, Religionists, and Communists."

Ngoko Set of Javanese words, a level of Javanese language, considered low, unrefined, and informal.

Ngremo Opening dance of ludruk.

NU Nahdatul Ulama, the conservative Muslim party.

Pélog Tuning system for gamelan consisting of seven non-equidistant tones, probably more ancient than sléndro.

Pemuda Rakjat "People's Youth," the youth branch of the Indonesian Communist party.

PKI The Indonesian Communist Party.

PNI The Indonesian Nationalist Party, more elitist than the Communists.

PSI The small Indonesian Socialist Party.

Rebab Two-stringed violin.

R.K. Headman of a kampung.

RKKS Surabaja City Kampung Association, the PKI-controlled system of kampung government.

Rupiah Indonesian monetary unit, equal to 1/45 United States dollar officially and 1/1,250 United States dollar on the black market in 1963.

R.T. Headman of an association of a dozen or so neighbors within a kampung.

Rukun To cooperate, to feel as one, to harmonize socially.

Sampak-Srepegan Two of the three parts of the Talu, a musical composition with a strong climax.

Santri Pious Muslims.

Saron Gamelan instrument composed of from seven to eleven metal keys lying on a rack.

Selingan Interlude between scenes of the ludruk melodrama, during which a female impersonator sings and dances.

Sembah Posture expressing respect, involving squatting with one's legs crossed, hands lying in the lap then slowly raised, palms pressed together, until the thumbs nearly touch the tip of ones' nose.

Siter Zither.

Slametan Feast, often among neighbors in a kampung, supposed to create harmony among the celebrants and thus make their souls calm and *slamet* (safe) from spirits.

Sléndro Tuning system for gamelan composed of five almost equidistant tones; was probably introduced into Java in the eighth century A.D.

SOBSI All-Indonesian Central Labor Organization, a Communist-controlled federation of trade unions.

Srimpi Stylized dance portraying courtly stories, at one time performed only in the courts of the royalty.

Suling   A flute.

Talèdèk   Female or transvestite dancer-singers, who are often also prostitutes.

THR   Taman Hiburan Rakjat (People's Amusement Park) of Surabaja, locale of a ludruk theater.

Tjarik   Assistant to a lurah.

Tjerita   Term literally meaning "story," used by ludruk participants to refer to the melodramatic story which each ludruk performance features.

TRIKORA   A catchword for the three commands which the people are supposed to have voiced to Sukarno — that the government should supply food, clothing, should establish security in the countryside, and should take possession of West New Guinea.

Wajang kulit   Puppet play produced by projecting the shadows of leather puppets on a transparent screen.

Wajang wong   Dance-drama, invented in the 18th century, portraying many of the stories of the wajang kulit (which are in part inspired by the Indian *Mahabharata*), but employing people instead of puppets as actors.

Warung   Concession stand selling coffee, rice and such; caters to lower classes.

Bibliography

Alkema, B., and Bezemer, T. J. *Concise Handbook of the Ethnology of the Netherlands East Indies.* Trans. Richard Neuse. New Haven: Human Relations Area File Press, 1961.

Anderson, Benedict R. O'G. *Mythology and the Tolerance of the Javanese.* Ithaca, N.Y.: Cornell University, Modern Indonesia Project, 1965.

Bateson, Gregory. "Bali: The Value System of a Steady State." In *Social Structure: Studies Presented to A. R. Radcliffe-Brown,* ed. Meyer Fortes. Oxford: Clarendon Press, 1949.

Bateson, Gregory, and Mead, Margaret. *Balinese Character: A Photographic Analysis.* New York: The New York Academy of Sciences, 1942.

Bellah, Robert N. "Some Suggestions for the Systematic Study of Religion," Unpublished paper. Cambridge, Mass.: Department of Social Relations, Harvard University, n.d.

————. *Tokugawa Religion.* Glencoe, Ill.: Free Press, 1957.

Brandon, James R. *Theatre in Southeast Asia.* Cambridge, Mass.: Harvard University Press, In press.

Burke, Kenneth. *The Philosophy of Literary Form.* New York: Vintage Books, 1957.

————. *A Grammar of Motives.* Cleveland: World, 1962.

Devereux, George. "Art and Mythology: a general theory." In *Studying Personality Cross-culturally,* ed. Bert Kaplan. Evanston: Row, Peterson, 1961.

Dewey, Alice G. *Peasant Marketing in Java.* New York: Free Press of Glencoe, 1962.

Dewey, John. *Art as Experience.* New York: Minton, Balch, 1934.

Durkheim, Emile. *The Elementary Forms of Religious Life.* Trans. Joseph Ward Swain. New York: Collier, 1961.

Durkheim, Emile, and Mauss, Marcel. *Primitive Classification.* Trans. Rodney Needham. Chicago: University of Chicago Press, 1963.

Erikson, Erik H. "The Legend of Hitler's Childhood." In *Childhood and Society.* New York: Norton, 1950.

Feith, Herbert. "Dynamics of Guided Democracy." In *Indonesia,* ed. Ruth T. McVey. New Haven: Human Relations Area File Press, 1963.

Firth, Raymond. *Essays on Social Organization and Values.* London: Athlone Press, 1964.

Frye, Northrop. *Anatomy of Criticism.* Princeton, N.J.: Princeton University Press, 1957.

Geertz, Clifford. *The Development of the Javanese Economy: A Sociocultural Approach.* Cambridge, Mass.: Massachusetts Institute of Technology Press, 1956.

————. "Ritual and Social Change: A Javanese Example." *American Anthropologist* 59 (1957):32–54.

————. "Form and Variation in Balinese Village Structure." *American Anthropologist* 61 (1959):991–1012.

————. "The Javanese Village." *Local, Ethnic, and National Loyalties in Village Indonesia: A Symposium,* ed. G. William Skinner. New Haven: Yale University, Southeast Asian Studies, 1959.

————. *The Religion of Java.* New York: Free Press of Glencoe, 1960.

————. "Religion as a Cultural System." In *Anthropological Approaches to the Study of Religion,* ed. Michael Banton. London: Tavistock, 1966.

Geertz, Hildred. *The Javanese Family.* New York: Free Press of Glencoe, 1961.

————. "Indonesian Cultures and Communities." In *Indonesia,* ed. Ruth T. McVey. New Haven: Human Relations Area File Press, 1963.

Gennep, Arnold van. *The Rites of Passage.* Trans. Monika B. Vizedom and Gabrielle L. Caffee. Chicago: University of Chicago Press, 1960.

Gluckman, Max. "Les Rites de Passage." In *Essays on the Ritual of Social Relations,* ed. Max Gluckman. Manchester: Manchester University Press, 1962.

Hadiwidjojo, H. "Fungsi Seni Ludruk dari Zaman ke Zaman" (Functions of Ludruk from Era to Era). In *Dwi Pantja-Warsa Jajasan Saraswati 28 Djuni 1952–28 Djuni 1962.* Surakarta, Java: 1962.

Hawkins, Everett D. "Labor in Transition." In *Indonesia,* ed. Ruth T. McVey. New Haven: Human Relations Area File Press, 1963.

Heyns, Roger W., and Lippit, Ronald. "Systematic Observational Techniques." In *Handbook of Social Psychology,* ed. Gardner Lindzéy. Cambridge, Mass.: Addison-Wesley, 1954.

Hindley, Donald. *The Communist Party of Indonesia 1951–1963.* Berkeley and Los Angeles: University of California Press, 1964.

Hood, Mantle. "Music and Theater in Java and Bali." In *Indonesia,* ed. Ruth T. McVey. New Haven: Human Relations Area File Press, 1963.

Hovland, Carl. I; Lumsdaine, Arthur A.; and Sheffield, Fred D. *Experiments on Mass Communication.* Princeton, N.J.: Princeton University Press, 1949.

Hymes, Dell. "Introduction: Toward Ethnographies of Communication." *American Anthropologist* 66 (1964):1–34.

Keil, Charles. *Urban Blues.* Chicago: University of Chicago Press, 1966.

Knight, G. Wilson. *The Wheel of Fire.* Cleveland: World, 1963.

Koentjaraningrat, R. M. "The Javanese of South Central Java." *Social Structure in Southeast Asia,* ed. George Peter Murdock. Chicago: Quadrangle Books, 1960.

Kracauer, Siegfried. *From Caligari to Hitler.* New York: Noonday Press, 1959.

Kunst, Jaap. *Music in Java.* 2 vols. Trans. Emile van Loo. The Hague: Nijhoff, 1949.

Lambert, William W. "Stimulus-Response Contiguity and Reinforcement Theory in Social Psychology." In *Handbook of Social Psychology,* ed. Gardner Lindzey. Cambridge, Mass.: Addison-Wesley, 1954.

Landon, Kenneth Perry. *Southeast Asia: Crossroad of Religions.* Chicago: University of Chicago Press, 1949.

Leach, E. R. *Political Systems of Highland Burma.* London: G. Bell and Sons, 1964.

Lévi-Strauss, Claude. "The Structural Study of Myth." In *Structural Anthropology.* Trans. Claire Jacobson and Brooke Grundfest Schoepfe. New York: Basic Books, 1963.

————. *The Savage Mind.* Chicago: University of Chicago Press, 1966.

Levy, Marion J., Jr. *Modernization and the Structure of Societies: A Setting for International Affairs.* 2 vols. Princeton, N.J.: Princeton University Press, 1966.

Lowenthal, Leo. *Literature, Popular Culture, and Society.* Englewood Cliffs, N.J.: Prentice-Hall, 1961.

Lukács, Georg. "Zur Soziologie des modernen Dramas." *Archiv für Sozialwissenschaft und Sozialpolitik* 38 (1914):303–45.

McLuhan, Marshall. *Understanding Media: The Extensions of Man.* New York: McGraw-Hill, 1965.

Malinowski, Bronislaw, "Myth in Primitive Psychology." In *Magic, Science, and Religion, and Other Essays.* Garden City, N.Y.: Doubleday, 1955.

Mangkunegara VII of Surakarta, K.G.P.A.A. *On the Wajang Kulit (Purwa) and Its Symbolic and Mystical Elements.* Trans. Claire Holt. Ithaca, N.Y.: Cornell University, Southeast Asia Program, 1957.

Mead, Margaret. *An Anthropologist at Work: Writings of Ruth Benedict.* Boston: Houghton Mifflin, 1959.

Mead, Margaret, and MacGregor, Frances Cooke. *Growth and Culture: A Photographic Study of Balinese Childhood.* New York, Putnam's Sons, 1951.

Merton, Robert K. *Social Theory and Social Structure.* Glencoe, Ill.: Free Press, 1957.

Moerdowo. *Reflections on Indonesian Arts and Culture.* Surabaja: Permata, 1958.

Needham, Rodney. *Structure and Sentiment: A Test Case in Social Anthropology.* Chicago: University of Chicago Press, 1962.

————. Introduction to *Primitive Classification,* by Durkheim and Mauss. Chicago: University of Chicago Press, 1963.

Ogan, Eugene. "Nasioi Marriage: An Essay in Model-Building." *Southwestern Journal of Anthropology* 22 (1966):172–93.

Overbeck, H. "Pantoens in het Javaansch." *Djawa: Tijdschrift van het Java-Instituut* 10 (1930):208–30.

Parsons, Talcott. *The Structure of Social Action.* Glencoe, Ill. Free Press, 1949.

Pauker, Guy J. "Indonesian Images of Their National Self." *Public Opinion Quarterly* 22 (1958):305–24.

Peacock, James L. "Javanese Folkdrama and Social Change." Unpublished doctoral thesis. Cambridge, Mass.: Harvard University, 1965.

————. "Javanese Clown and Transvestite Songs: Relations between 'Primitive Classification' and 'Communicative Events.'" In *Essays on the Verbal and Visual Arts: Proceedings of the 1966 Annual Spring Meeting, American Ethnological Society,* ed. June Helm. Seattle: University of Washington Press, 1967.

————. "Anti-Dutch Anti-Muslim, Drama among Surabaja Proletarians: A Description of Performances and Responses," forthcoming in *Indonesia.*

————. "Ritual, Entertainment and Modernization: A Javanese Case," forthcoming in *Comparative Studies in Society and History.*

Pelzer, Karl J. "Physical and Human Resource Patterns." In *Indonesia,* ed. Ruth T. McVey. New Haven: Human Relations Area File Press, 1963.

Pigeaud, Th. *Javaanse Volksvertoningen.* Batavia: Volkslectuur, 1938.

_____. *Javaans-Nederlands Handwoordenboek.* Groningen: Wolters, 1938.

Poerbokoesoemo, L. "Ludruk dari Segi Sedjarah serta Perkembangannja" (Ludruk from the Viewpoint of its Development and History). Paper delivered at the Seminar Ludruk, Balai Pemuda in Surabaja, December 25–28, 1960.

Poerwadarminta, W. J. S. *Kamus Umum Bahasa Indonesia* (General Indonesian Dictionary). Djakarta: Dinas Penerbitan Balai Pustaka, 1961.

Rassers, W. H. *Panji, the Culture Hero: A Structural Study of Religion in Java.* The Hague: Nijhoff, 1959.

Reed, Stephen W., ed. *Indonesia.* New Haven: Human Relations Area File Press, 1956.

"Of Rice and Rats." *Time* 83 (February 28, 1964): 40

Romney, A. Kimball, and D'Andrade, Roy Goodwin, eds. *Transcultural Studies in Cognition. American Anthropologist,* (Special Publication) 66 (1964), no. 2.

Shamsudin, J. "Prasaran: Peranan Ludruk dalam Masjarakat" (Working Paper: The Role of Ludruk in Society). Paper delivered at the Seminar Ludruk, Balai Pemuda in Surabaja, December 25–28, 1960.

Soemadj, Ki Adj. "Penjanggah Umum Ki Soemadji Adj. Untuk Prasaran Sdr. Lesmonodewa Poebokoesoemo" (General Protest by Ki Soemadji Adj. Regarding the Working Paper of Brother Lesmonodewa Poebokoesoemo). Paper delivered at the Seminar Ludruk, Balai Pemuda in Surabaja, December 25–28, 1960.

Soemady. "Kesenian Ludruk dan Siaran Radio" (Ludruk and Radio Broadcasting), Unpublished paper. Surabaja: Radio Republik Indonesia, 1961.

Sukarno. *Res Publica! Once More Res Publica!* Djakarta: Ministry of Information, 1959.

_____. *Moluccas Speeches.* Djakarta: Ministry of Information, 1960.

_____. "Youth Pledge," *PIA News Bulletin.* Djakarta, December 14, 1960.

_____. "Laksana Malaekat Jang Menjerbu dari Langit: Djalannja Revolusi Kita" (Like Angels that Strike from the Skies: The March of Our Revolution). In *Dari Proklamasi sampai Resopim.* Djakarta: Departemèn Penerangan, 1962.

_____. "Penemuan Kembali Revolusi Kita" (The Rediscovery of Our Revolution). In *Dari Proklamasi sampai Resopim.* Djakarta: Departemèn Penerangan, 1962.

Topping, Seymour, "A 'New' Indonesia Faces Huge Tasks." *The New York Times* 115 (August 25, 1966): 4.

Turner, Victor, "Three Symbols of Passage in Ndembu Circumcision Ritual," In *Essays on the Ritual of Social Relations,* ed. Max Gluckman. Manchester: Manchester University Press, 1962.

————. "Witchcraft and Sorcery: Taxonomy versus Dynamics," *Africa* 34 (1964):314–24.

Van der Kroef, J. M. "The Realist Convergence in Indonesian Political Life." *Journal of East Asiatic Studies* 5 (1956):279–97.

Weber, Max. *The Theory of Social and Economic Organization.* Trans. A. M. Henderson and Talcott Parsons. New York: Oxford University Press, 1947.

————. *The Protestant Ethic and the Spirit of Capitalism.* Trans. Talcott Parsons. New York: Charles Scribner's Sons, 1958.

————. "On Religious Rejections of the World." In *Theories of Society: Foundations of Modern Sociological Theory,* 2 vols., ed. Talcott Parsons, Edward Shils, Kaspar D. Naegele, and Jesse R. Pitts. New York: Free Press of Glencoe, 1961.

Wertheim, W. F. "Changes in Indonesia's Social Stratification," *Pacific Affairs* 28 (1955):41–52.

————. *East-West Parallels.* Chicago: Quadrangle Books, 1965.

Wilken, G. A. *Manual for the Comparative Ethnology of the Netherlands East Indies.* Trans. S. Dumas Kaan and ed. C. M. Pleyte. New Haven: Human Relations Area File Press, 1961.

Wongsosewojo, R. Ahmad. "Loedroek." *Djawa: Tijdschrift van het Java-Instituut* 10 (1930):204–7.

Zoete, Beryl de, and Spies, Walter. *Dance and Drama in Bali.* London: Faber and Faber, n.d.

Index

Abangan, defined, 18, 19, 293
Alus, defined, 7, 293
Amplifying effect, 254
Animism, 35–36; relation to ludruk, 37; relation to modernization, 219–27 *passim.* See also *Bersih désa; Danjang; Slametan*
Aristocrats of Java: portrayed in ludruk, 151–55; traits of, 17. *See also* Transvestites
Army: basis for jokes, 163; opponent of Communists, 25; relation to ludruk, 34, 41–45
Art: affected by modernization, 230; contrasted to religion, 211, 243–45; its social influence, 244–45
Artistic influences on ludruk: Indonesian, 56–58; Javanese, 50–56

Audience response, 241–55; to clowns, 177, 179–80; empathetic qualities, 65–70; method of recording, 278–79; relation to political sponsorship, xvi, 45, 241; study of as aid to social prediction, 254–55; to transvestites, 197

Bateson, Gregory, theories of Javanese personality, 169*n*, 222*n*
Bersih désa, 97, 219–20, 294
Besut, 30, 35–37, 123
Brandon, James R., on Southeast Asian theatrical pattern, 3–4, 60–61
Bureaucratization of Java: as butt of jokes, 161–63; influenced by ludruk, 231